Symbiote Spider-Man: Crossroads

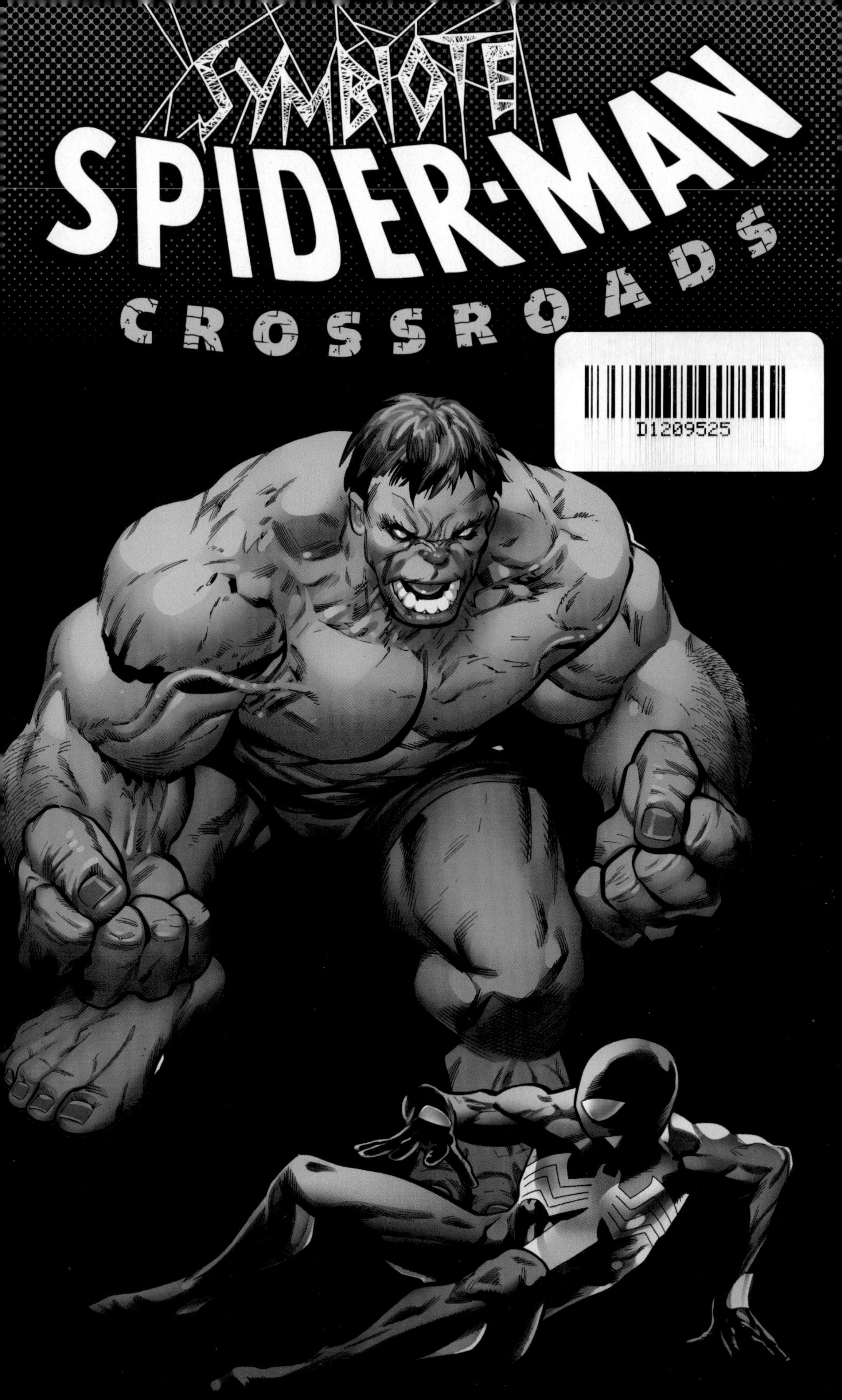

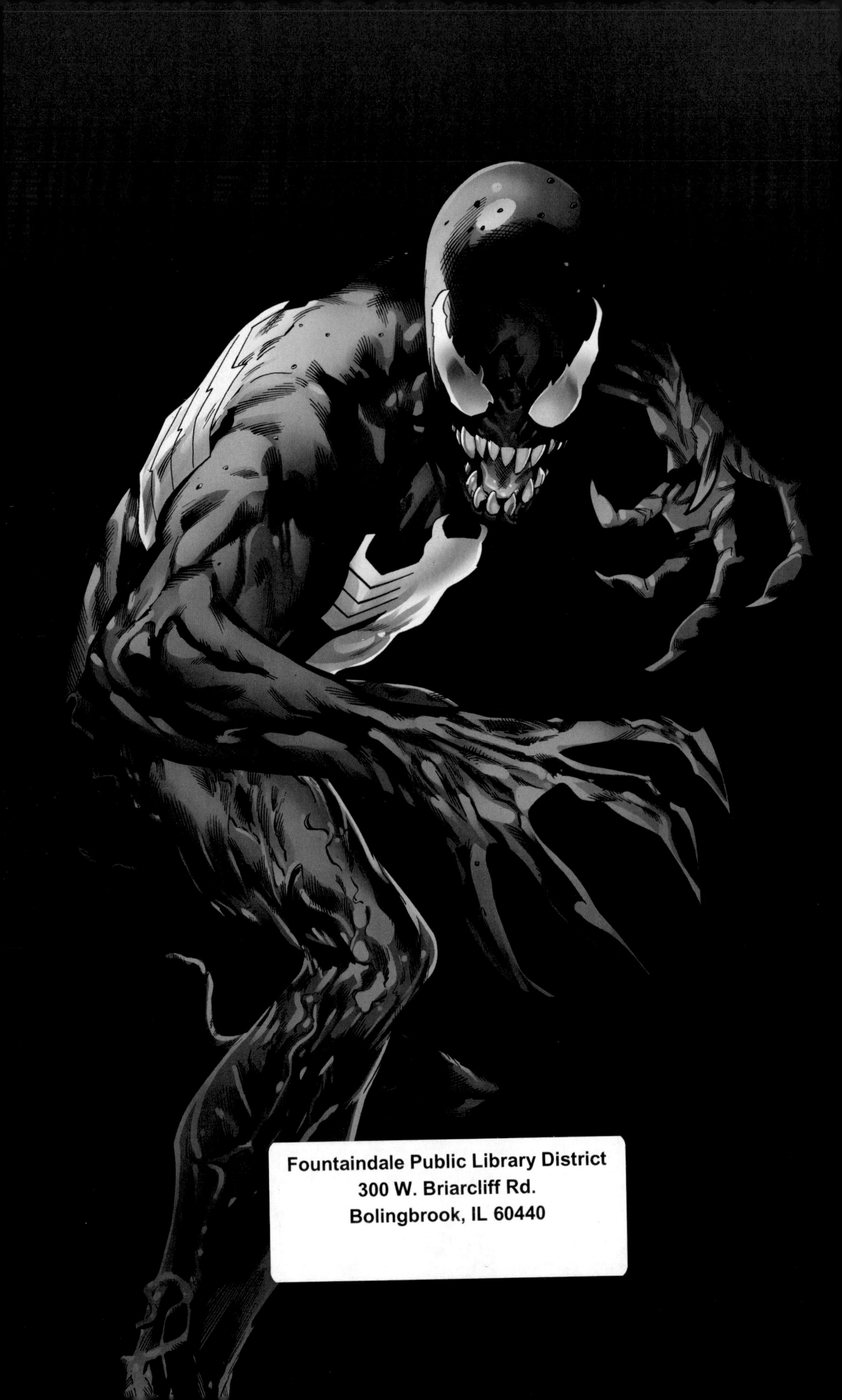

SYMBIOTE SPIDER-MAN CROSSROADS

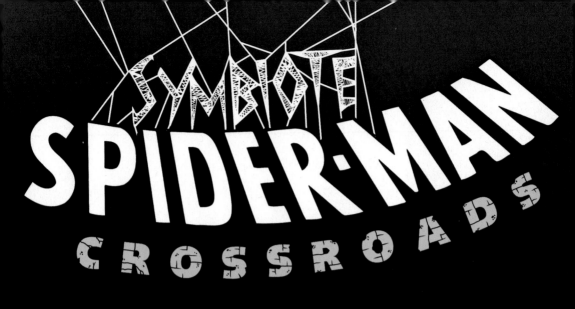

PETER DAVID
WRITER

GREG LAND
PENCILER

JAY LEISTEN
INKER

FRANK D'ARMATA
COLORIST

VC's JOE SABINO
LETTERER

GREG LAND & **FRANK D'ARMATA**
COVER ART

DANNY KHAZEM
ASSISTANT EDITOR

DEVIN LEWIS
EDITOR

NICK LOWE
EXECUTIVE EDITOR

SPIDER-MAN *CREATED BY* **STAN LEE** & **STEVE DITKO**

Collection Editor: DANIEL KIRCHHOFFER
Associate Managing Editor: MAIA LOY
Associate Managing Editor: LISA MONTALBANO
Senior Editor, Special Projects: JENNIFER GRÜNWALD

VP Production & Special Projects: JEFF YOUNGQUIST
Book Designers: SARAH SPADACCINI WITH SALENA MAHINA
SVP Print, Sales & Marketing: DAVID GABRIEL
Editor in Chief: C.B. CEBULSKI

MBIOTE SPIDER-MAN: CROSSROADS. Contains material originally published in magazine form as SYMBIOTE SPIDER-MAN: CROSSROADS (2021) #1-5. First printing 2021. ISBN 978-1-302-92800-1. Published MARVEL WORLDWIDE, INC., a subsidiary of MARVEL ENTERTAINMENT, LLC. OFFICE OF PUBLICATION: 1290 Avenue of the Americas, New York, NY 10104. © 2021 MARVEL No similarity between any of the names, racters, persons, and/or institutions in this book with those of any living or dead person or institution is intended, and any such similarity which may exist is purely coincidental. **Printed in Canada.** KEVIN FEIGE, ef Creative Officer; DAN BUCKLEY, President, Marvel Entertainment; JOE QUESADA, EVP & Creative Director; DAVID BOGART, Associate Publisher & SVP of Talent Affairs; TOM BREVOORT, VP, Executive Editor; NICK VE, Executive Editor, VP of Content, Digital Publishing; DAVID GABRIEL, VP of Print & Digital Publishing; JEFF YOUNGQUIST, VP of Production & Special Projects; ALEX MORALES, Director of Publishing Operations; EDINGTON, Managing Editor; RICKEY PURDIN, Director of Talent Relations; JENNIFER GRÜNWALD, Senior Editor, Special Projects; SUSAN CRESPI, Production Manager; STAN LEE, Chairman Emeritus. For rmation regarding advertising in Marvel Comics or on Marvel.com, please contact Vit DeBellis, Custom Solutions & Integrated Advertising Manager, at

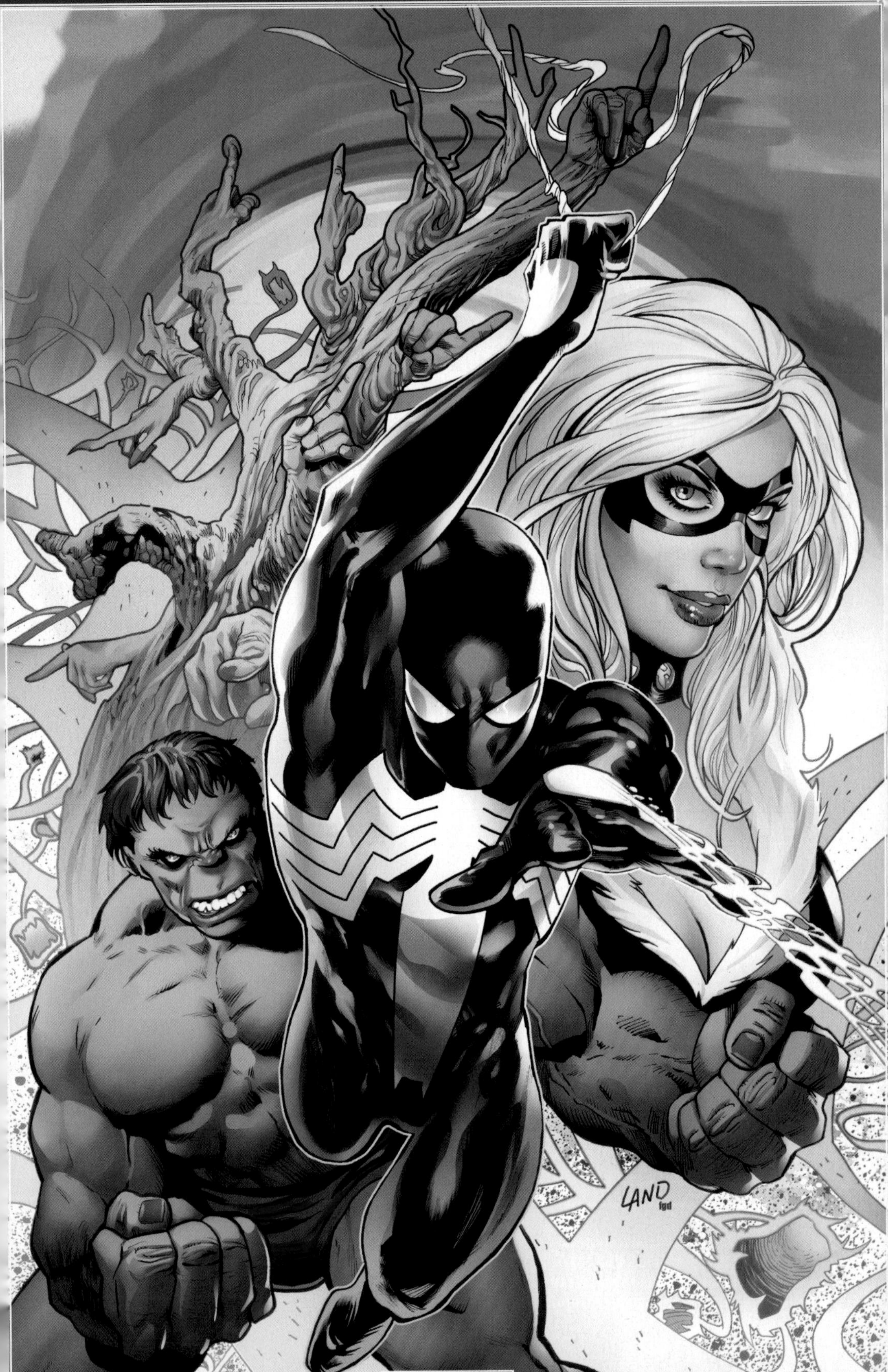
LAND

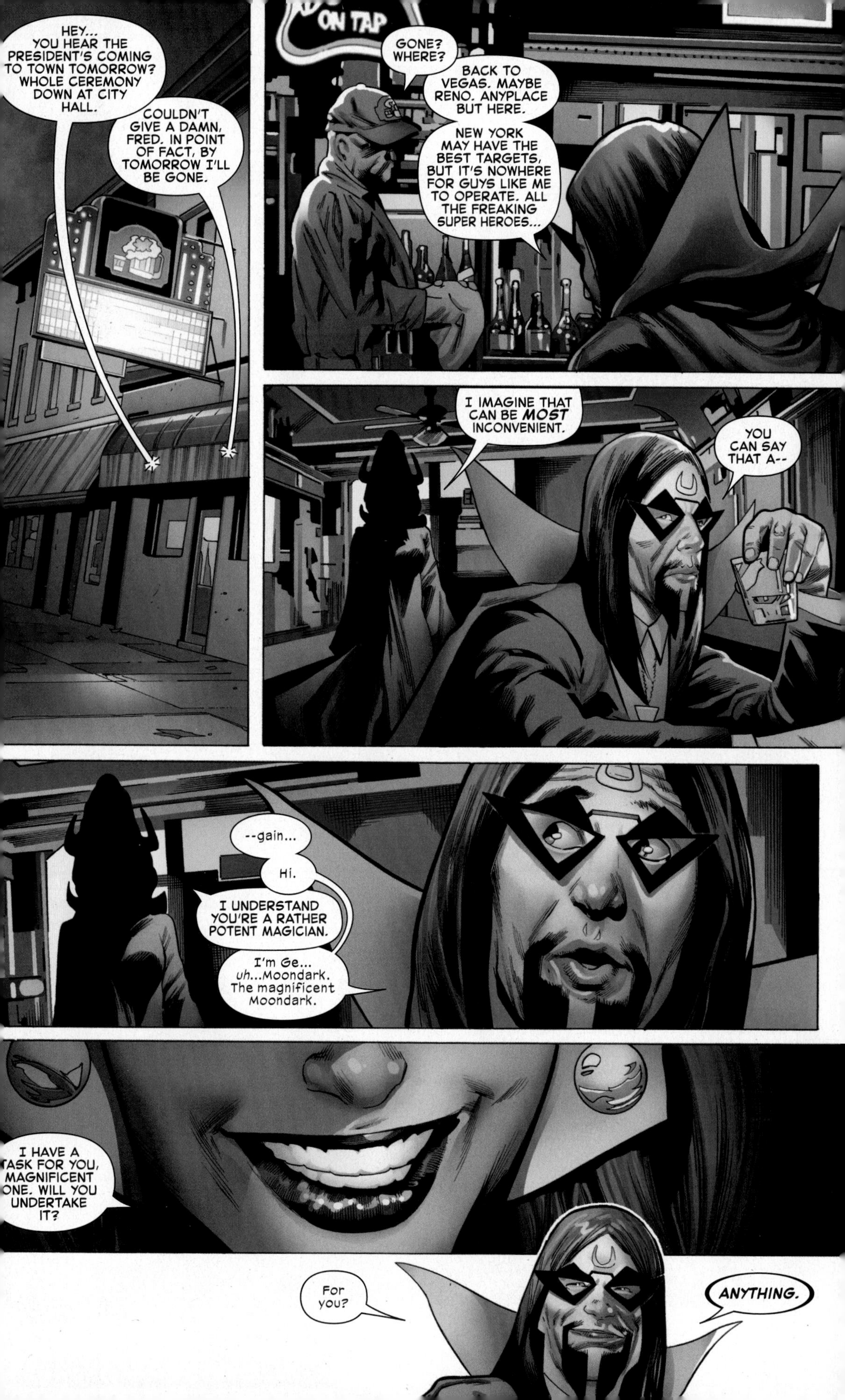
ON TAP
HEY... YOU HEAR THE PRESIDENT'S COMING TO TOWN TOMORROW? WHOLE CEREMONY DOWN AT CITY HALL.
COULDN'T GIVE A DAMN, FRED. IN POINT OF FACT, BY TOMORROW I'LL BE GONE.
GONE? WHERE?
BACK TO VEGAS. MAYBE RENO. ANYPLACE BUT HERE.
NEW YORK MAY HAVE THE BEST TARGETS, BUT IT'S NOWHERE FOR GUYS LIKE ME TO OPERATE. ALL THE FREAKING SUPER HEROES...
I IMAGINE THAT CAN BE MOST INCONVENIENT.
YOU CAN SAY THAT A--
--gain...
Hi.
I UNDERSTAND YOU'RE A RATHER POTENT MAGICIAN.
I'm Ge... uh...Moondark. The magnificent Moondark.
I HAVE A TASK FOR YOU, MAGNIFICENT ONE. WILL YOU UNDERTAKE IT?
For you?
ANYTHING.

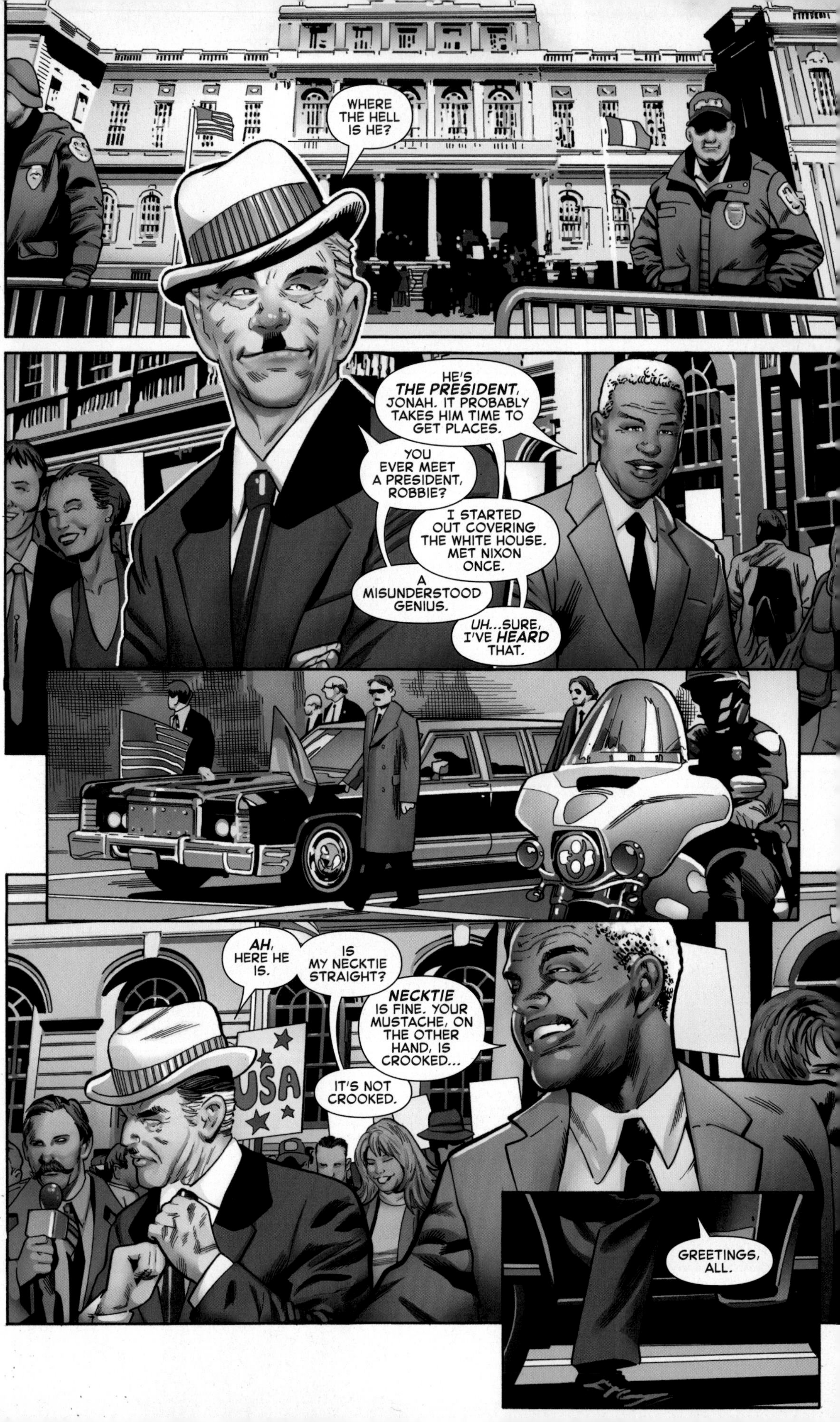
WHERE THE HELL IS HE?
HE'S *THE PRESIDENT*, JONAH. IT PROBABLY TAKES HIM TIME TO GET PLACES.
YOU EVER MEET A PRESIDENT, ROBBIE?
I STARTED OUT COVERING THE WHITE HOUSE. MET NIXON ONCE.
A MISUNDERSTOOD GENIUS.
UH...SURE, I'VE *HEARD* THAT.
AH, HERE HE IS.
IS MY NECKTIE STRAIGHT?
NECKTIE IS FINE. YOUR MUSTACHE, ON THE OTHER HAND, IS CROOKED...
IT'S NOT CROOKED.
USA
GREETINGS, ALL.

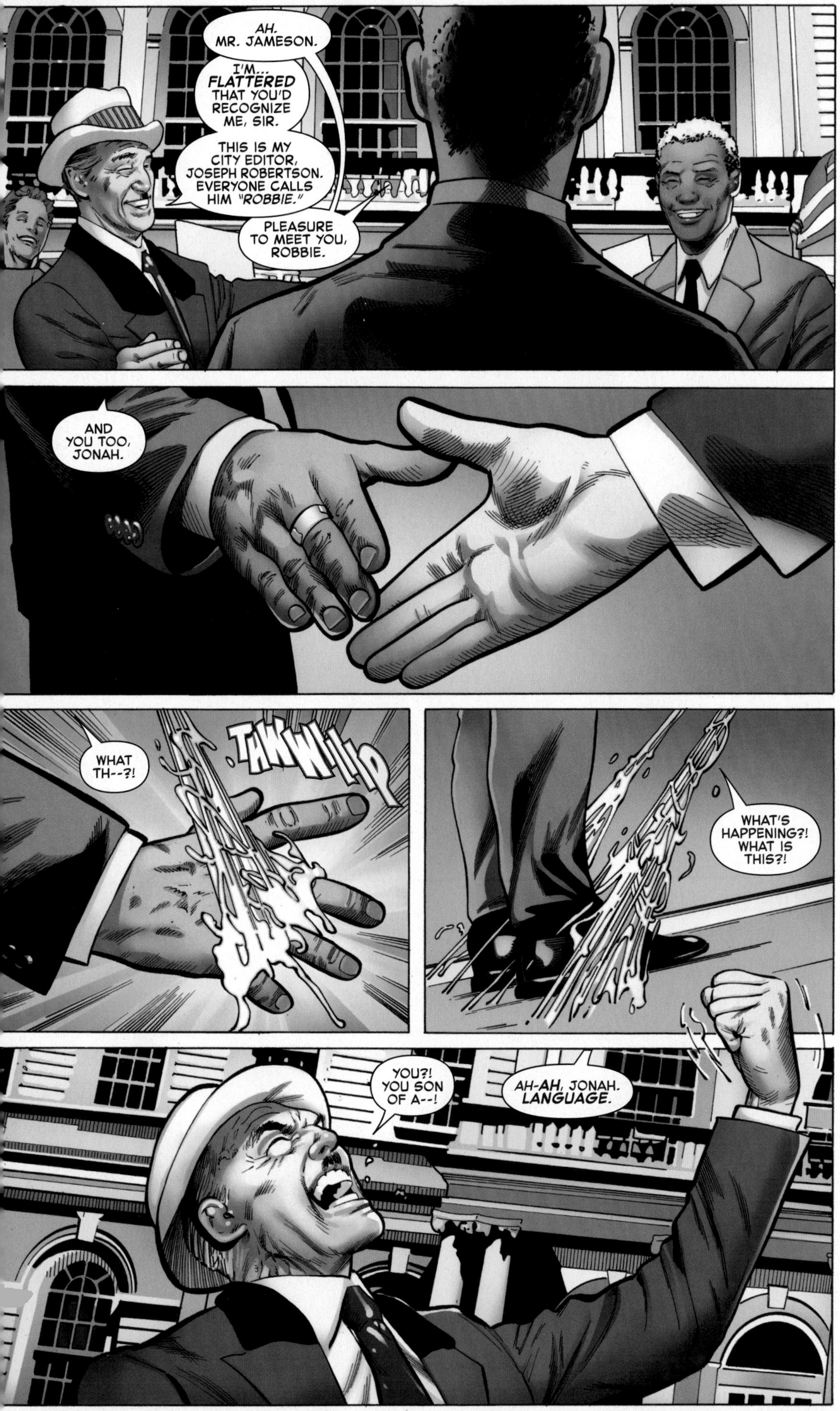
AH. MR. JAMESON.
I'M... FLATTERED THAT YOU'D RECOGNIZE ME, SIR.
THIS IS MY CITY EDITOR, JOSEPH ROBERTSON. EVERYONE CALLS HIM "ROBBIE."
PLEASURE TO MEET YOU, ROBBIE.
AND YOU TOO, JONAH.
WHAT TH--?!
THWIP
WHAT'S HAPPENING?! WHAT IS THIS?!
YOU?! YOU SON OF A--!
AH-AH, JONAH. LANGUAGE.

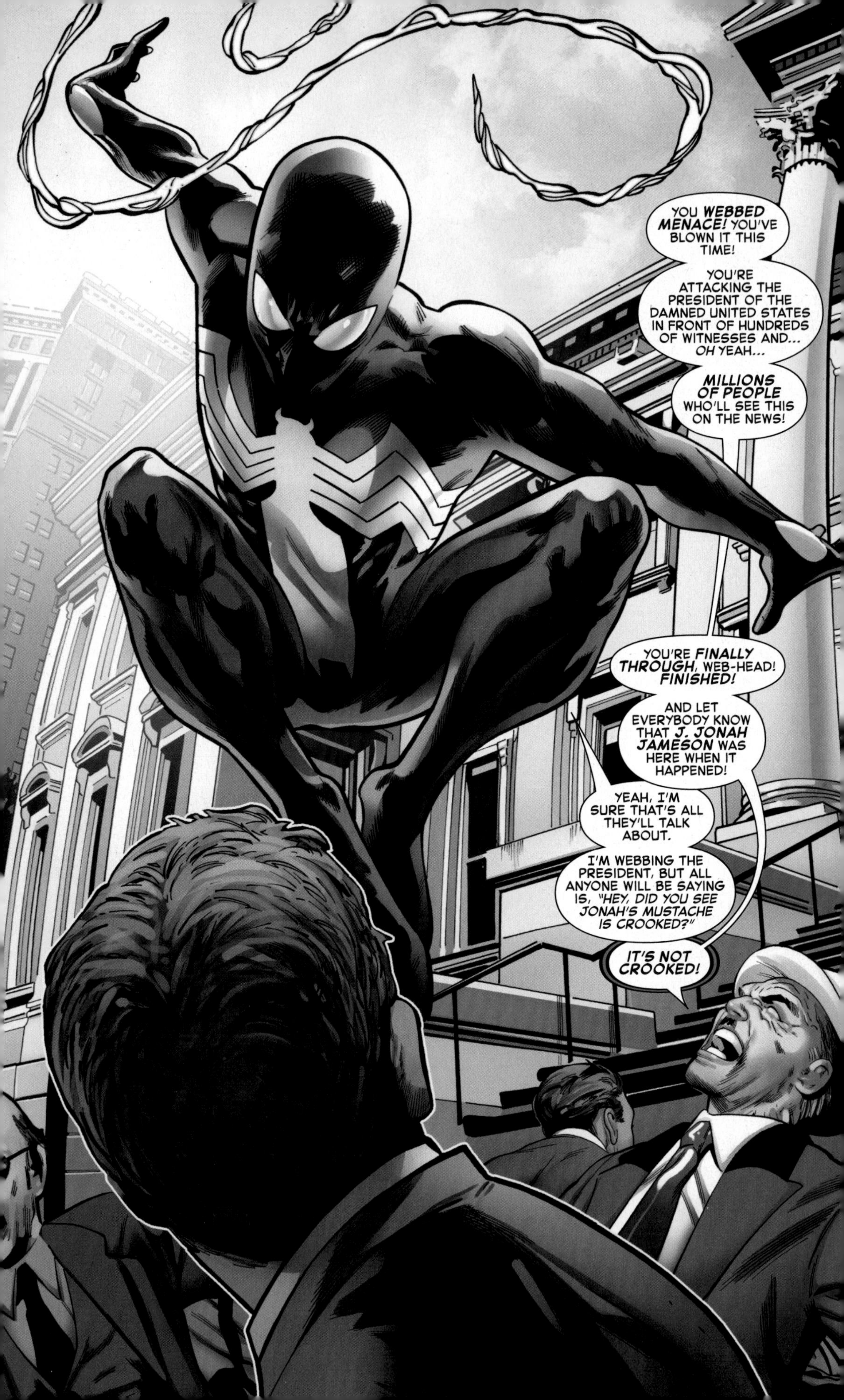
YOU **WEBBED MENACE!** YOU'VE BLOWN IT THIS TIME!
YOU'RE ATTACKING THE PRESIDENT OF THE DAMNED UNITED STATES IN FRONT OF HUNDREDS OF WITNESSES AND... *OH* YEAH...
MILLIONS OF PEOPLE WHO'LL SEE THIS ON THE NEWS!
YOU'RE ***FINALLY THROUGH***, WEB-HEAD! ***FINISHED!***
AND LET EVERYBODY KNOW THAT ***J. JONAH JAMESON*** WAS HERE WHEN IT HAPPENED!
YEAH, I'M SURE THAT'S ALL THEY'LL TALK ABOUT.
I'M WEBBING THE PRESIDENT, BUT ALL ANYONE WILL BE SAYING IS, "HEY, DID YOU SEE JONAH'S MUSTACHE IS CROOKED?"
IT'S NOT CROOKED!

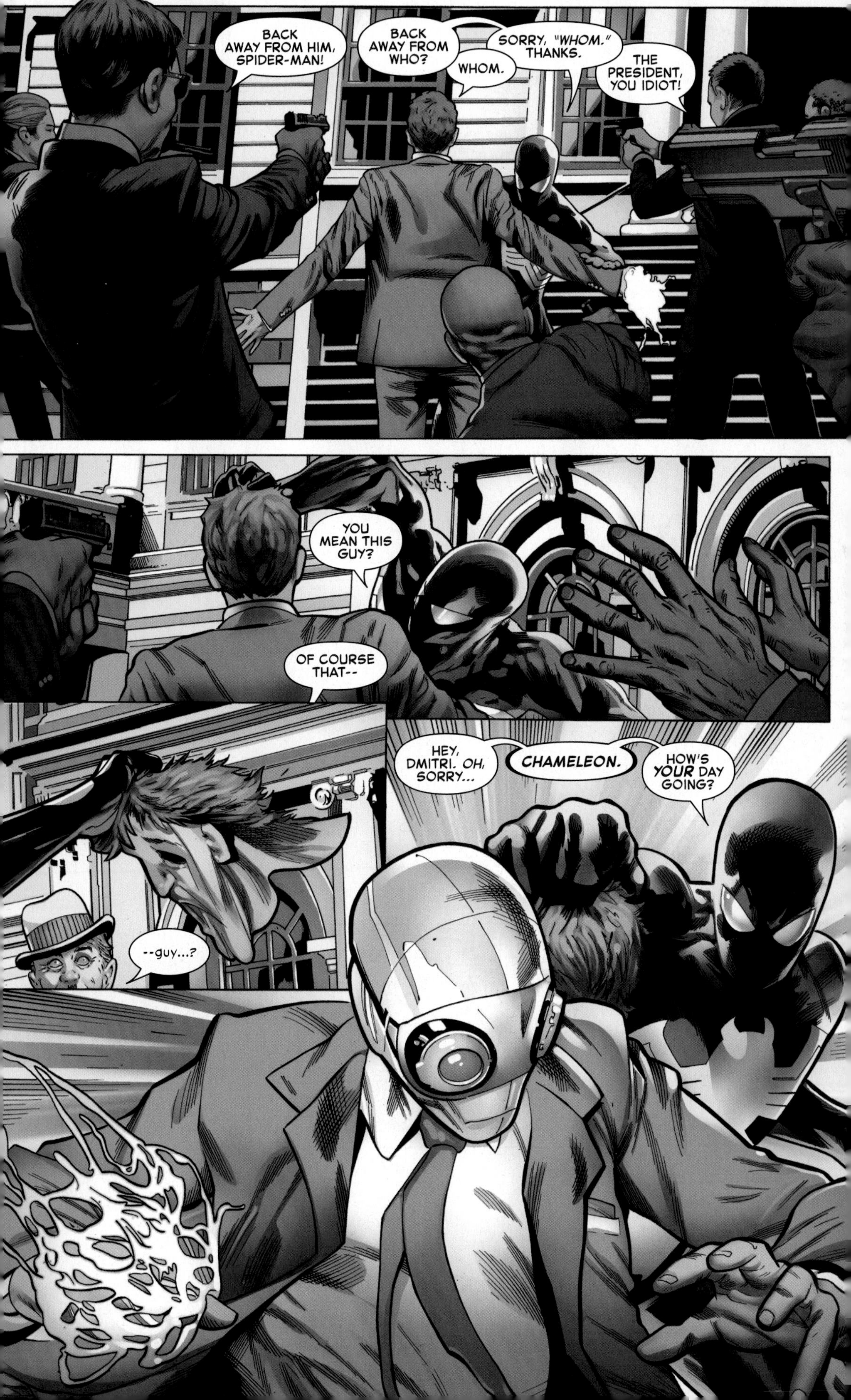

BACK AWAY FROM HIM, SPIDER-MAN!
BACK AWAY FROM WHO?
WHOM.
SORRY, "WHOM." THANKS.
THE PRESIDENT, YOU IDIOT!
YOU MEAN THIS GUY?
OF COURSE THAT--
--guy...?
HEY, DMITRI. OH, SORRY...
CHAMELEON.
HOW'S YOUR DAY GOING?

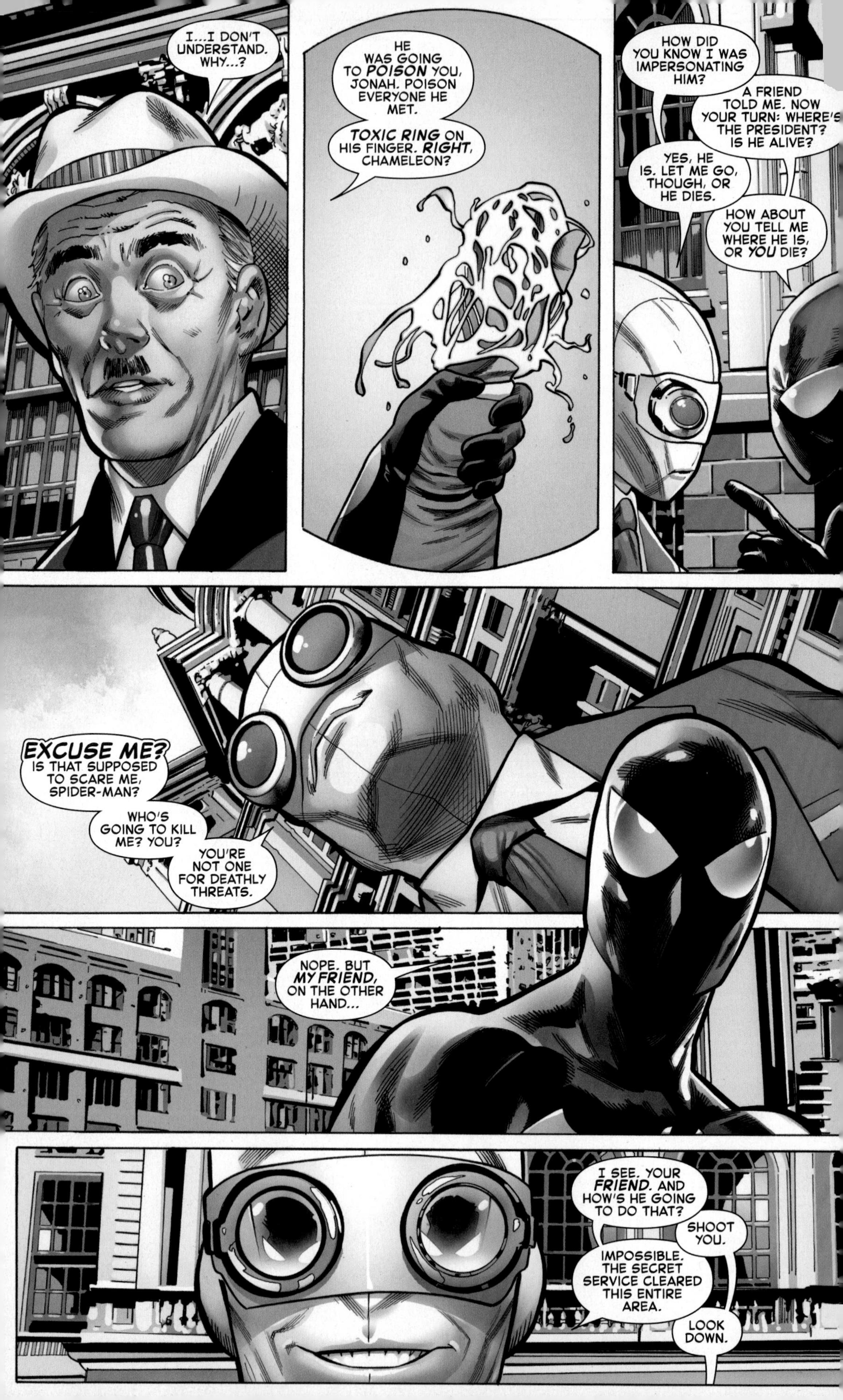

I...I DON'T UNDERSTAND. WHY...?
HE WAS GOING TO POISON YOU, JONAH. POISON EVERYONE HE MET.
TOXIC RING ON HIS FINGER. RIGHT, CHAMELEON?
HOW DID YOU KNOW I WAS IMPERSONATING HIM?
A FRIEND TOLD ME. NOW YOUR TURN: WHERE'S THE PRESIDENT? IS HE ALIVE?
YES, HE IS. LET ME GO, THOUGH, OR HE DIES.
HOW ABOUT YOU TELL ME WHERE HE IS, OR YOU DIE?
EXCUSE ME? IS THAT SUPPOSED TO SCARE ME, SPIDER-MAN?
WHO'S GOING TO KILL ME? YOU?
YOU'RE NOT ONE FOR DEATHLY THREATS.
NOPE. BUT MY FRIEND, ON THE OTHER HAND...
I SEE. YOUR FRIEND. AND HOW'S HE GOING TO DO THAT?
SHOOT YOU.
IMPOSSIBLE. THE SECRET SERVICE CLEARED THIS ENTIRE AREA.
LOOK DOWN.

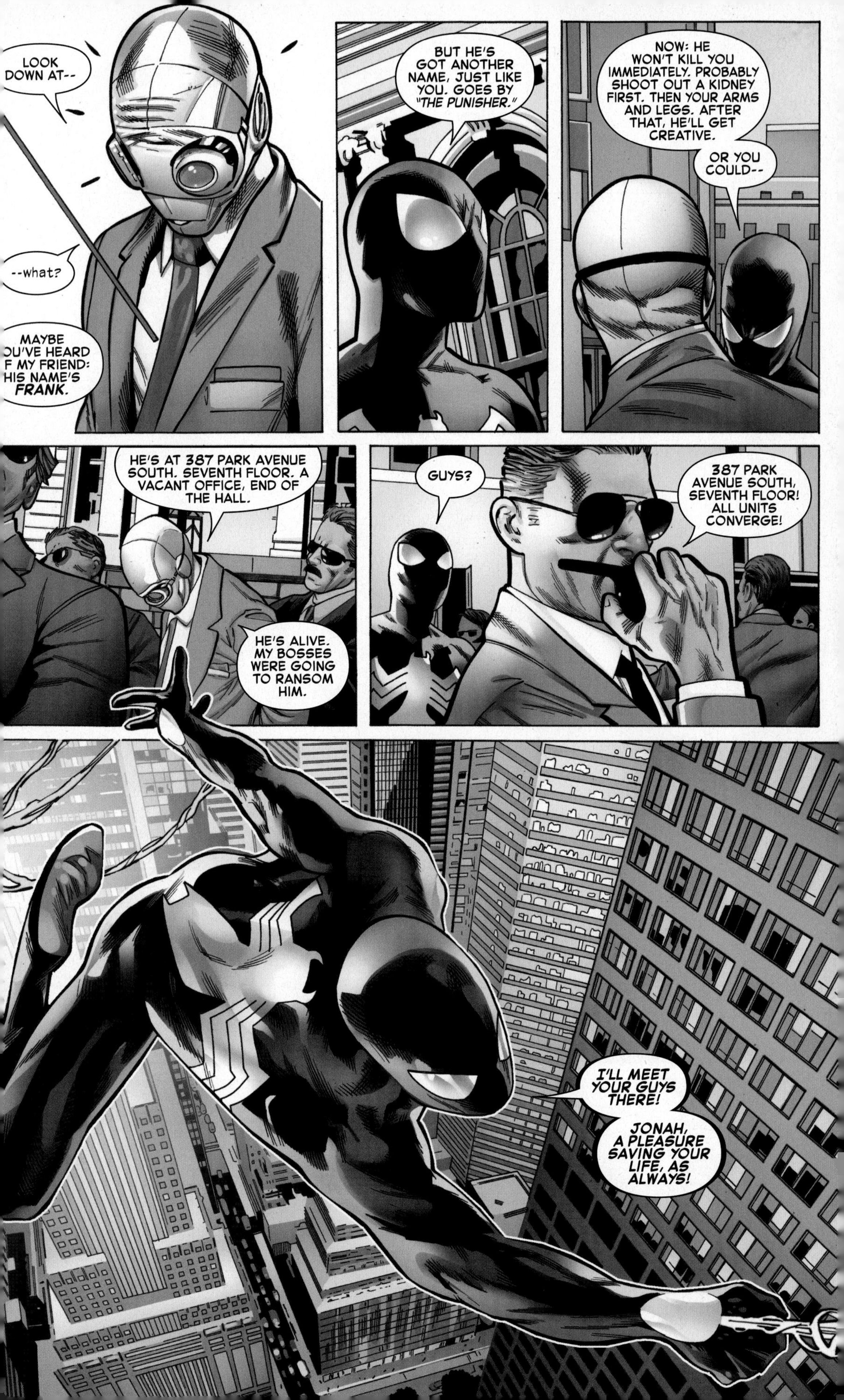
LOOK DOWN AT--
--what?
MAYBE OU'VE HEARD F MY FRIEND: HIS NAME'S *FRANK.*
BUT HE'S GOT ANOTHER NAME, JUST LIKE YOU. GOES BY *"THE PUNISHER."*
NOW: HE WON'T KILL YOU IMMEDIATELY. PROBABLY SHOOT OUT A KIDNEY FIRST. THEN YOUR ARMS AND LEGS. AFTER THAT, HE'LL GET CREATIVE.
OR YOU COULD--
HE'S AT 387 PARK AVENUE SOUTH. SEVENTH FLOOR. A VACANT OFFICE, END OF THE HALL.
HE'S ALIVE. MY BOSSES WERE GOING TO RANSOM HIM.
GUYS?
387 PARK AVENUE SOUTH, SEVENTH FLOOR! ALL UNITS CONVERGE!
I'LL MEET YOUR GUYS THERE!
JONAH, A PLEASURE SAVING YOUR LIFE, AS ALWAYS!

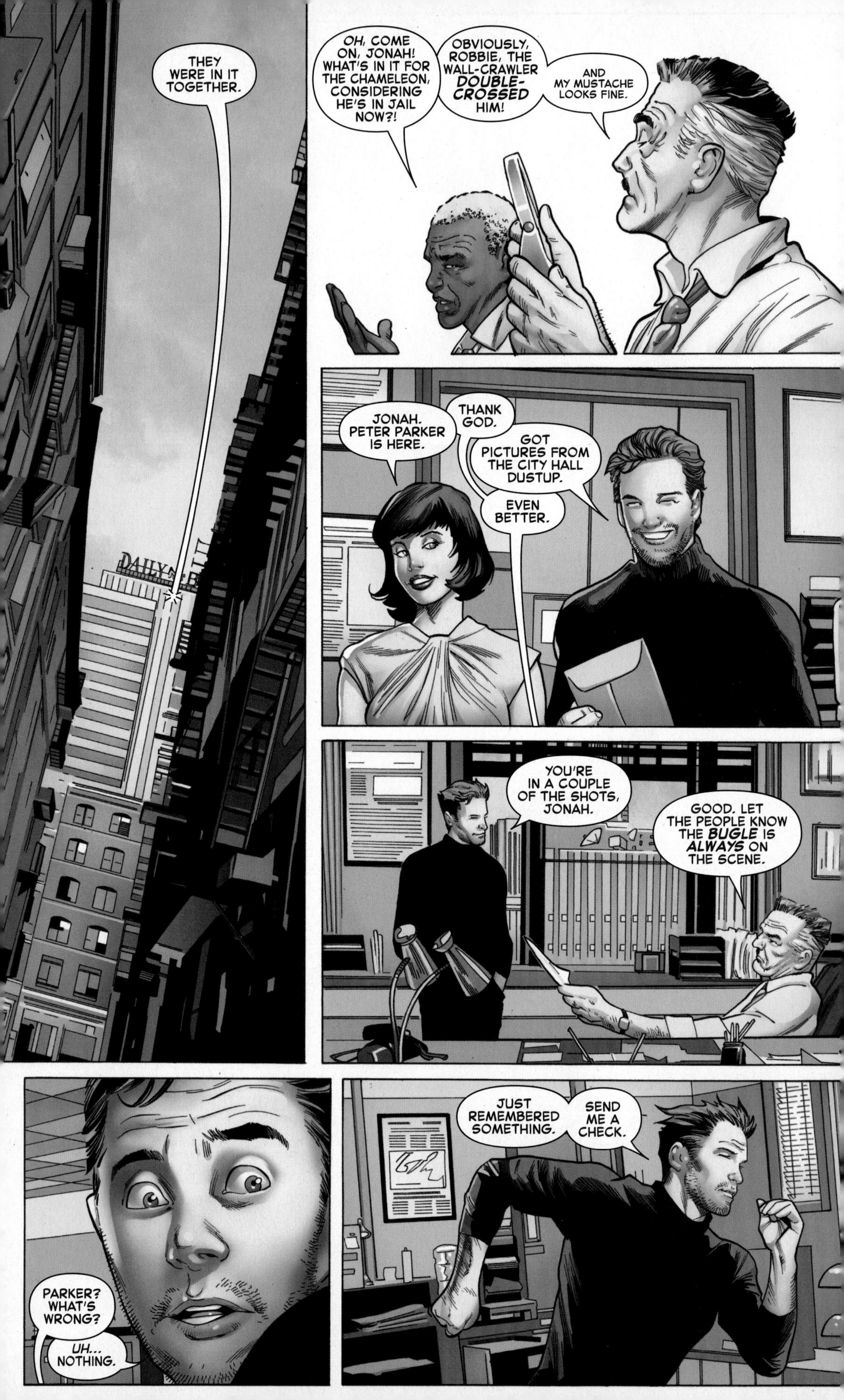

THEY WERE IN IT TOGETHER.
OH, COME ON, JONAH! WHAT'S IN IT FOR THE CHAMELEON, CONSIDERING HE'S IN JAIL NOW?!
OBVIOUSLY, ROBBIE, THE WALL-CRAWLER *DOUBLE-CROSSED* HIM!
AND MY MUSTACHE LOOKS FINE.
JONAH. PETER PARKER IS HERE.
THANK GOD.
GOT PICTURES FROM THE CITY HALL DUSTUP.
EVEN BETTER.
YOU'RE IN A COUPLE OF THE SHOTS, JONAH.
GOOD. LET THE PEOPLE KNOW THE *BUGLE* IS *ALWAYS* ON THE SCENE.
PARKER? WHAT'S WRONG?
UH... NOTHING.
JUST REMEMBERED SOMETHING.
SEND ME A CHECK.

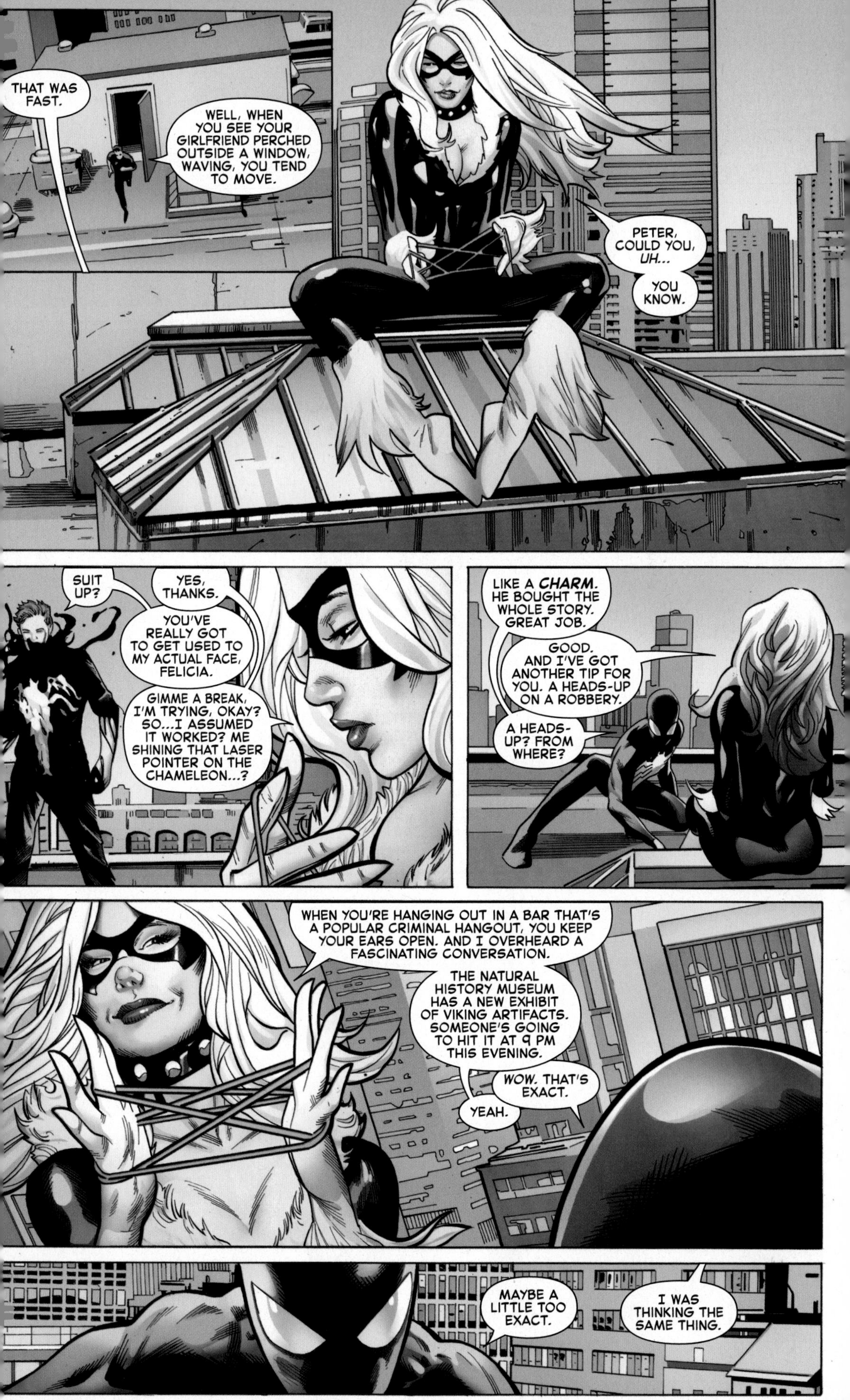
THAT WAS FAST.
WELL, WHEN YOU SEE YOUR GIRLFRIEND PERCHED OUTSIDE A WINDOW, WAVING, YOU TEND TO MOVE.
PETER, COULD YOU, *UH...*
YOU KNOW.
SUIT UP?
YES, THANKS.
YOU'VE REALLY GOT TO GET USED TO MY ACTUAL FACE, FELICIA.
GIMME A BREAK, I'M TRYING, OKAY? SO...I ASSUMED IT WORKED? ME SHINING THAT LASER POINTER ON THE CHAMELEON...?
LIKE A ***CHARM.*** HE BOUGHT THE WHOLE STORY. GREAT JOB.
GOOD. AND I'VE GOT ANOTHER TIP FOR YOU. A HEADS-UP ON A ROBBERY.
A HEADS-UP? FROM WHERE?
WHEN YOU'RE HANGING OUT IN A BAR THAT'S A POPULAR CRIMINAL HANGOUT, YOU KEEP YOUR EARS OPEN. AND I OVERHEARD A FASCINATING CONVERSATION.
THE NATURAL HISTORY MUSEUM HAS A NEW EXHIBIT OF VIKING ARTIFACTS. SOMEONE'S GOING TO HIT IT AT 9 PM THIS EVENING.
WOW. THAT'S EXACT.
YEAH.
MAYBE A LITTLE TOO EXACT.
I WAS THINKING THE SAME THING.

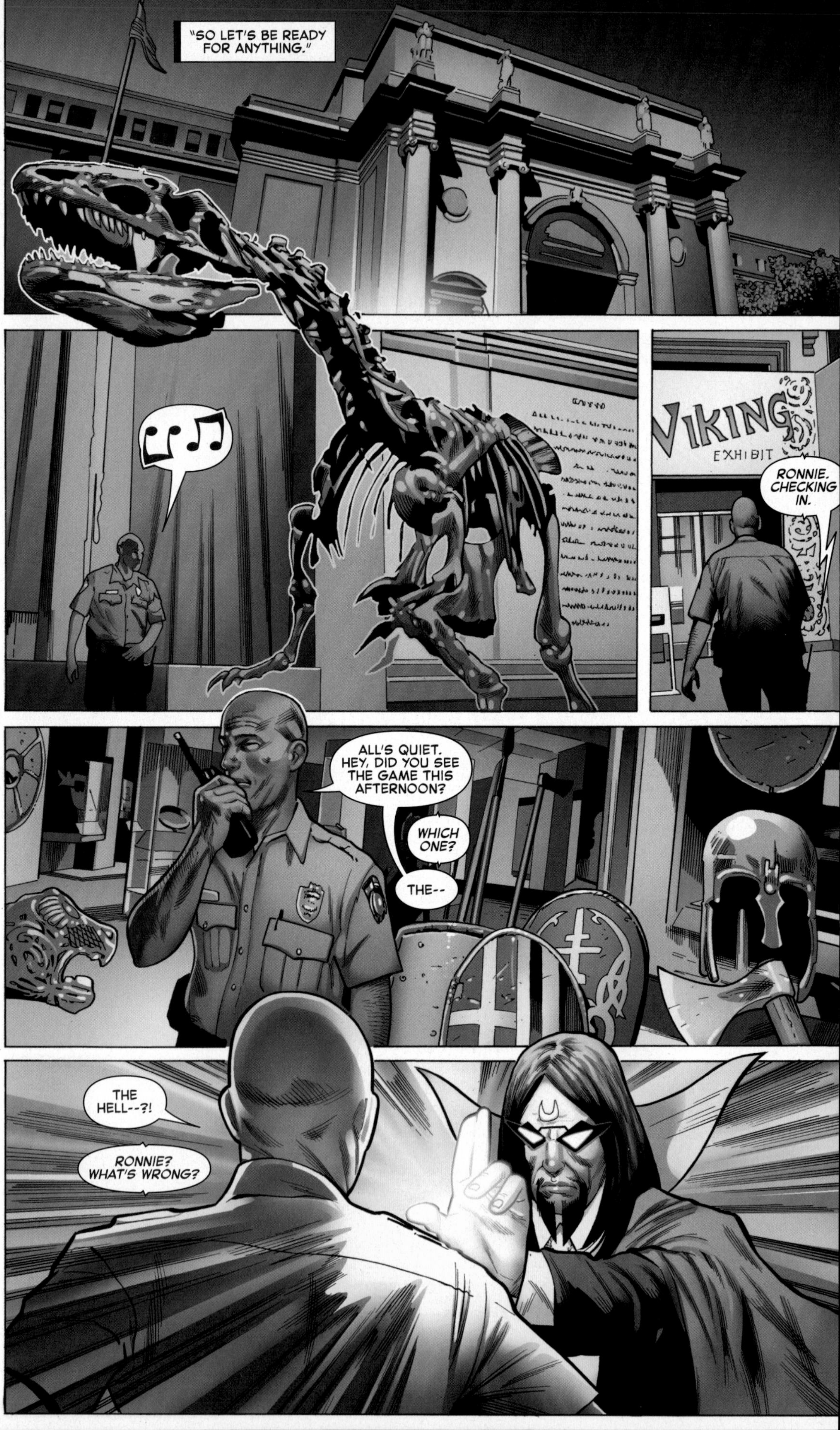
"SO LET'S BE READY FOR ANYTHING."
VIKING EXHIBIT
RONNIE. CHECKING IN.
ALL'S QUIET. HEY, DID YOU SEE THE GAME THIS AFTERNOON?
WHICH ONE?
THE--
THE HELL--?!
RONNIE? WHAT'S WRONG?

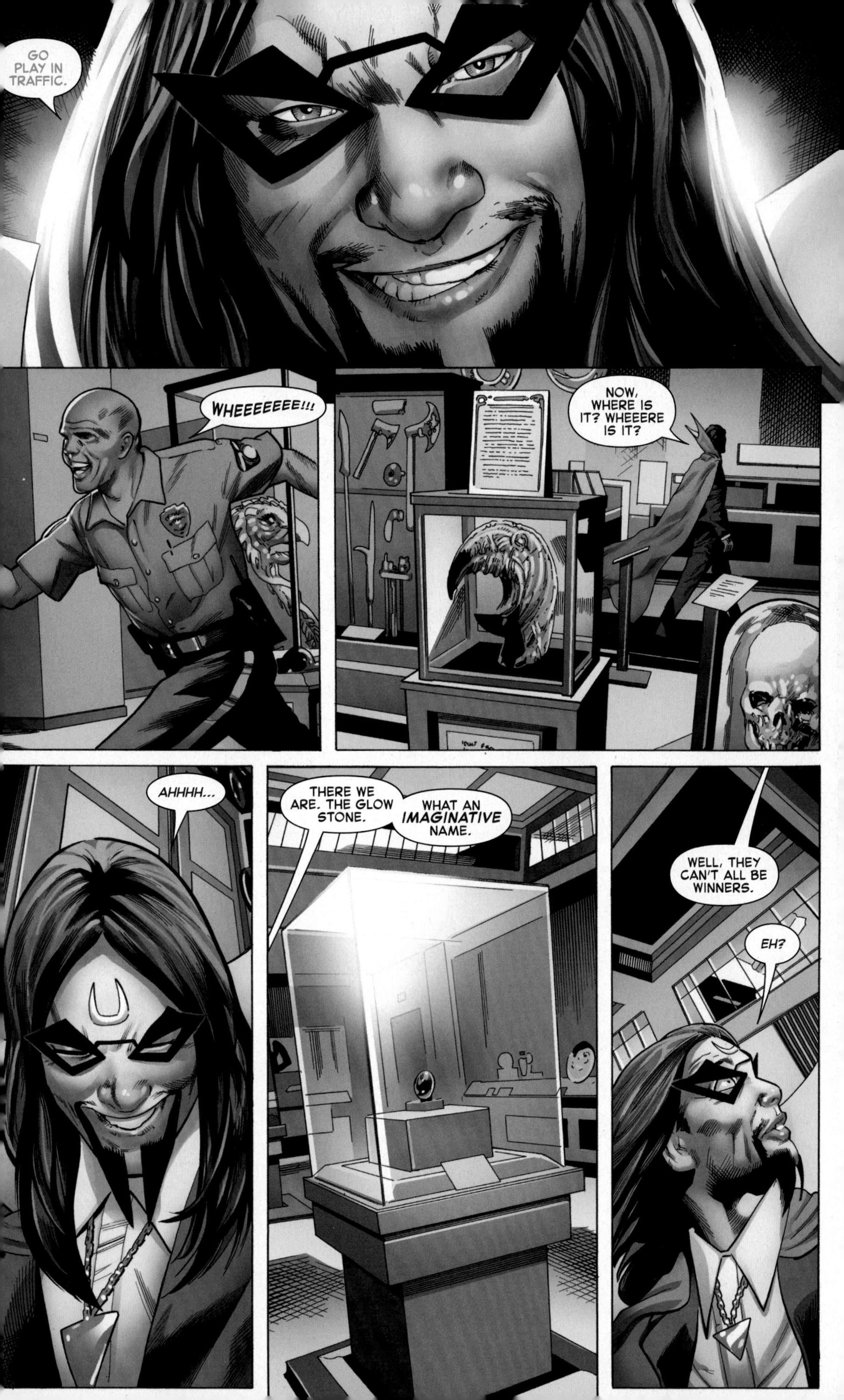
GO PLAY IN TRAFFIC.
WHEEEEEEE!!!
NOW, WHERE IS IT? WHEEERE IS IT?
AHHHH...
THERE WE ARE. THE GLOW STONE.
WHAT AN *IMAGINATIVE* NAME.
WELL, THEY CAN'T ALL BE WINNERS.
EH?

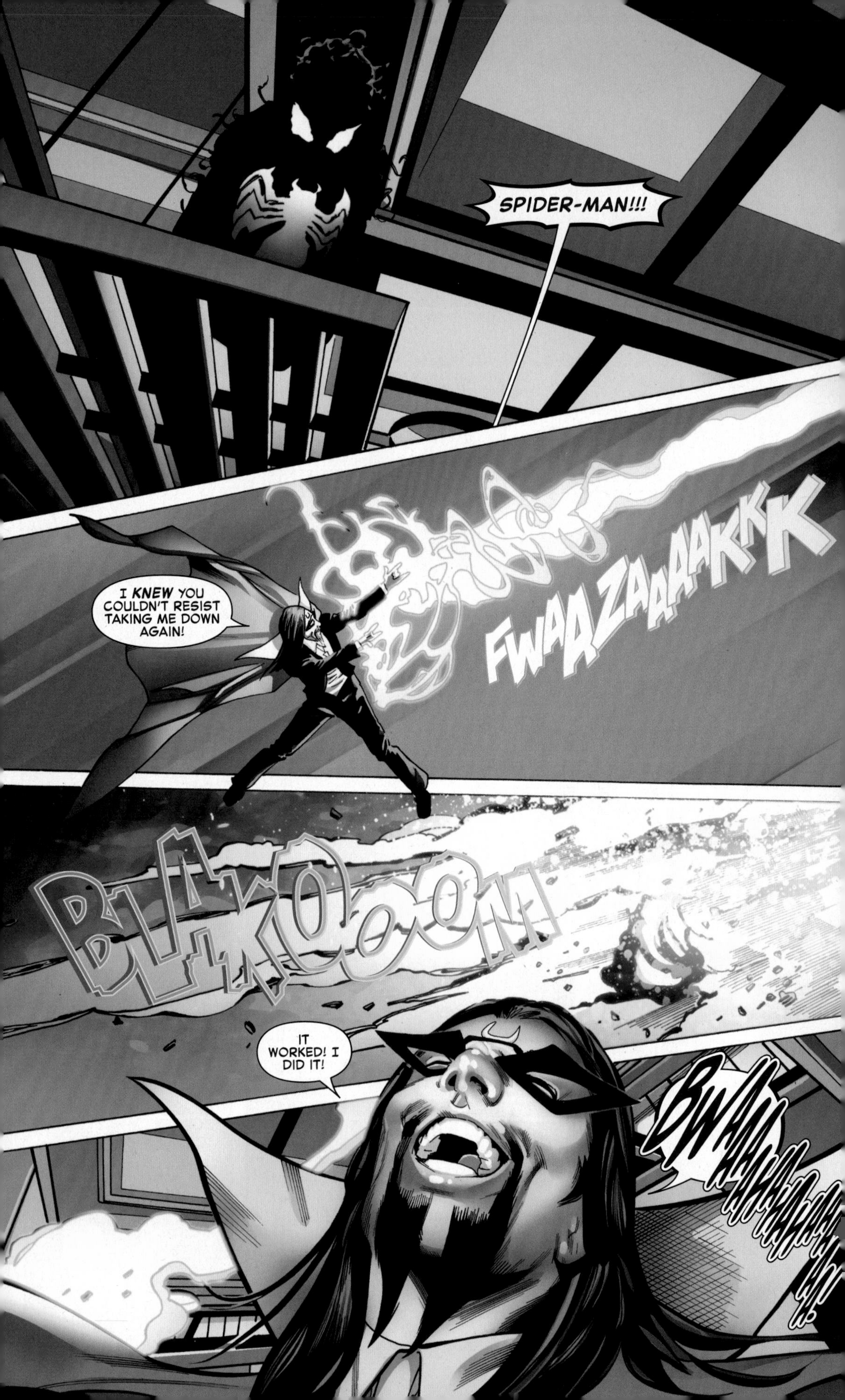
SPIDER-MAN!!!
I KNEW YOU COULDN'T RESIST TAKING ME DOWN AGAIN!
FWAAZAAAAKKK
BLAKOOOM
IT WORKED! I DID IT!

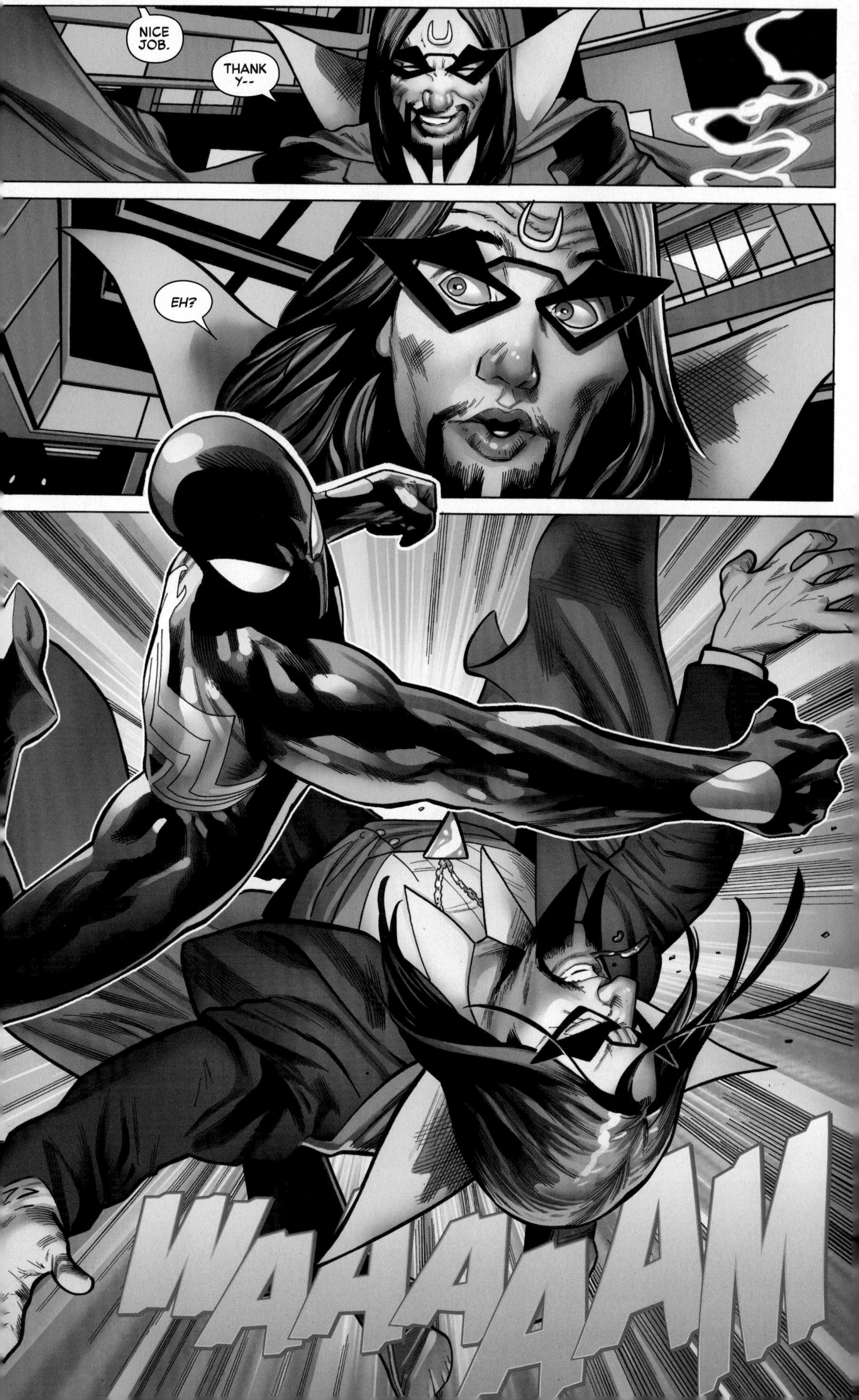

NICE JOB.
THANK Y--
EH?
WHAAAM

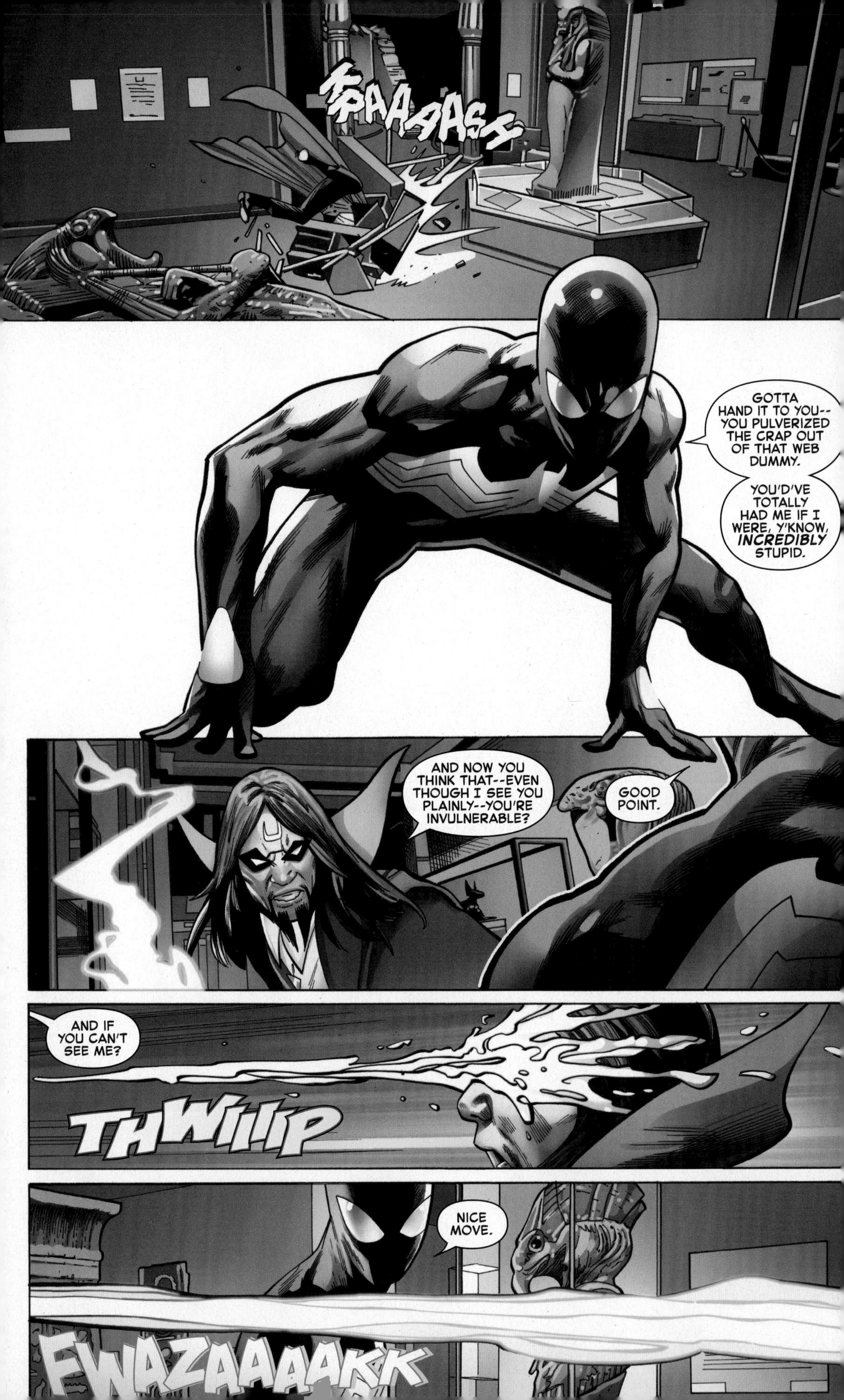
KRRAAAASH
GOTTA HAND IT TO YOU--YOU PULVERIZED THE CRAP OUT OF THAT WEB DUMMY.
YOU'D'VE TOTALLY HAD ME IF I WERE, Y'KNOW, *INCREDIBLY* STUPID.
AND NOW YOU THINK THAT--EVEN THOUGH I SEE YOU PLAINLY--YOU'RE INVULNERABLE?
GOOD POINT.
AND IF YOU CAN'T SEE ME?
THWIIIP
NICE MOVE.
FWAZAAAAKK

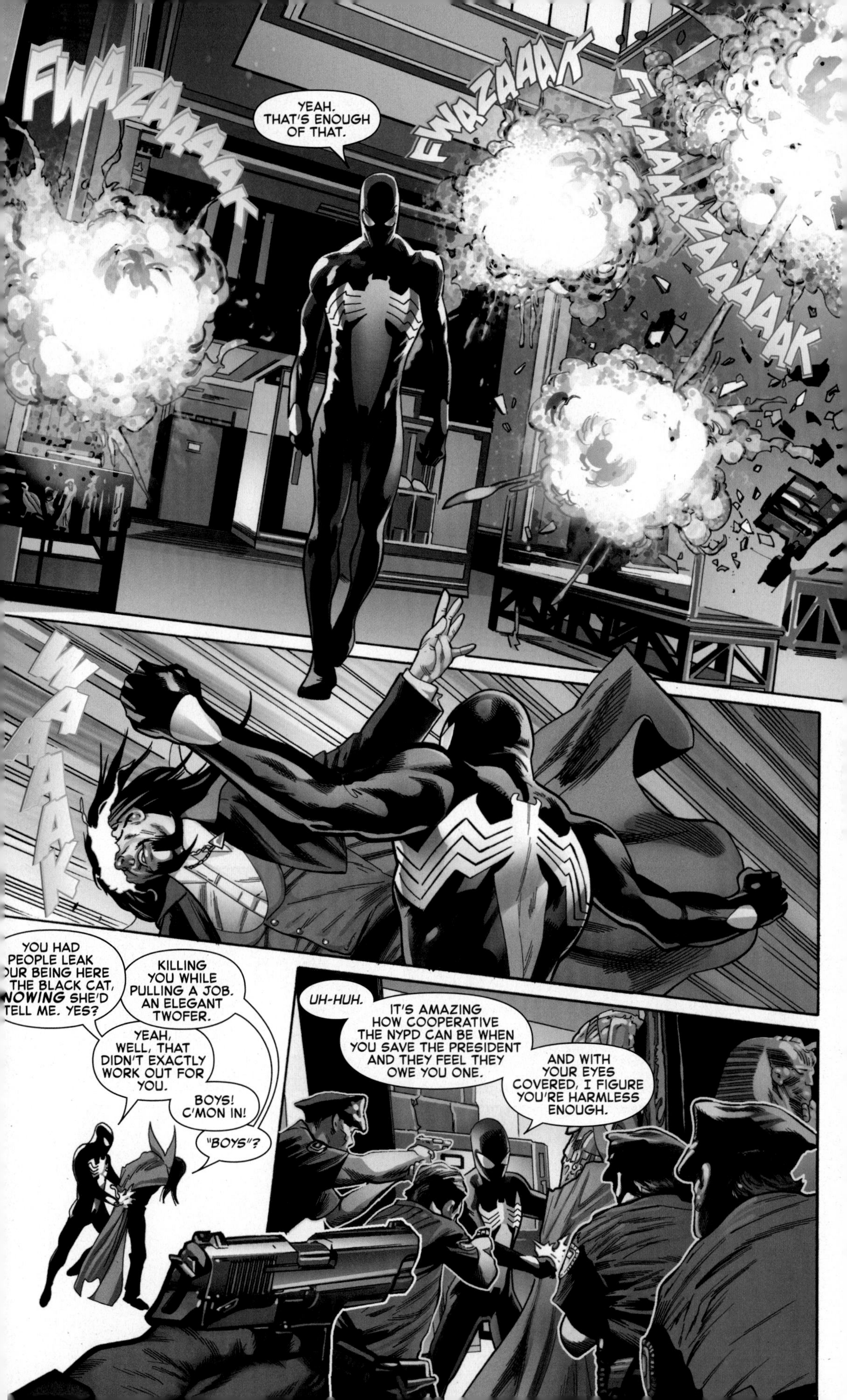
FWAZAAAAAK
YEAH. THAT'S ENOUGH OF THAT.
FWAZAAAK
FWAAAZAAAAAAK
WAAAAAK
YOU HAD PEOPLE LEAK OUR BEING HERE THE BLACK CAT, NOWING SHE'D TELL ME. YES?
KILLING YOU WHILE PULLING A JOB. AN ELEGANT TWOFER.
YEAH, WELL, THAT DIDN'T EXACTLY WORK OUT FOR YOU.
BOYS! C'MON IN!
"BOYS"?
UH-HUH.
IT'S AMAZING HOW COOPERATIVE THE NYPD CAN BE WHEN YOU SAVE THE PRESIDENT AND THEY FEEL THEY OWE YOU ONE.
AND WITH YOUR EYES COVERED, I FIGURE YOU'RE HARMLESS ENOUGH.

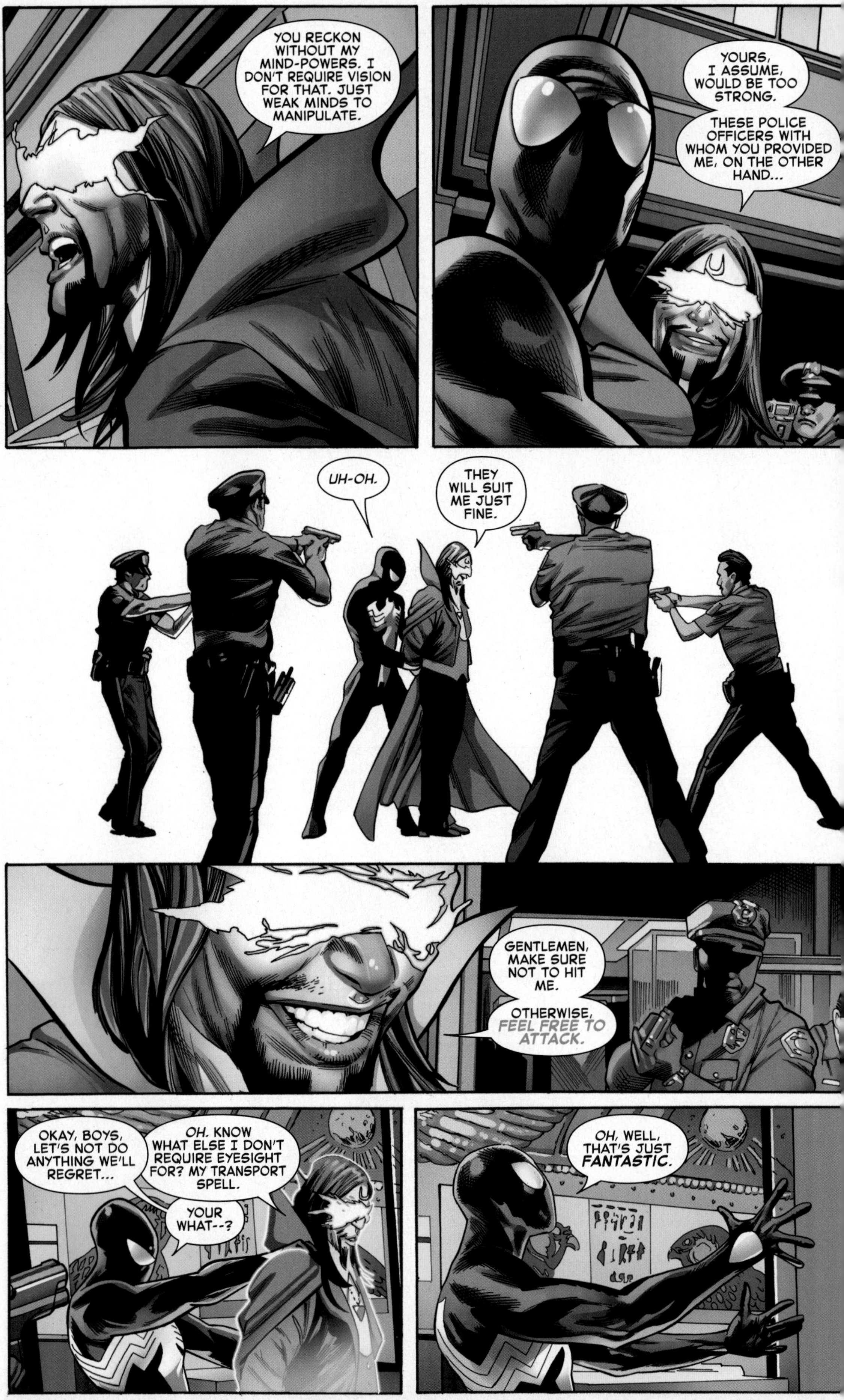
YOU RECKON WITHOUT MY MIND-POWERS. I DON'T REQUIRE VISION FOR THAT. JUST WEAK MINDS TO MANIPULATE.
YOURS, I ASSUME, WOULD BE TOO STRONG.
THESE POLICE OFFICERS WITH WHOM YOU PROVIDED ME, ON THE OTHER HAND...
UH-OH.
THEY WILL SUIT ME JUST FINE.
GENTLEMEN, MAKE SURE NOT TO HIT ME.
OTHERWISE, FEEL FREE TO ATTACK.
OKAY, BOYS, LET'S NOT DO ANYTHING WE'LL REGRET...
OH. KNOW WHAT ELSE I DON'T REQUIRE EYESIGHT FOR? MY TRANSPORT SPELL.
YOUR WHAT--?
OH, WELL, THAT'S JUST FANTASTIC.

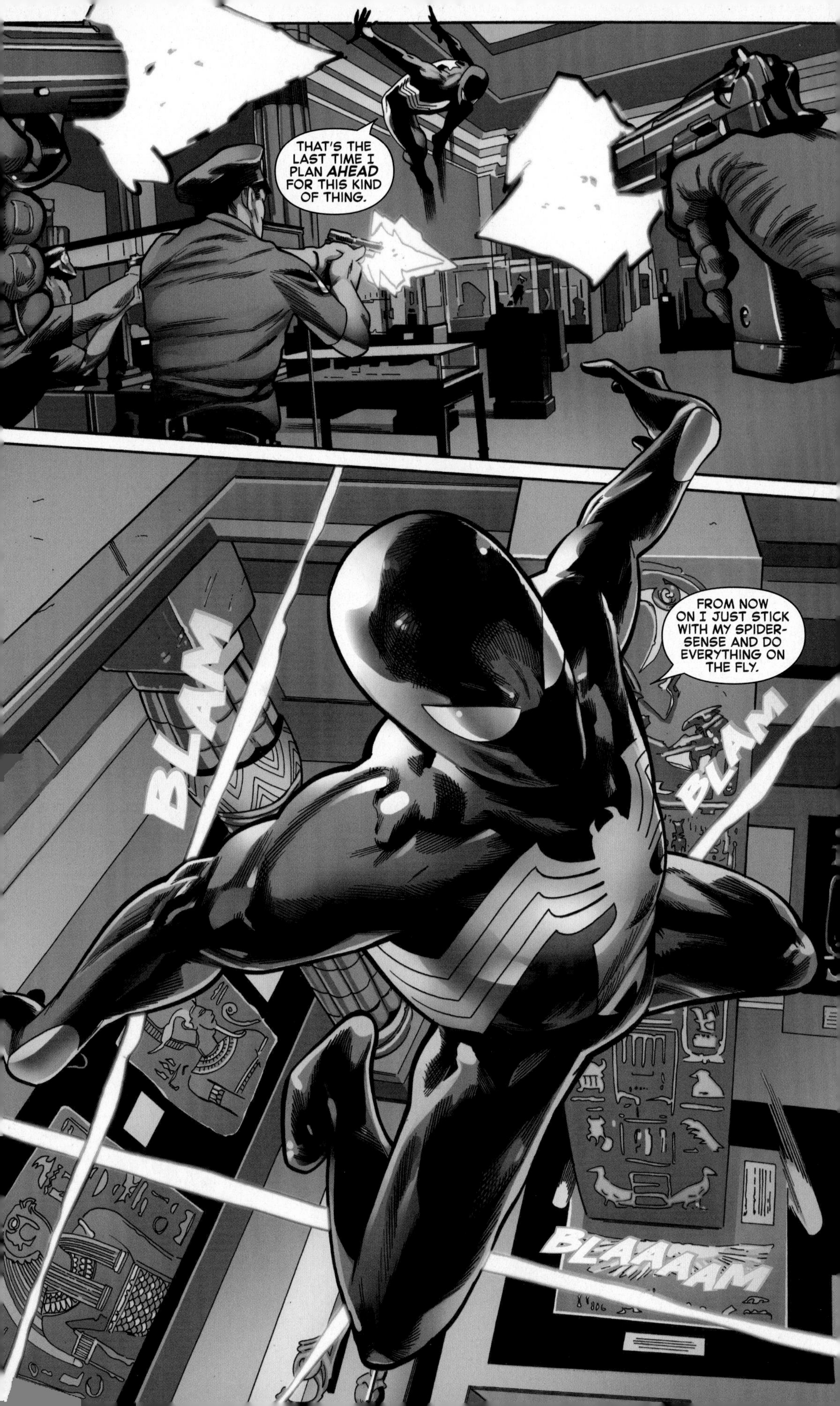
THAT'S THE LAST TIME I PLAN AHEAD FOR THIS KIND OF THING.
FROM NOW ON I JUST STICK WITH MY SPIDER-SENSE AND DO EVERYTHING ON THE FLY.
BLAM
BLAM
BLAAAAAM

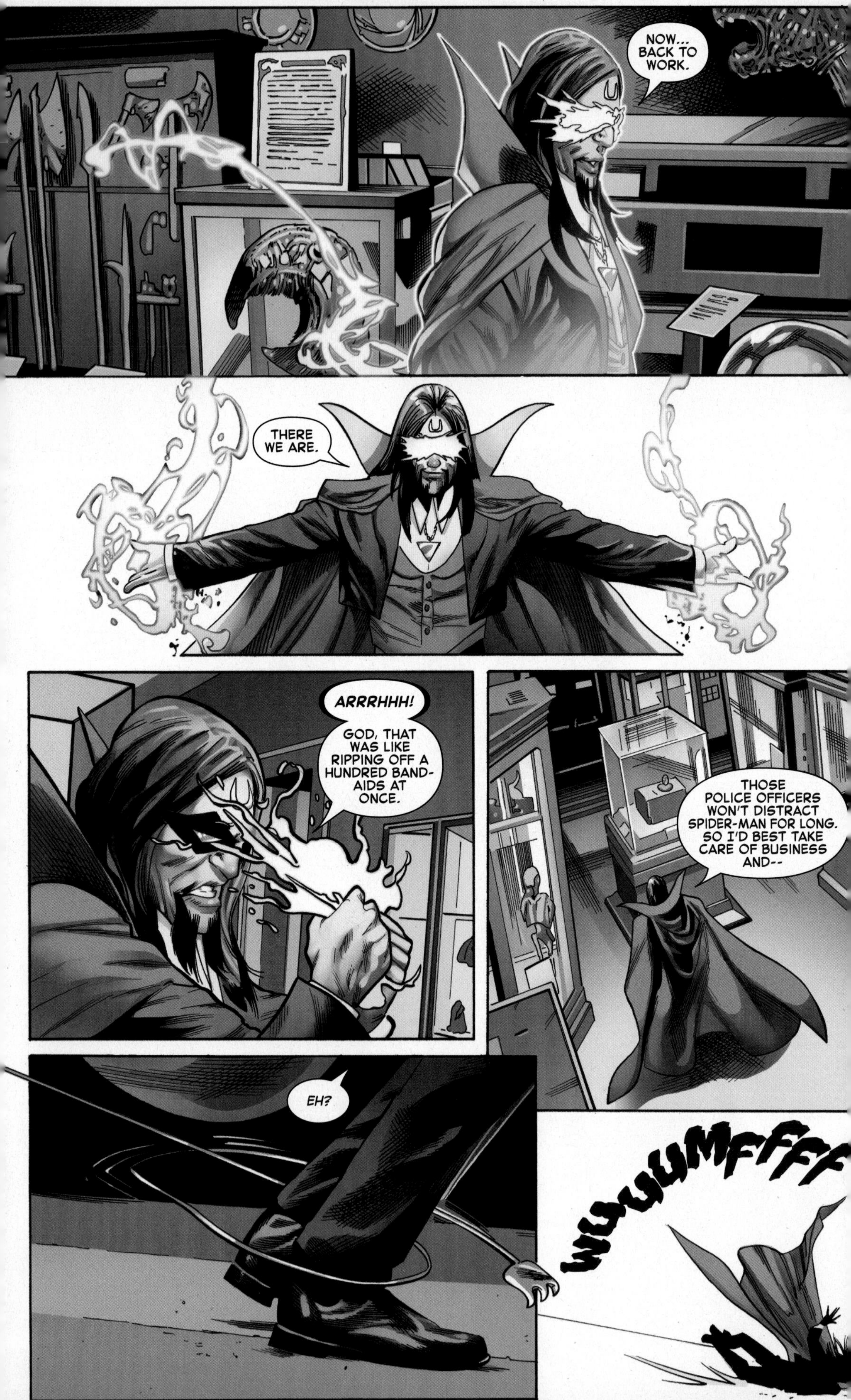
NOW... BACK TO WORK.
THERE WE ARE.
ARRRHHH!
GOD, THAT WAS LIKE RIPPING OFF A HUNDRED BAND-AIDS AT ONCE.
THOSE POLICE OFFICERS WON'T DISTRACT SPIDER-MAN FOR LONG. SO I'D BEST TAKE CARE OF BUSINESS AND--
EH?
WUUUMFFFF

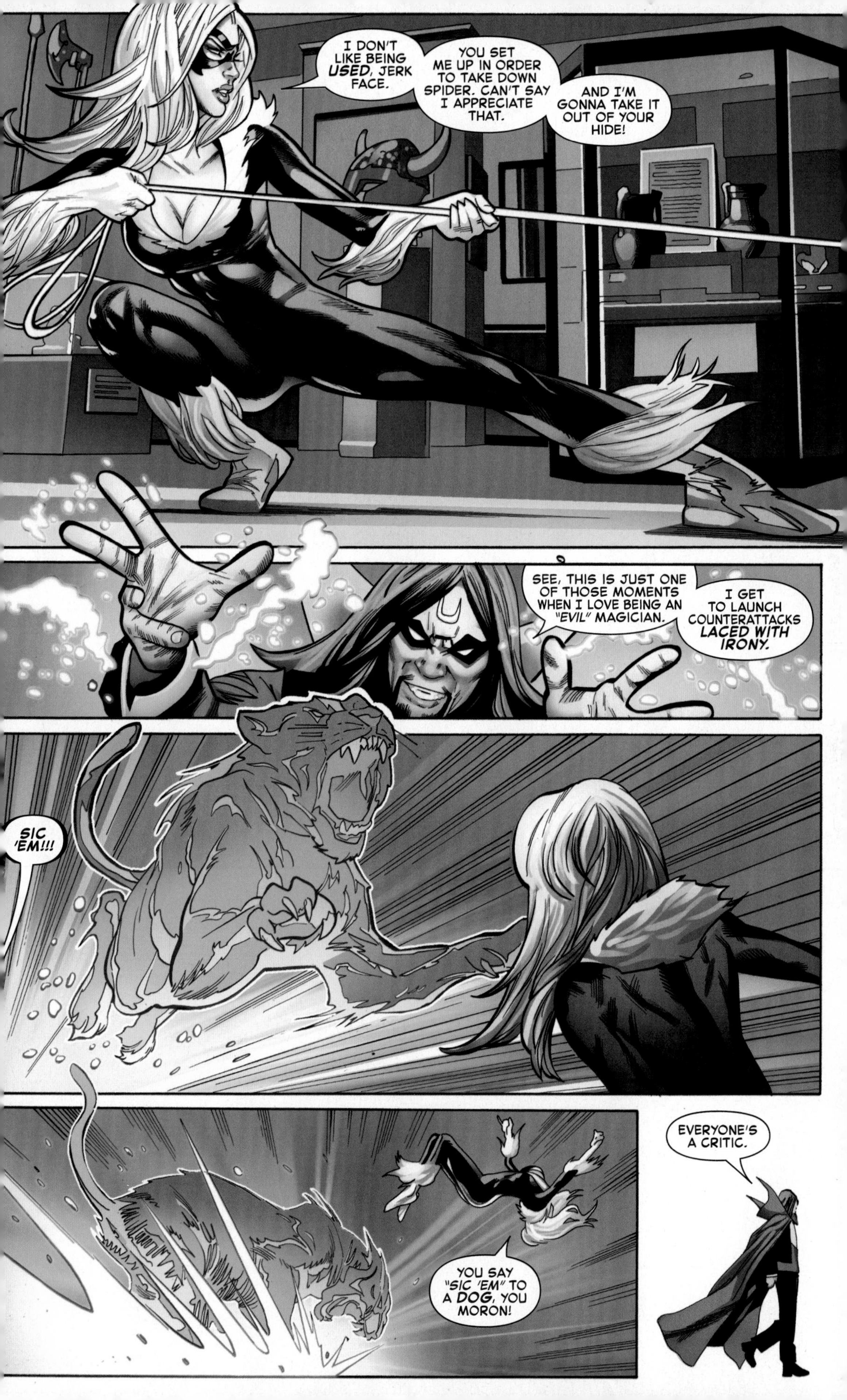
I DON'T LIKE BEING USED, JERK FACE.
YOU SET ME UP IN ORDER TO TAKE DOWN SPIDER. CAN'T SAY I APPRECIATE THAT.
AND I'M GONNA TAKE IT OUT OF YOUR HIDE!
SEE, THIS IS JUST ONE OF THOSE MOMENTS WHEN I LOVE BEING AN "EVIL" MAGICIAN.
I GET TO LAUNCH COUNTERATTACKS LACED WITH IRONY.
SIC 'EM!!!
YOU SAY "SIC 'EM" TO A DOG, YOU MORON!
EVERYONE'S A CRITIC.

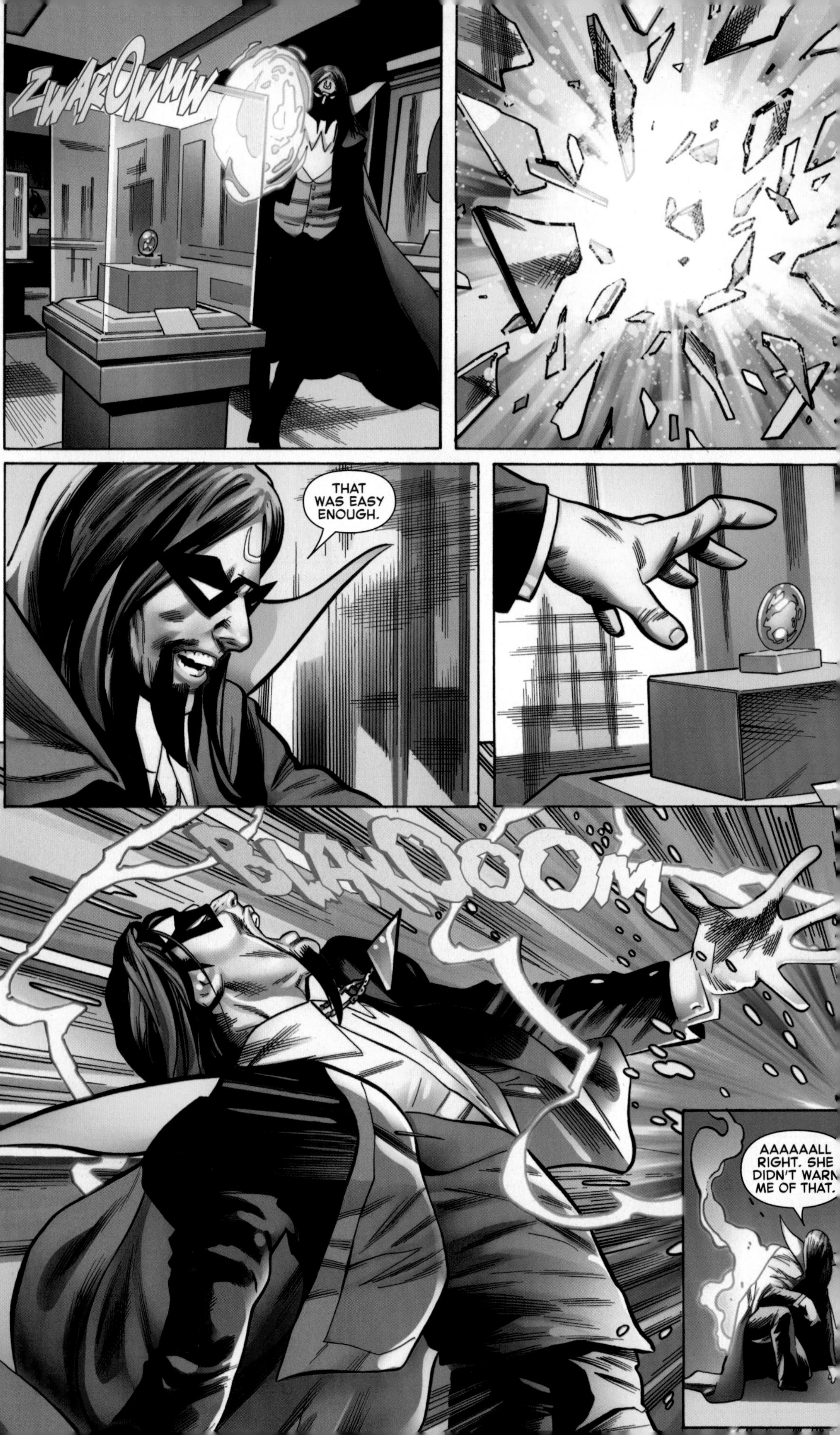
ZWAKOWWW
THAT WAS EASY ENOUGH.
BLAKOOOM
AAAAAALL RIGHT. SHE DIDN'T WARN ME OF THAT.

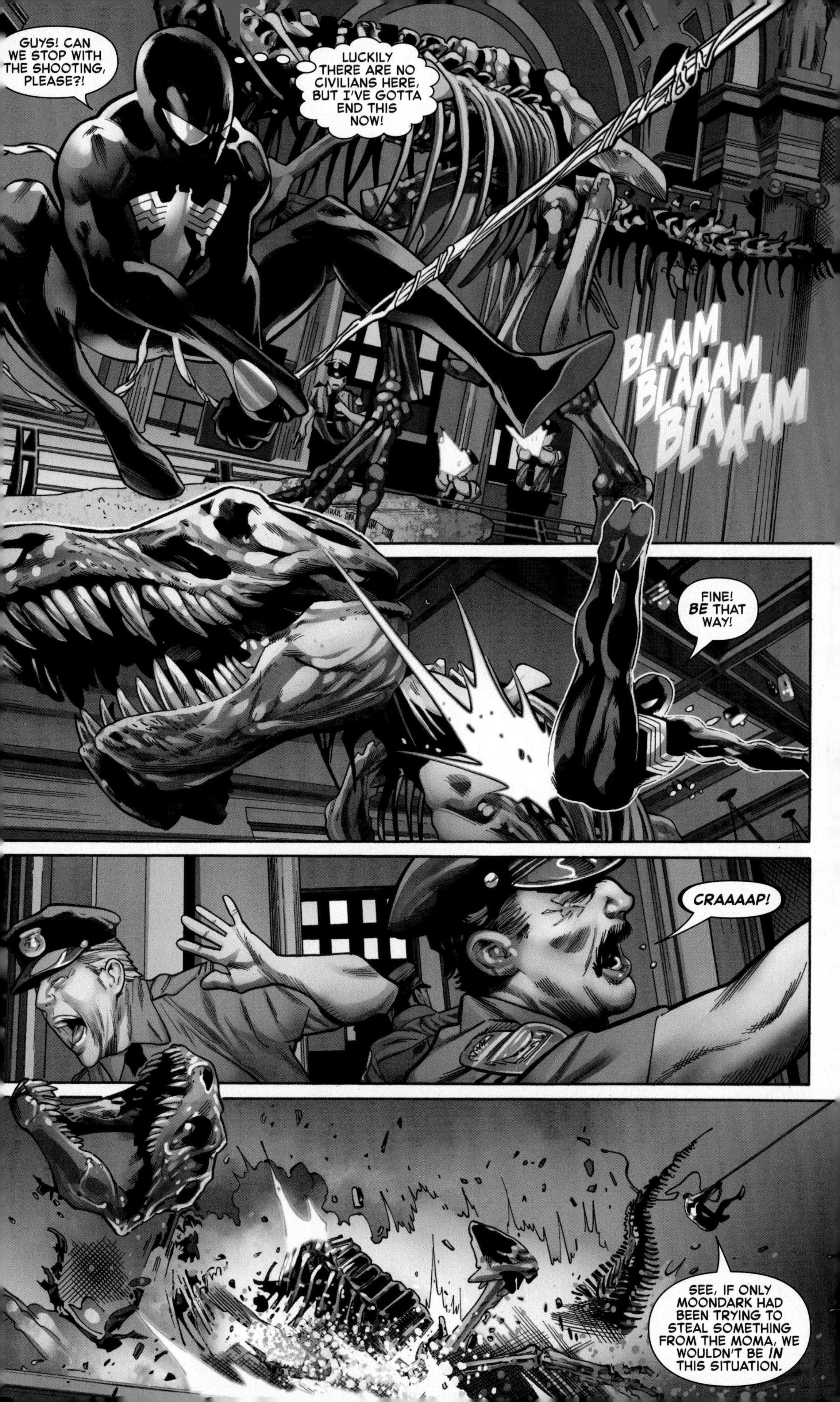
GUYS! CAN WE STOP WITH THE SHOOTING, PLEASE?!
LUCKILY THERE ARE NO CIVILIANS HERE, BUT I'VE GOTTA END THIS NOW!
BLAAM BLAAAM BLAAAM
FINE! BE THAT WAY!
CRAAAAP!
SEE, IF ONLY MOONDARK HAD BEEN TRYING TO STEAL SOMETHING FROM THE MOMA, WE WOULDN'T BE IN THIS SITUATION.

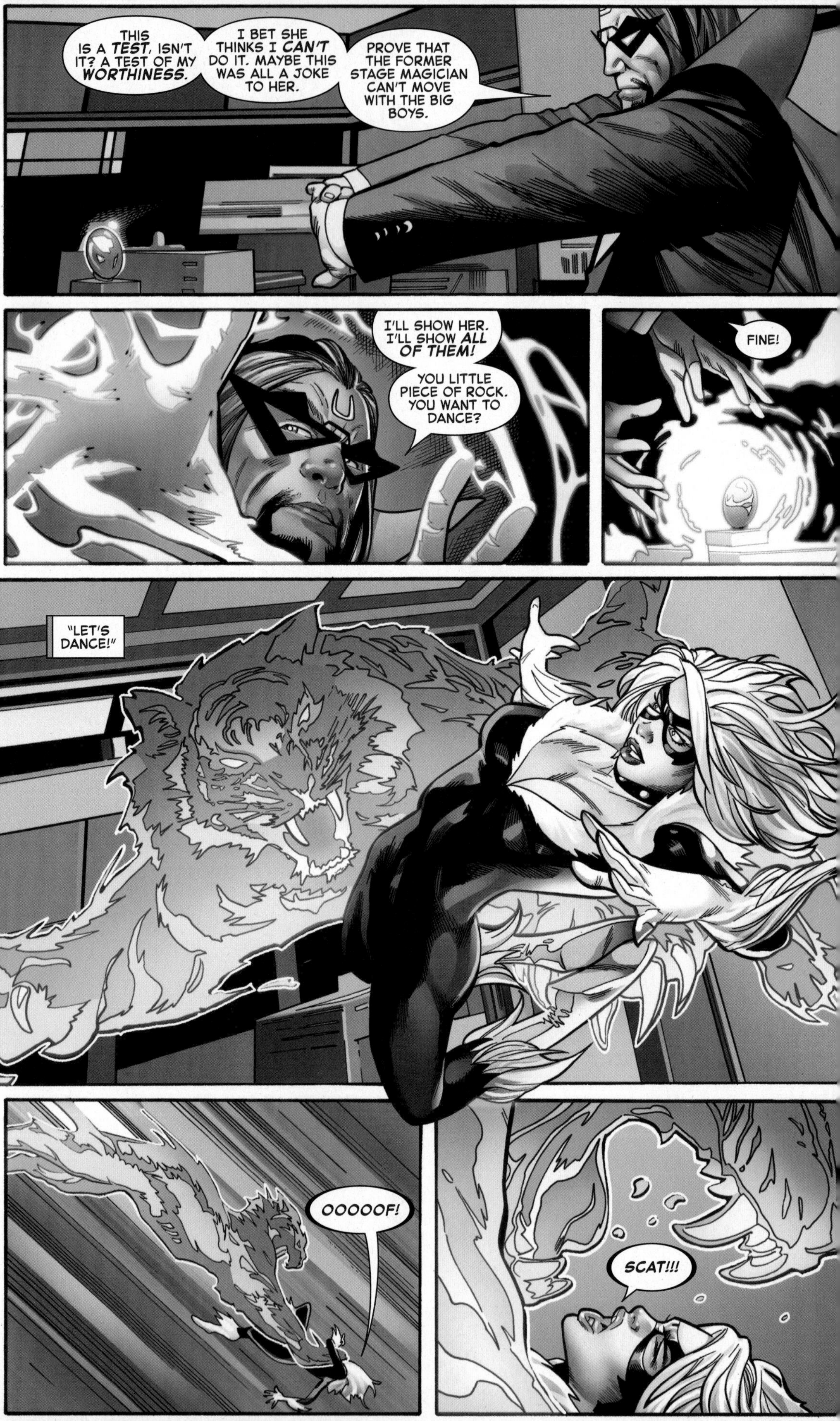

THIS IS A *TEST*, ISN'T IT? A TEST OF MY *WORTHINESS*.
I BET SHE THINKS I *CAN'T* DO IT. MAYBE THIS WAS ALL A JOKE TO HER.
PROVE THAT THE FORMER STAGE MAGICIAN CAN'T MOVE WITH THE BIG BOYS.
I'LL SHOW HER. I'LL SHOW *ALL OF THEM!*
YOU LITTLE PIECE OF ROCK. YOU WANT TO DANCE?
FINE!
"LET'S DANCE!"
OOOOOF!
SCAT!!!

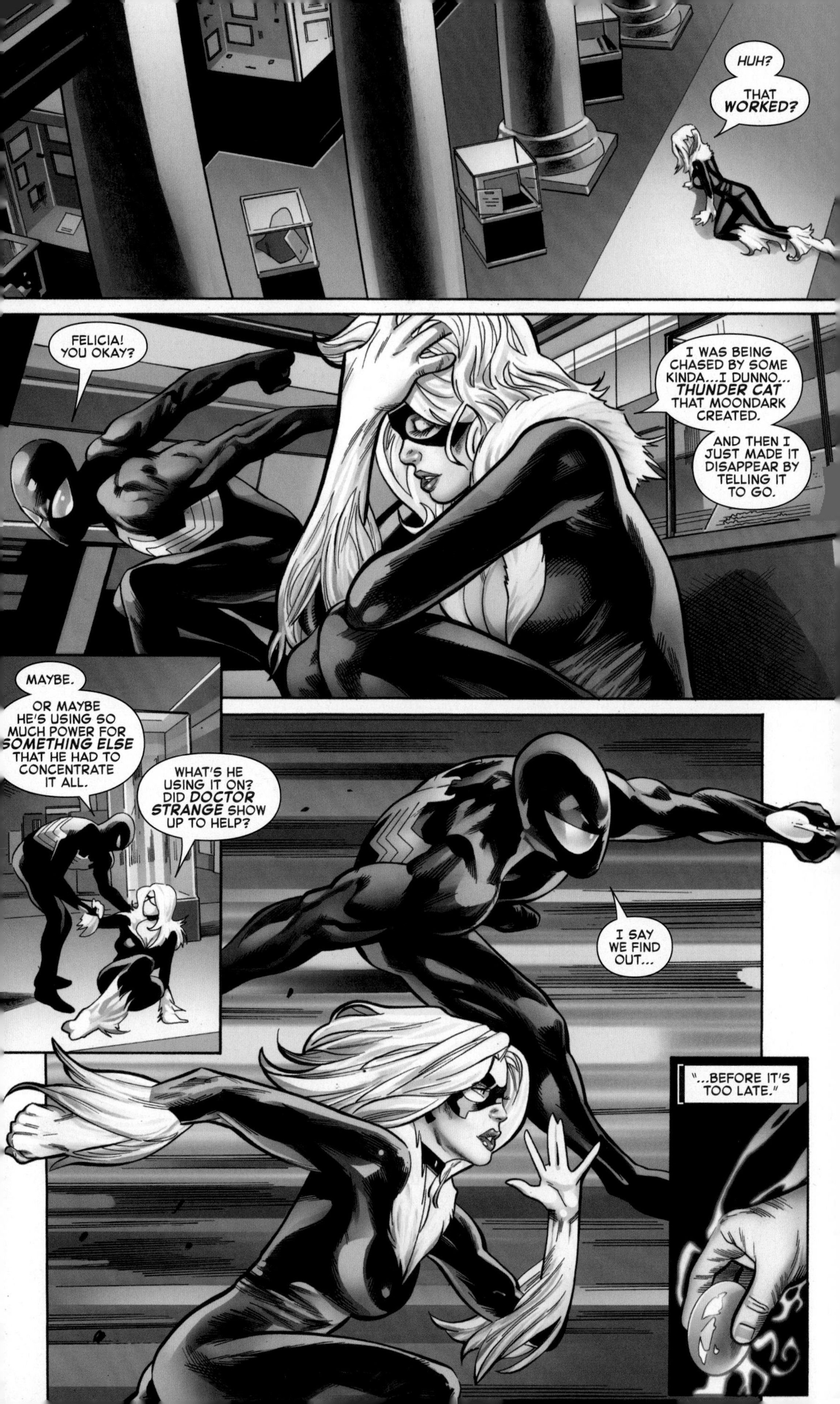
HUH?
THAT WORKED?
FELICIA! YOU OKAY?
I WAS BEING CHASED BY SOME KINDA...I DUNNO... THUNDER CAT THAT MOONDARK CREATED.
AND THEN I JUST MADE IT DISAPPEAR BY TELLING IT TO GO.
MAYBE.
OR MAYBE HE'S USING SO MUCH POWER FOR SOMETHING ELSE THAT HE HAD TO CONCENTRATE IT ALL.
WHAT'S HE USING IT ON? DID DOCTOR STRANGE SHOW UP TO HELP?
I SAY WE FIND OUT...
"...BEFORE IT'S TOO LATE."

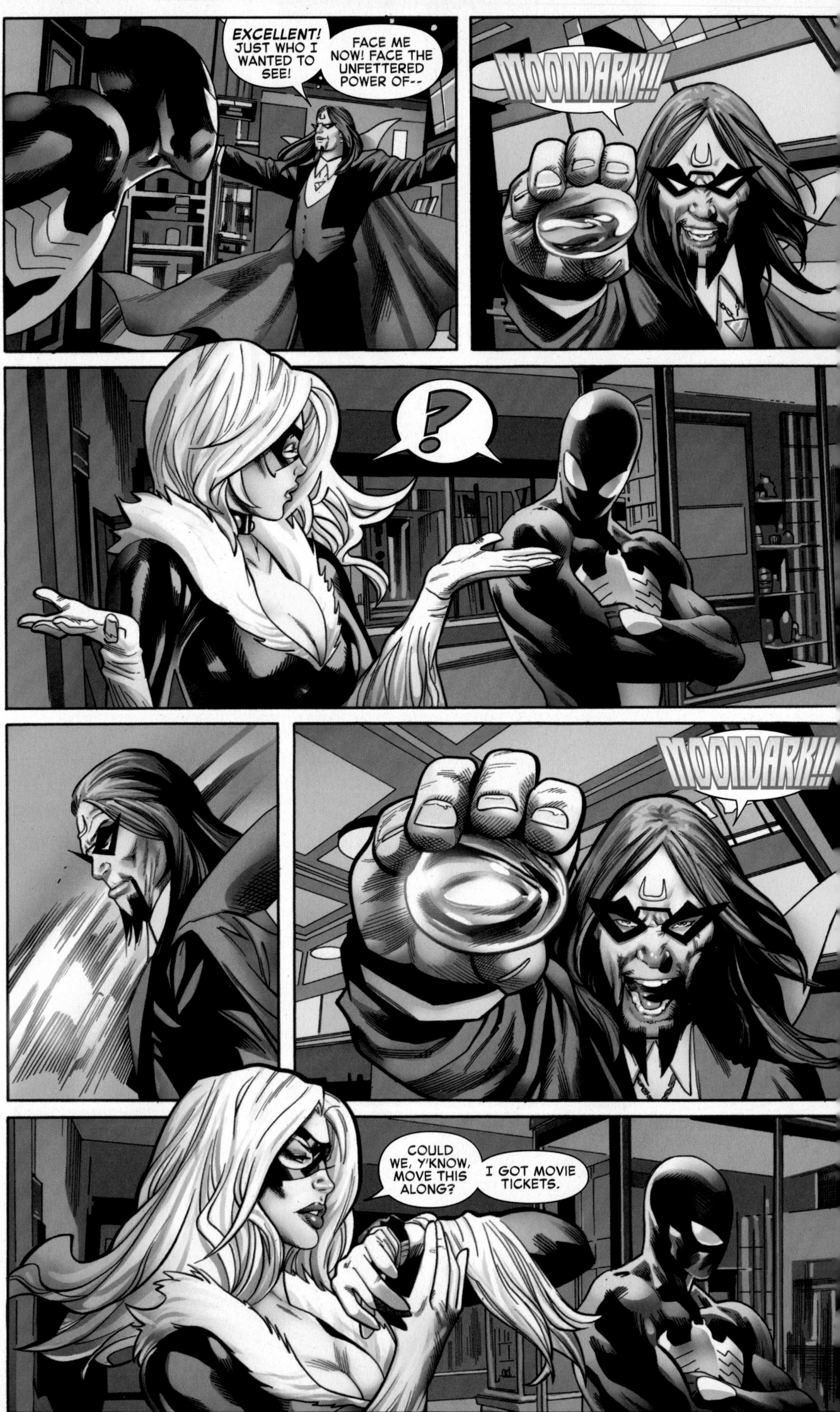
EXCELLENT! JUST WHO I WANTED TO SEE!
FACE ME NOW! FACE THE UNFETTERED POWER OF--
MOONDARK!!!
?
MOONDARK!!!
COULD WE, Y'KNOW, MOVE THIS ALONG?
I GOT MOVIE TICKETS.

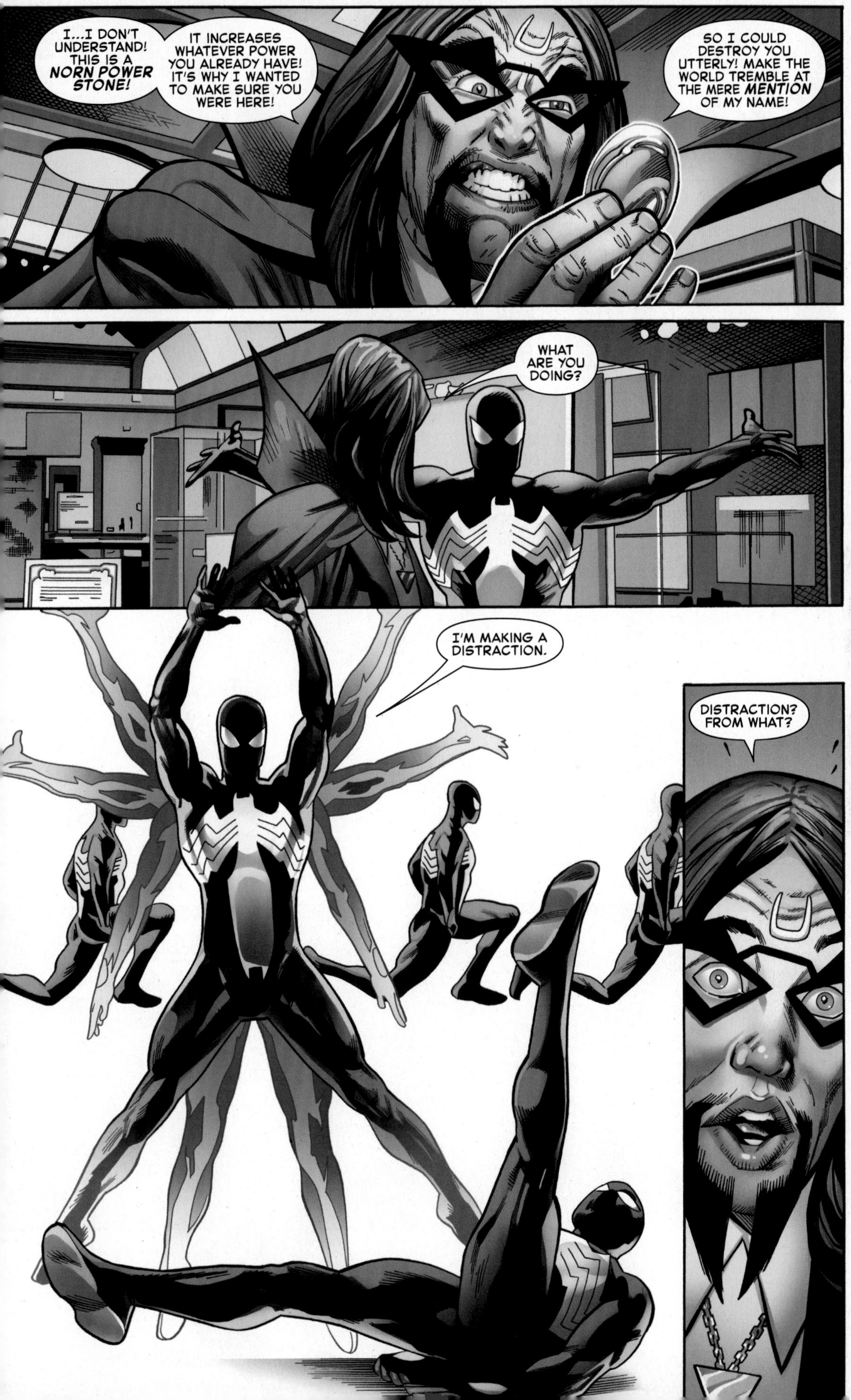
I...I DON'T UNDERSTAND! THIS IS A NORN POWER STONE!
IT INCREASES WHATEVER POWER YOU ALREADY HAVE! IT'S WHY I WANTED TO MAKE SURE YOU WERE HERE!
SO I COULD DESTROY YOU UTTERLY! MAKE THE WORLD TREMBLE AT THE MERE MENTION OF MY NAME!
WHAT ARE YOU DOING?
I'M MAKING A DISTRACTION.
DISTRACTION? FROM WHAT?

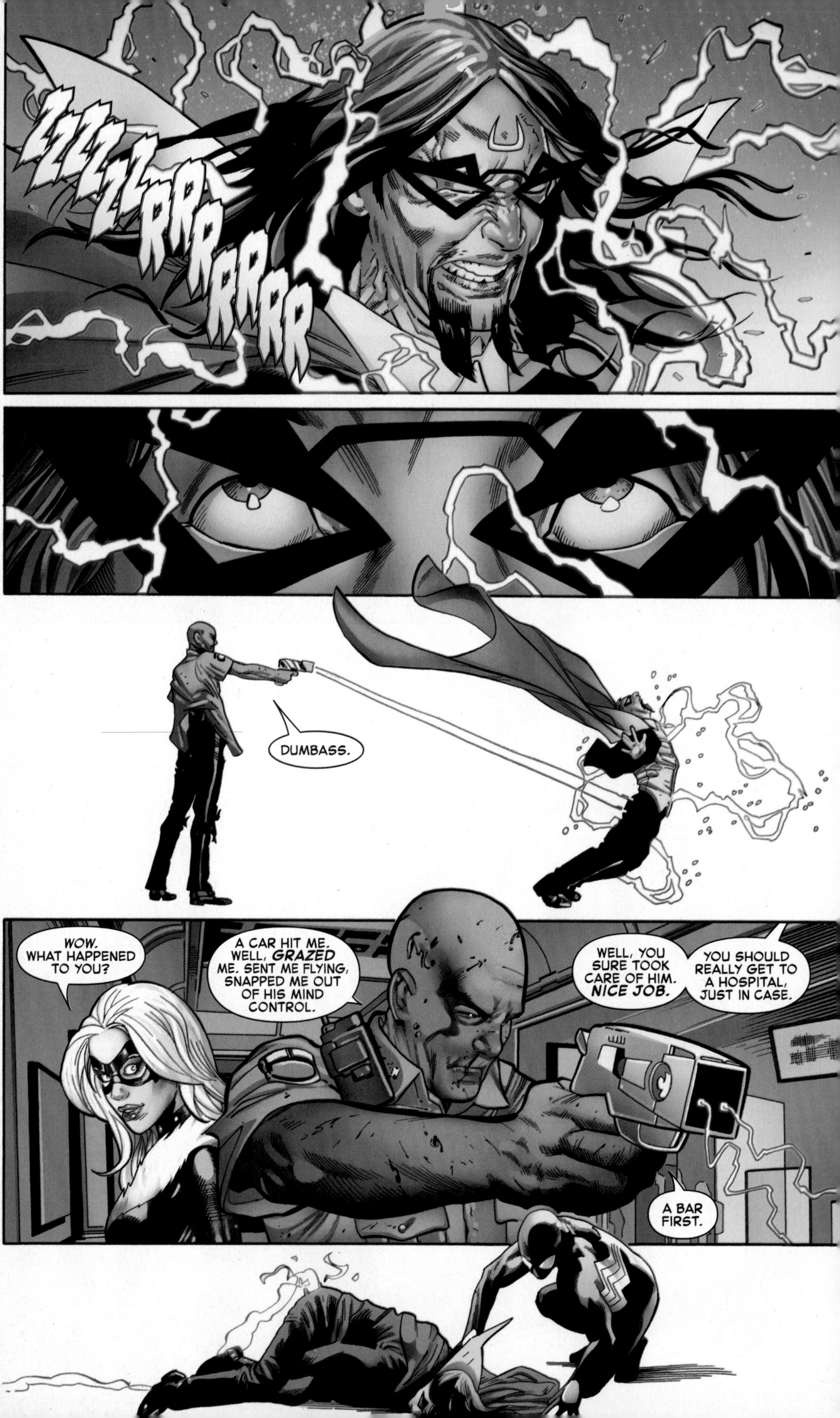
ZZZZZZRRRRRRRR
DUMBASS.
WOW. WHAT HAPPENED TO YOU?
A CAR HIT ME. WELL, GRAZED ME. SENT ME FLYING, SNAPPED ME OUT OF HIS MIND CONTROL.
WELL, YOU SURE TOOK CARE OF HIM. NICE JOB.
YOU SHOULD REALLY GET TO A HOSPITAL, JUST IN CASE.
A BAR FIRST.

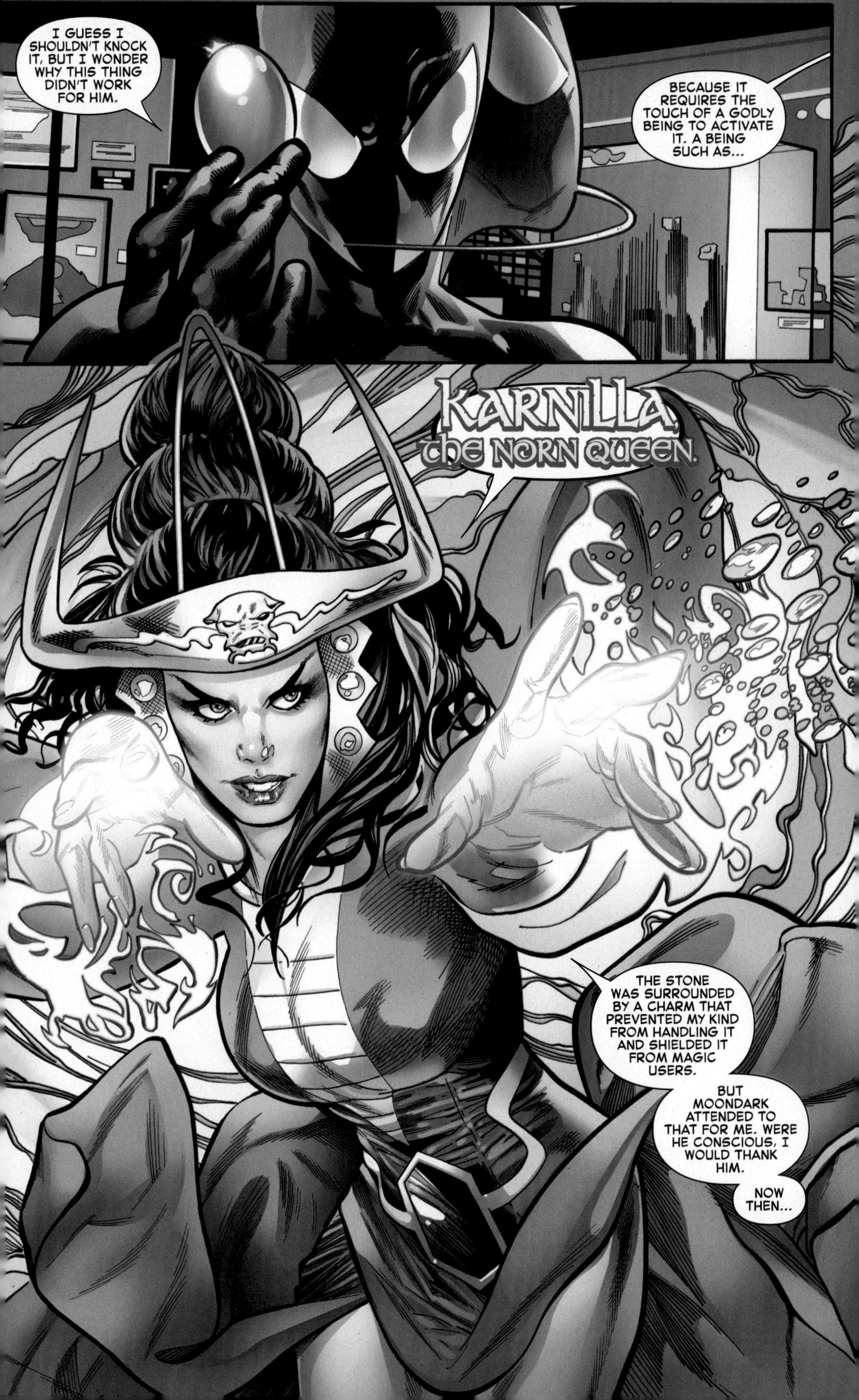

I GUESS I SHOULDN'T KNOCK IT, BUT I WONDER WHY THIS THING DIDN'T WORK FOR HIM.
BECAUSE IT REQUIRES THE TOUCH OF A GODLY BEING TO ACTIVATE IT. A BEING SUCH AS...
KARNILLA, THE NORN QUEEN.
THE STONE WAS SURROUNDED BY A CHARM THAT PREVENTED MY KIND FROM HANDLING IT AND SHIELDED IT FROM MAGIC USERS.
BUT MOONDARK ATTENDED TO THAT FOR ME. WERE HE CONSCIOUS, I WOULD THANK HIM.
NOW THEN...

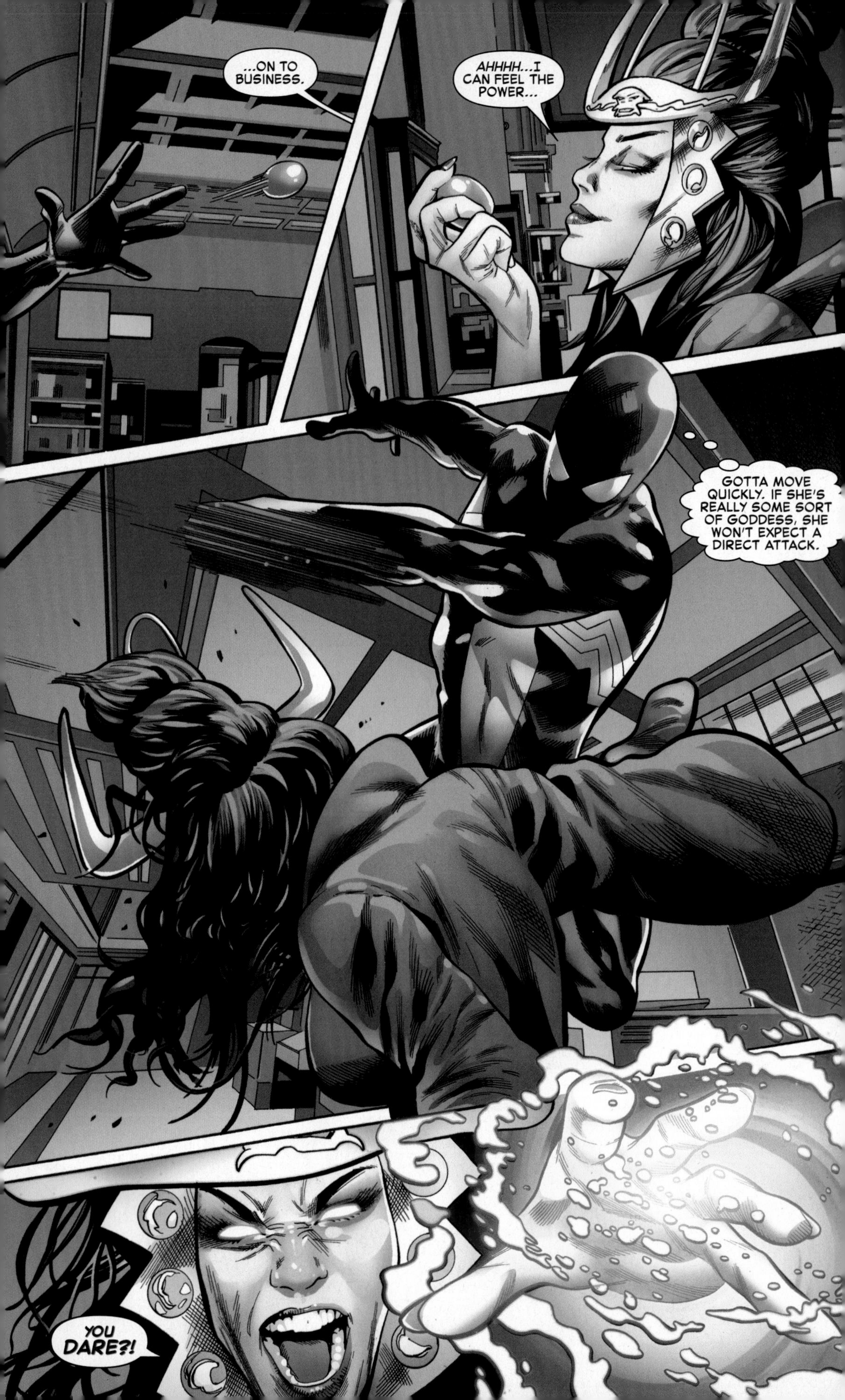
...ON TO BUSINESS.
AHHHH...I CAN FEEL THE POWER...
GOTTA MOVE QUICKLY. IF SHE'S REALLY SOME SORT OF GODDESS, SHE WON'T EXPECT A DIRECT ATTACK.
YOU DARE?!

UH-OH.

SPIDER!!! LOOK OUT!

I'M NOT EVEN GOING TO BOTHER BATTLING YOU.

FAREWELLL, YOU PATHETIC MORT--

WHAT?! NO!!!

THWIP

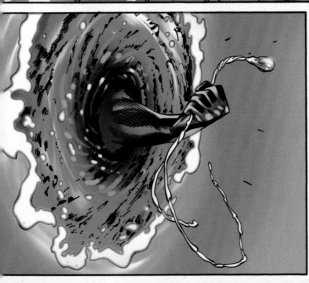

NOOOO!!!

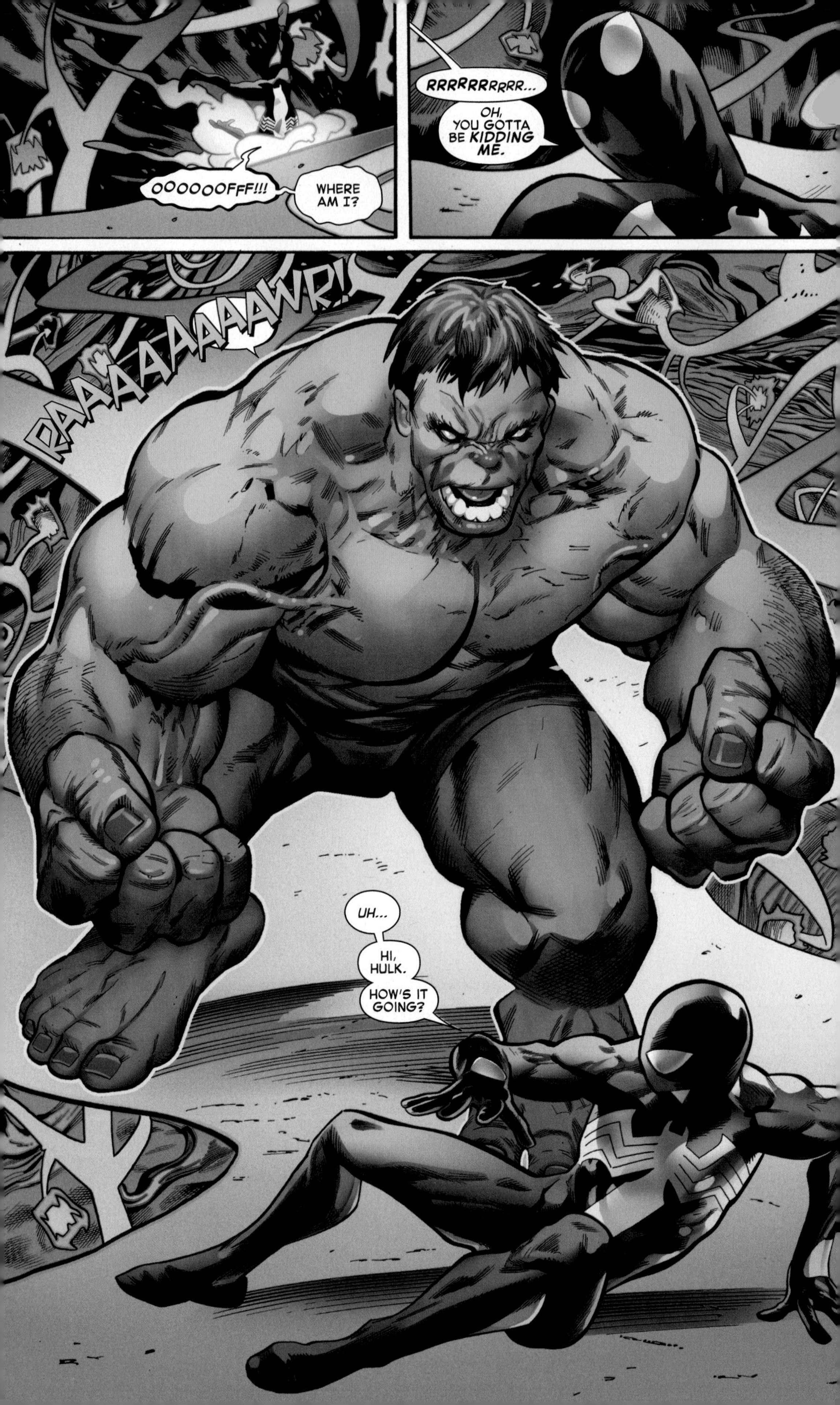
OOOOOOFFF!!!
WHERE AM I?
RRRRRRRRRR...
OH, YOU GOTTA BE KIDDING ME.
RAAAAAAAAAWR!
UH...
HI, HULK.
HOW'S IT GOING?

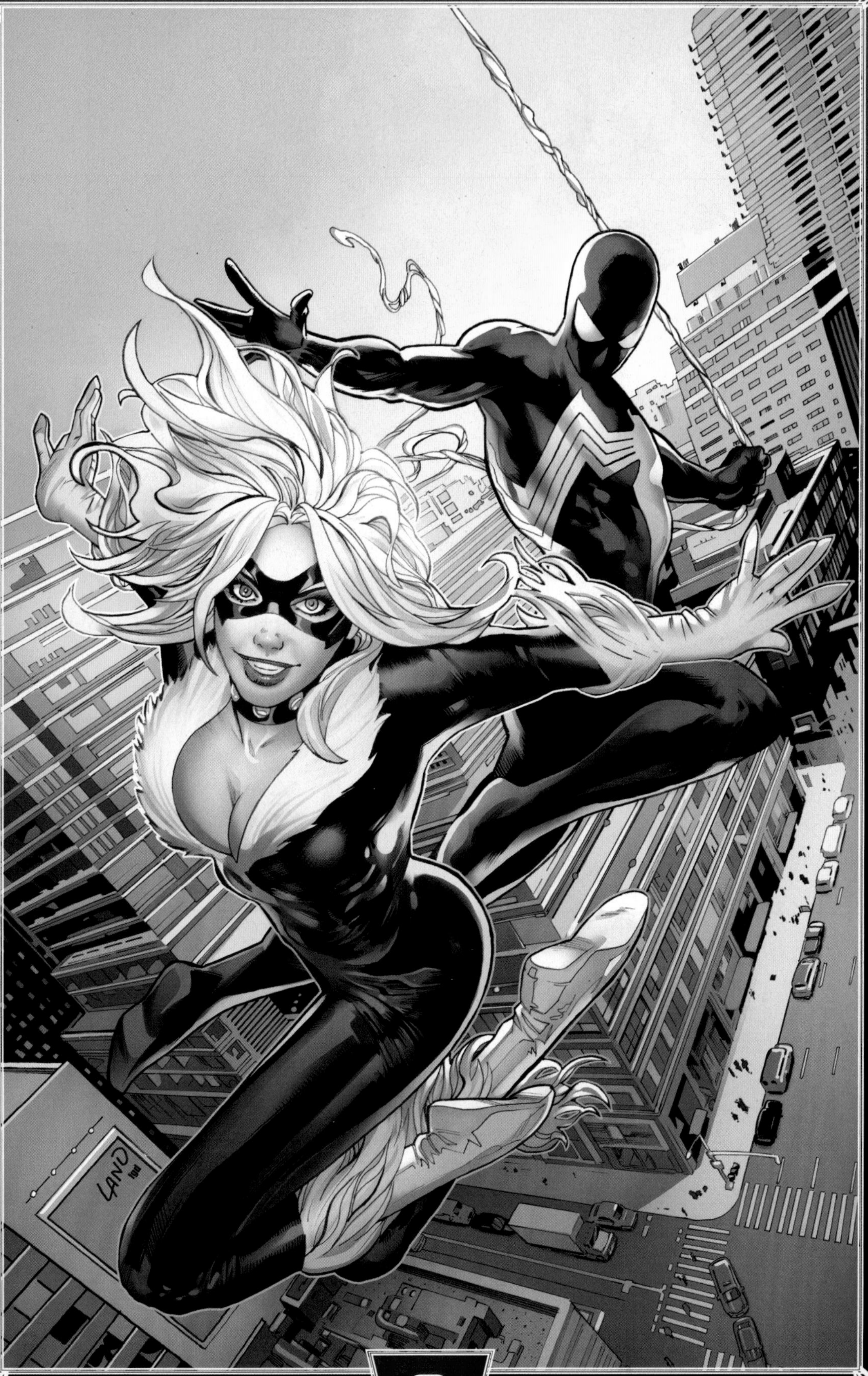

2

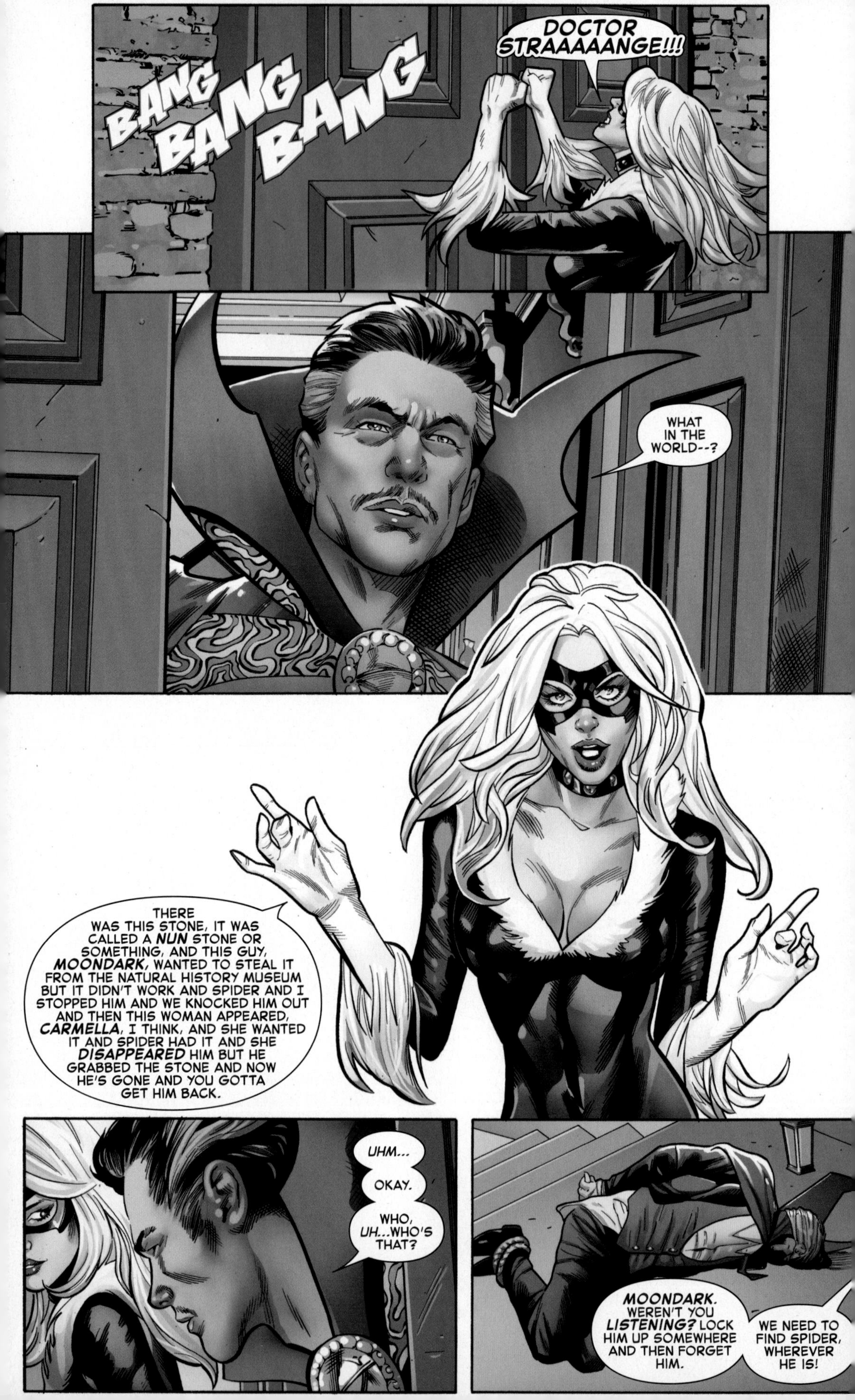

BANG BANG BANG
DOCTOR STRAAAAANGE!!!
WHAT IN THE WORLD--?
THERE WAS THIS STONE, IT WAS CALLED A NUN STONE OR SOMETHING, AND THIS GUY, MOONDARK, WANTED TO STEAL IT FROM THE NATURAL HISTORY MUSEUM BUT IT DIDN'T WORK AND SPIDER AND I STOPPED HIM AND WE KNOCKED HIM OUT AND THEN THIS WOMAN APPEARED, CARMELLA, I THINK, AND SHE WANTED IT AND SPIDER HAD IT AND SHE DISAPPEARED HIM BUT HE GRABBED THE STONE AND NOW HE'S GONE AND YOU GOTTA GET HIM BACK.
UHM...
OKAY.
WHO, UH...WHO'S THAT?
MOONDARK. WEREN'T YOU LISTENING? LOCK HIM UP SOMEWHERE AND THEN FORGET HIM.
WE NEED TO FIND SPIDER, WHEREVER HE IS!

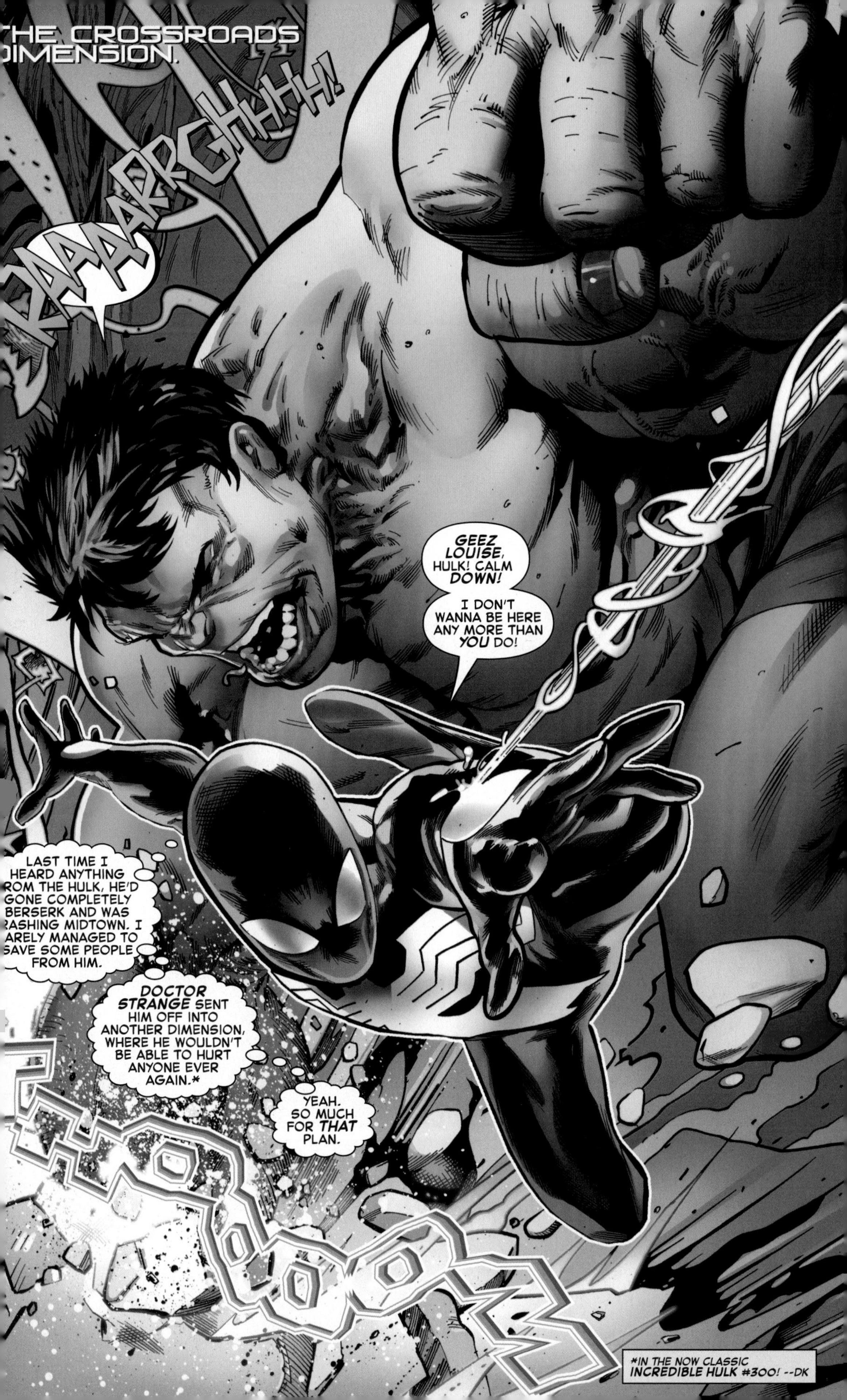
THE CROSSROADS DIMENSION.
KRAAARRGHHHH!
GEEZ LOUISE, HULK! CALM DOWN!
I DON'T WANNA BE HERE ANY MORE THAN YOU DO!
LAST TIME I HEARD ANYTHING FROM THE HULK, HE'D GONE COMPLETELY BERSERK AND WAS TRASHING MIDTOWN. I BARELY MANAGED TO SAVE SOME PEOPLE FROM HIM.
DOCTOR STRANGE SENT HIM OFF INTO ANOTHER DIMENSION, WHERE HE WOULDN'T BE ABLE TO HURT ANYONE EVER AGAIN.*
YEAH. SO MUCH FOR THAT PLAN.
*IN THE NOW CLASSIC INCREDIBLE HULK #300! --DK

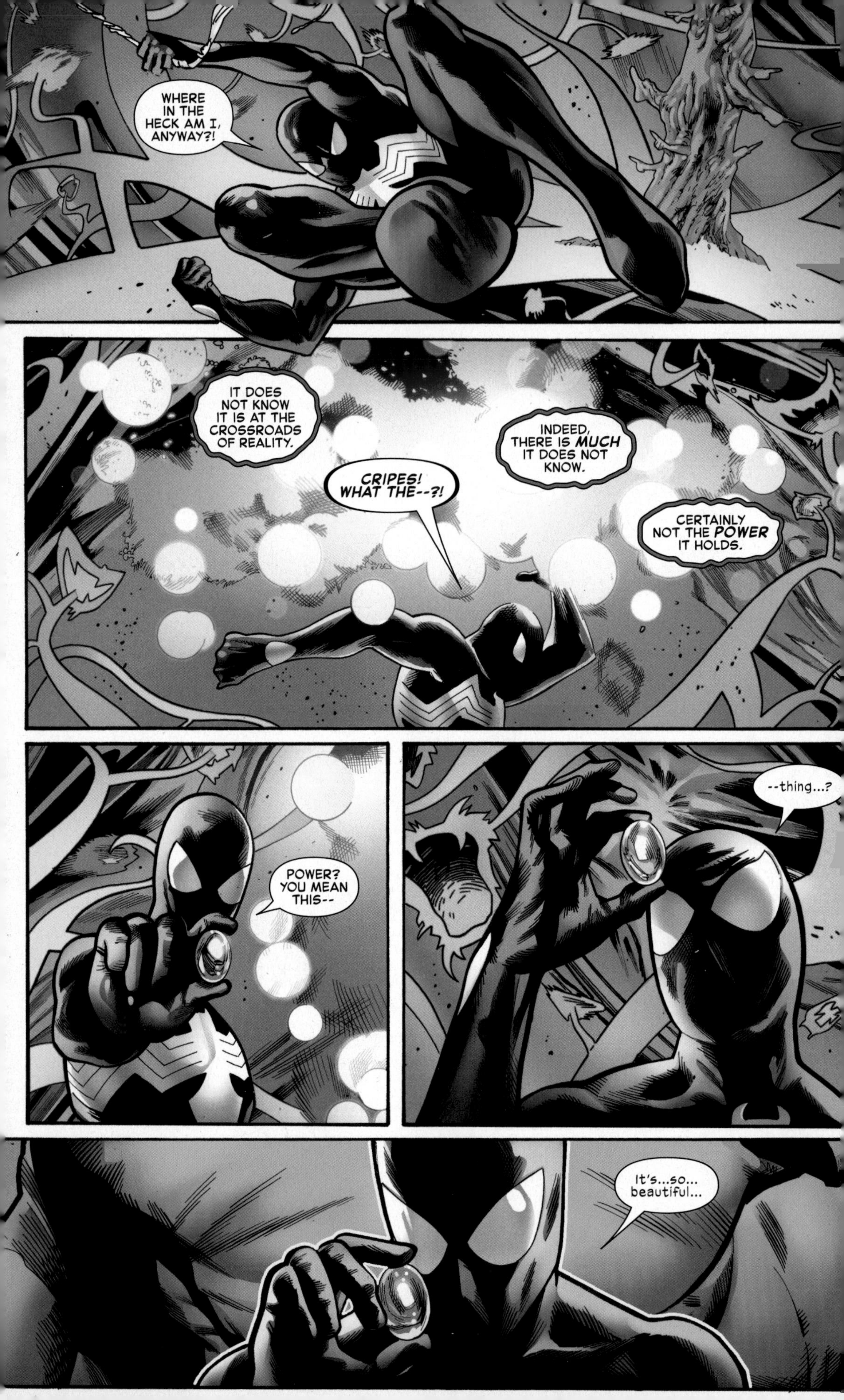
WHERE IN THE HECK AM I, ANYWAY?!
IT DOES NOT KNOW IT IS AT THE CROSSROADS OF REALITY.
INDEED, THERE IS *MUCH* IT DOES NOT KNOW.
CRIPES! WHAT THE--?!
CERTAINLY NOT THE *POWER* IT HOLDS.
POWER? YOU MEAN THIS--
--thing...?
It's...so... beautiful...

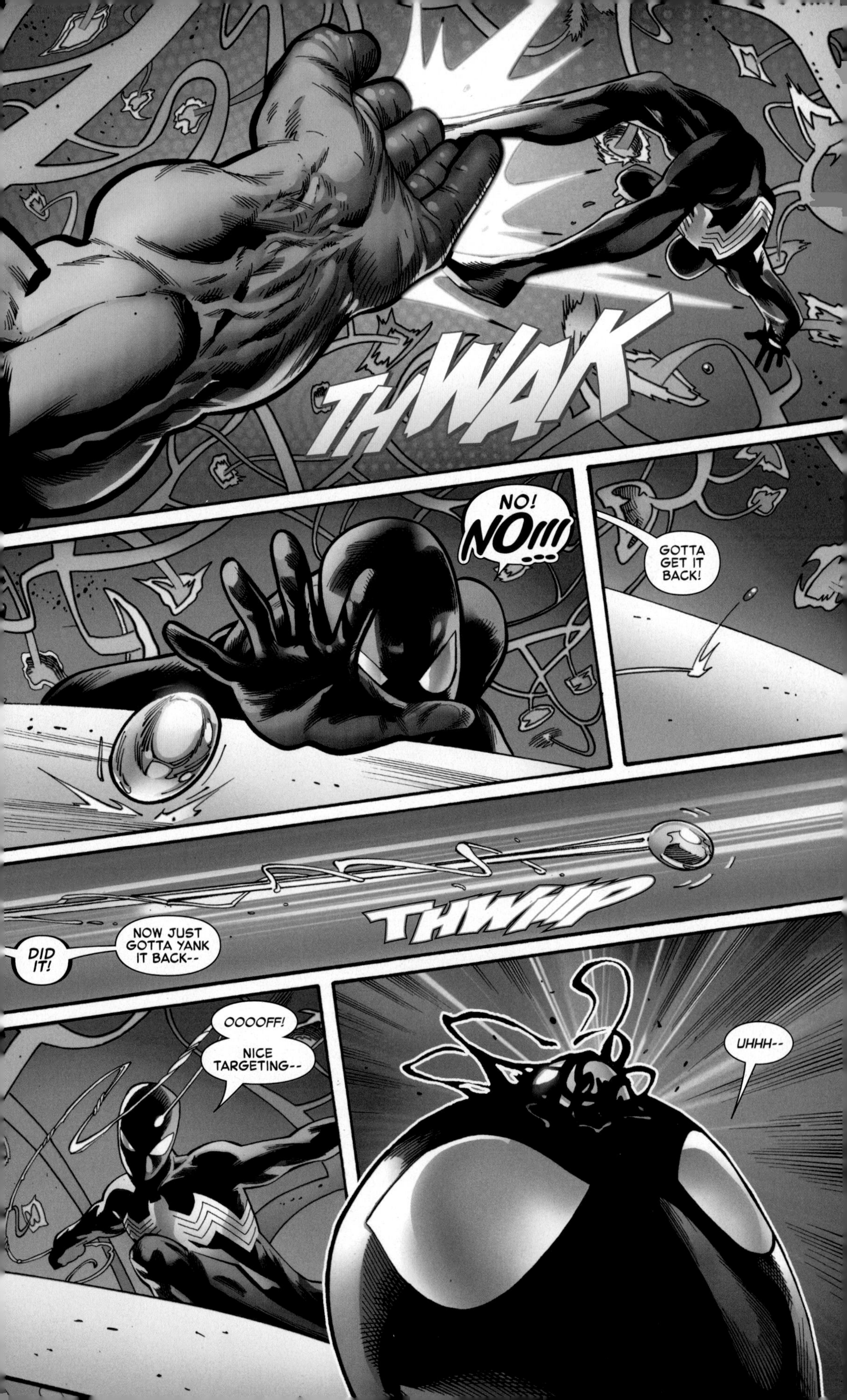
THWAK
NO! NO!!!...
GOTTA GET IT BACK!
THWIIP
DID IT!
NOW JUST GOTTA YANK IT BACK--
OOOOFF!
NICE TARGETING--
UHHH--

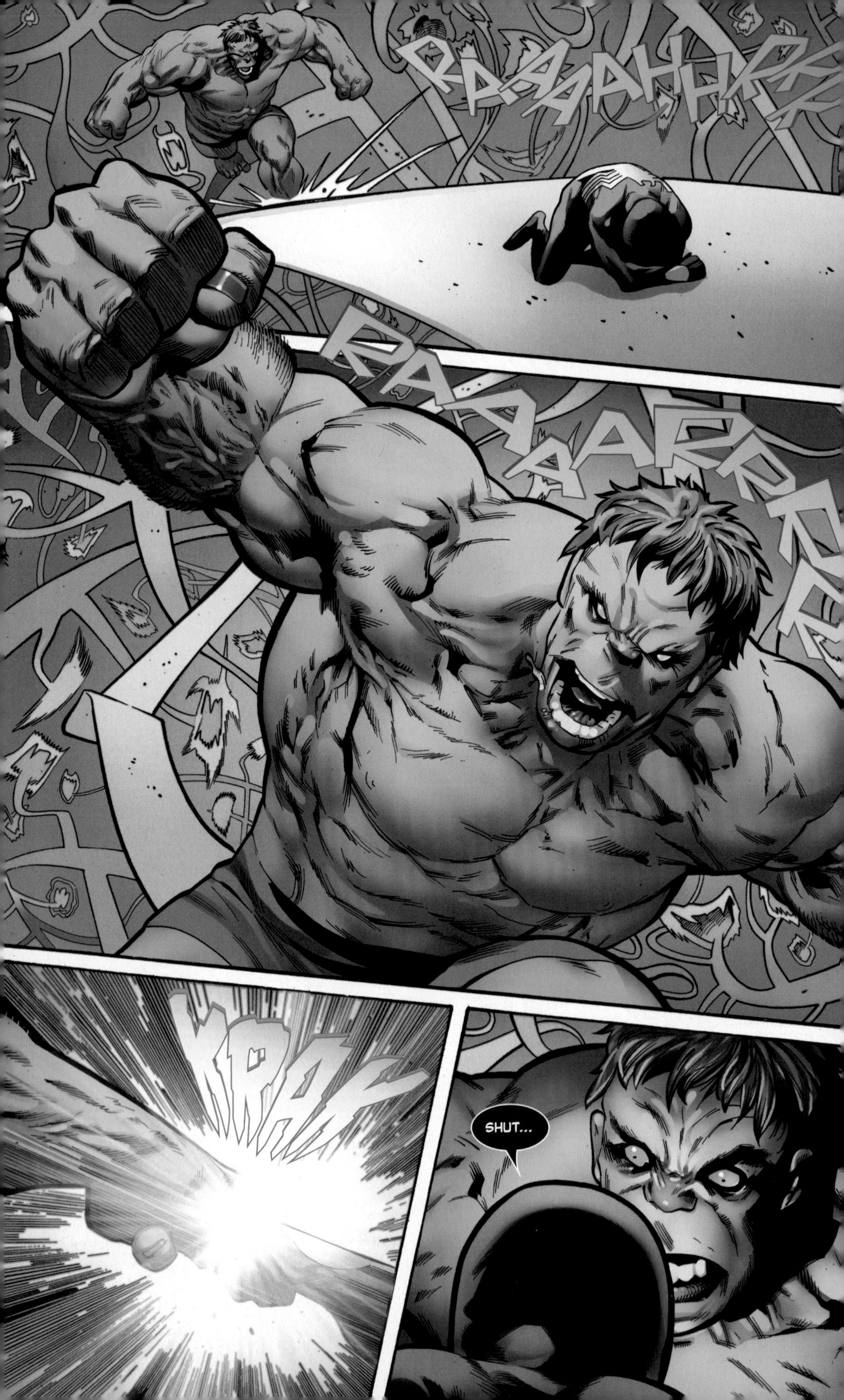
SHUT...

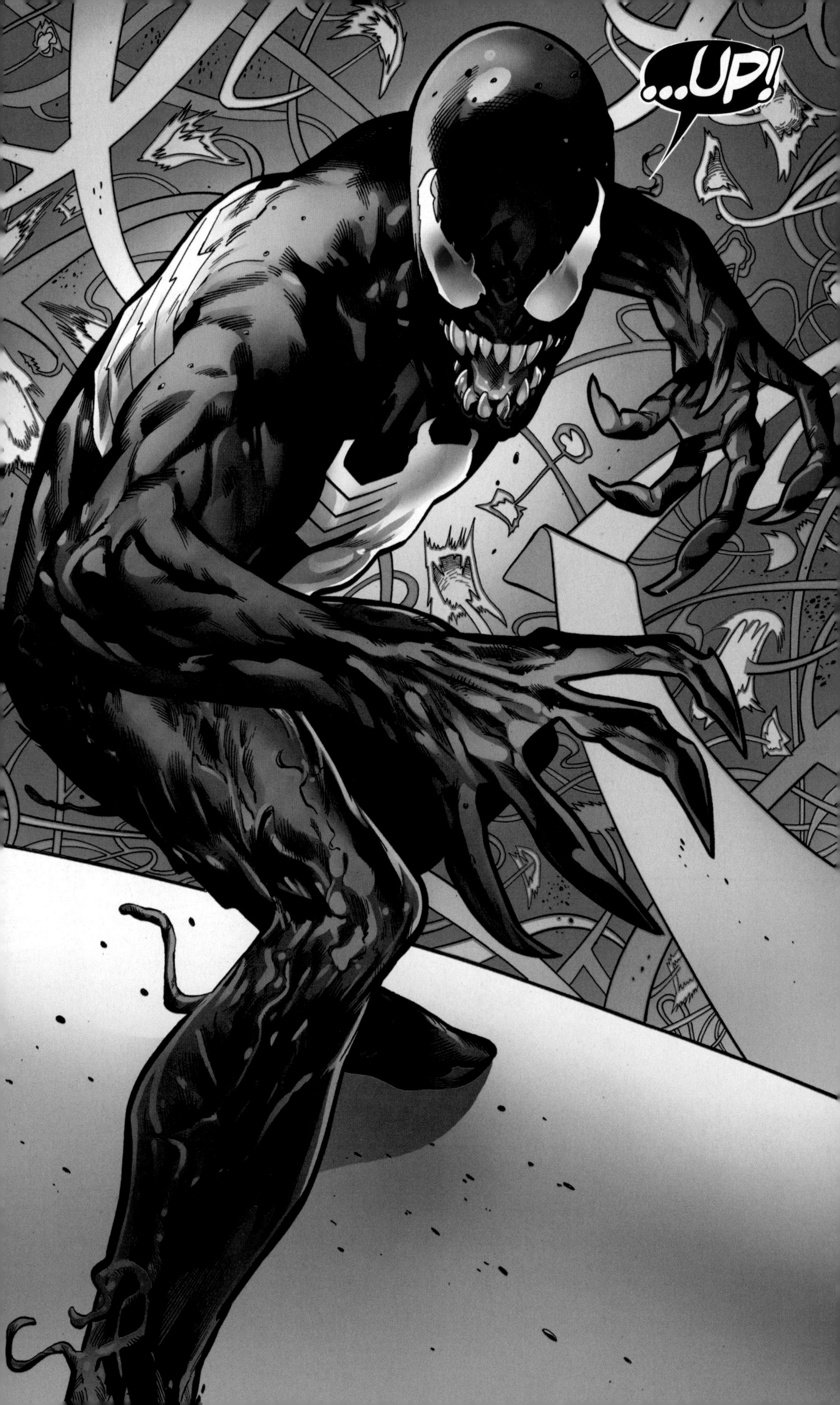
...UP!

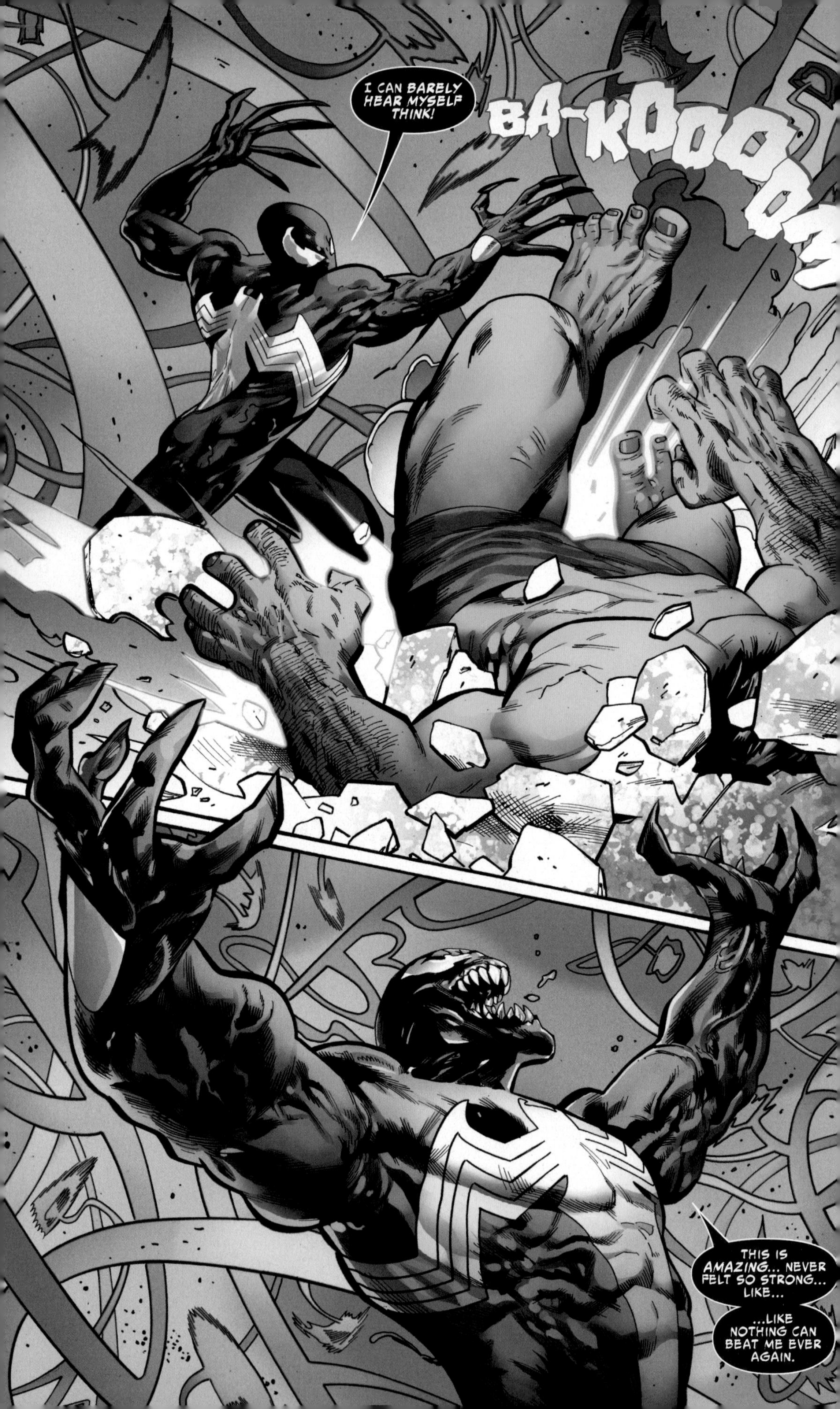
I CAN BARELY HEAR MYSELF THINK!
BA-KOOOOOM
THIS IS AMAZING... NEVER FELT SO STRONG... LIKE...
...LIKE NOTHING CAN BEAT ME EVER AGAIN.

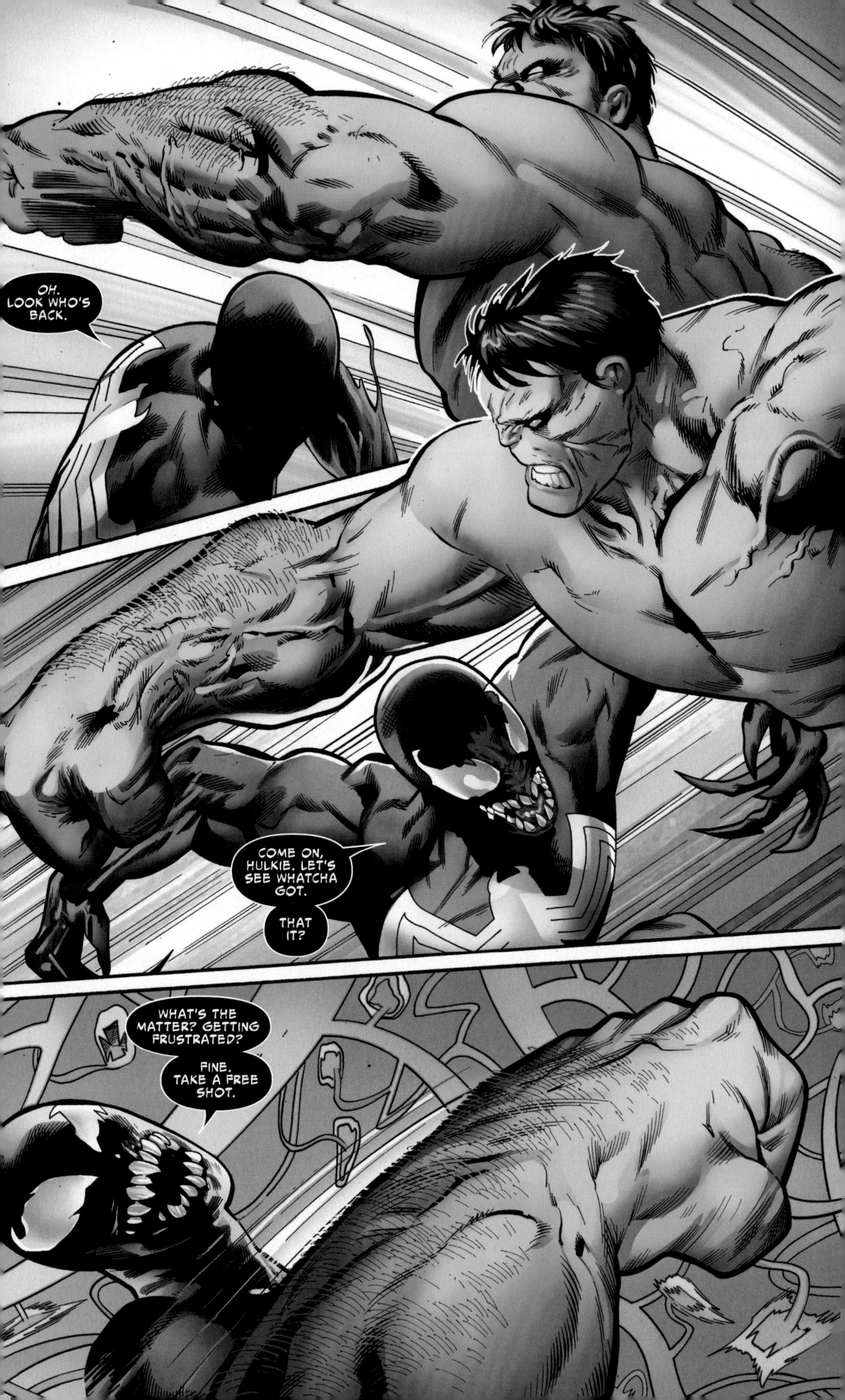
OH. LOOK WHO'S BACK.
COME ON, HULKIE. LET'S SEE WHATCHA GOT.
THAT IT?
WHAT'S THE MATTER? GETTING FRUSTRATED?
FINE. TAKE A FREE SHOT.

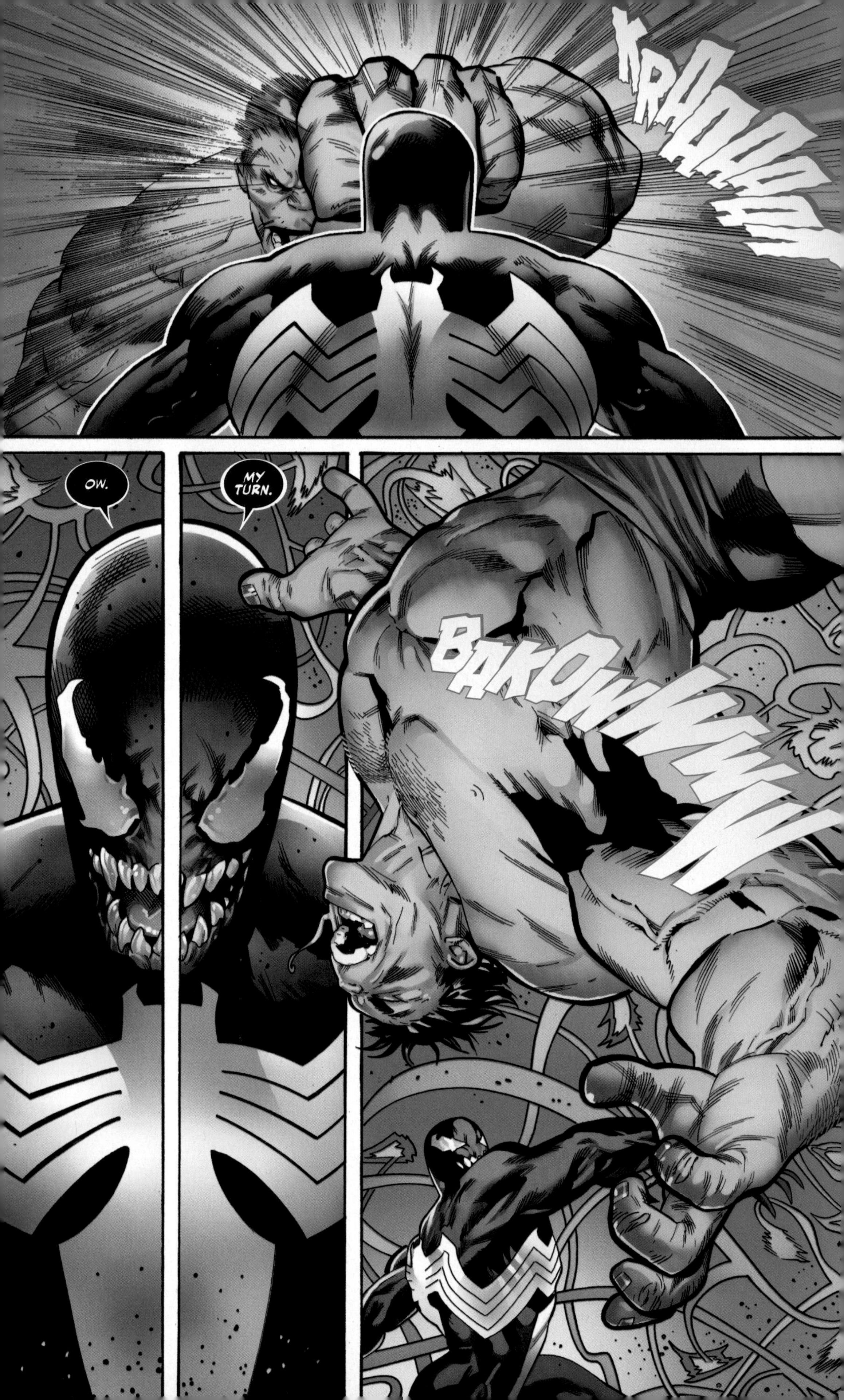
OW.
MY TURN.

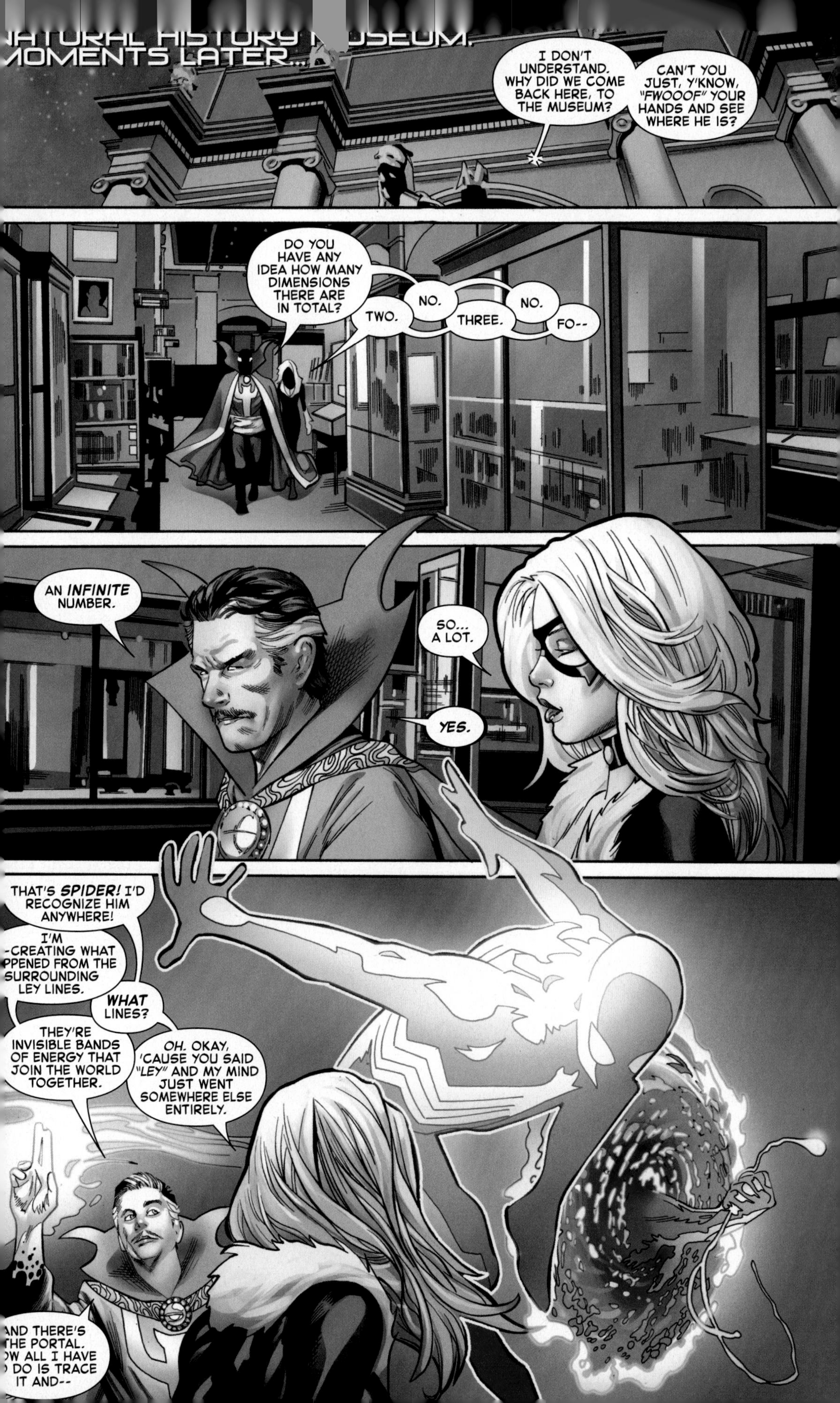
NATURAL HISTORY MUSEUM. MOMENTS LATER...
I DON'T UNDERSTAND. WHY DID WE COME BACK HERE, TO THE MUSEUM?
CAN'T YOU JUST, Y'KNOW, "FWOOOF" YOUR HANDS AND SEE WHERE HE IS?
DO YOU HAVE ANY IDEA HOW MANY DIMENSIONS THERE ARE IN TOTAL?
TWO.
NO.
THREE.
NO.
FO--
AN INFINITE NUMBER.
SO... A LOT.
YES.
THAT'S SPIDER! I'D RECOGNIZE HIM ANYWHERE!
I'M -CREATING WHAT PPENED FROM THE SURROUNDING LEY LINES.
WHAT LINES?
THEY'RE INVISIBLE BANDS OF ENERGY THAT JOIN THE WORLD TOGETHER.
OH. OKAY, 'CAUSE YOU SAID "LEY" AND MY MIND JUST WENT SOMEWHERE ELSE ENTIRELY.
AND THERE'S THE PORTAL. W ALL I HAVE DO IS TRACE IT AND--

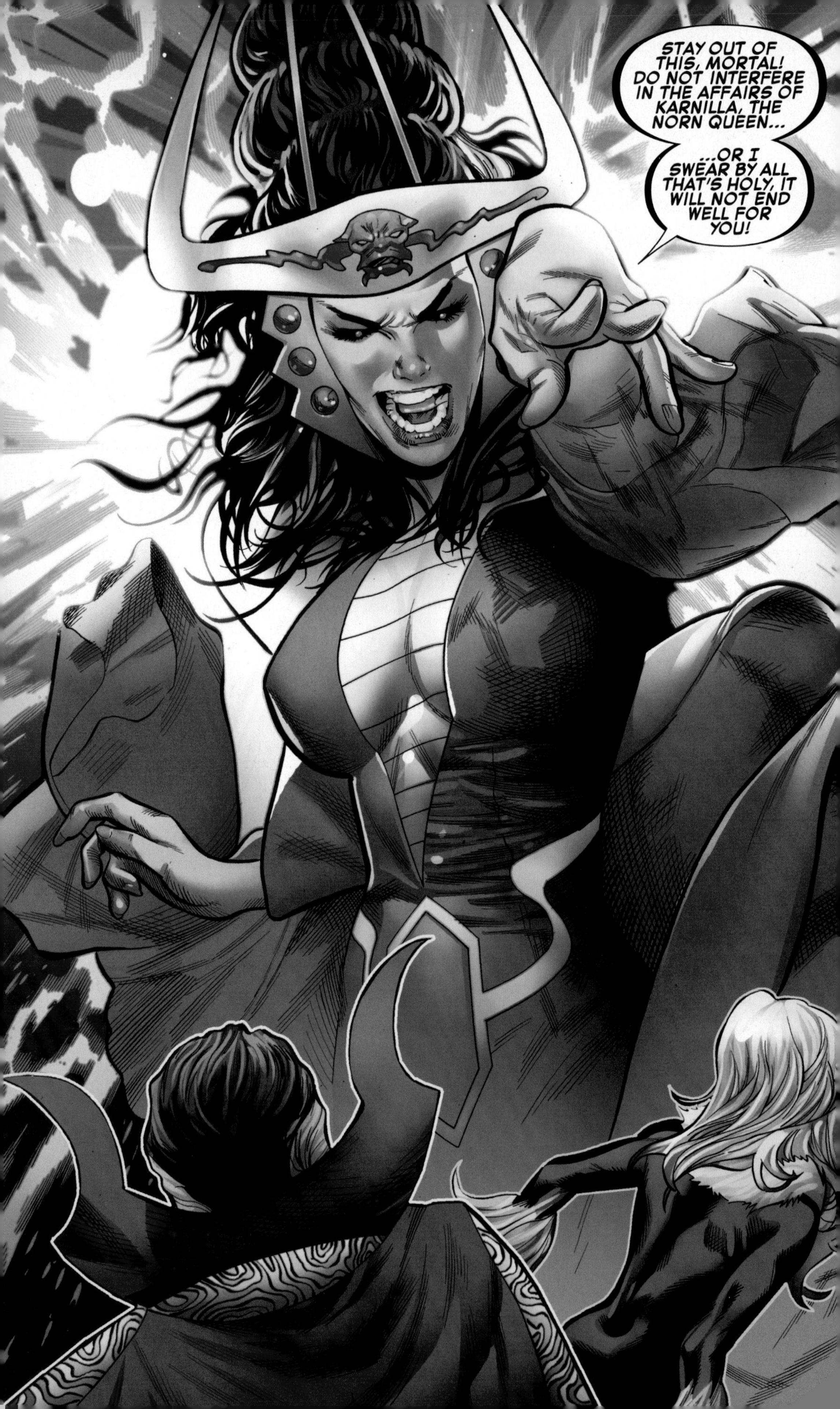

STAY OUT OF THIS, MORTAL! DO NOT INTERFERE IN THE AFFAIRS OF KARNILLA, THE NORN QUEEN...
...OR I SWEAR BY ALL THAT'S HOLY, IT WILL NOT END WELL FOR YOU!

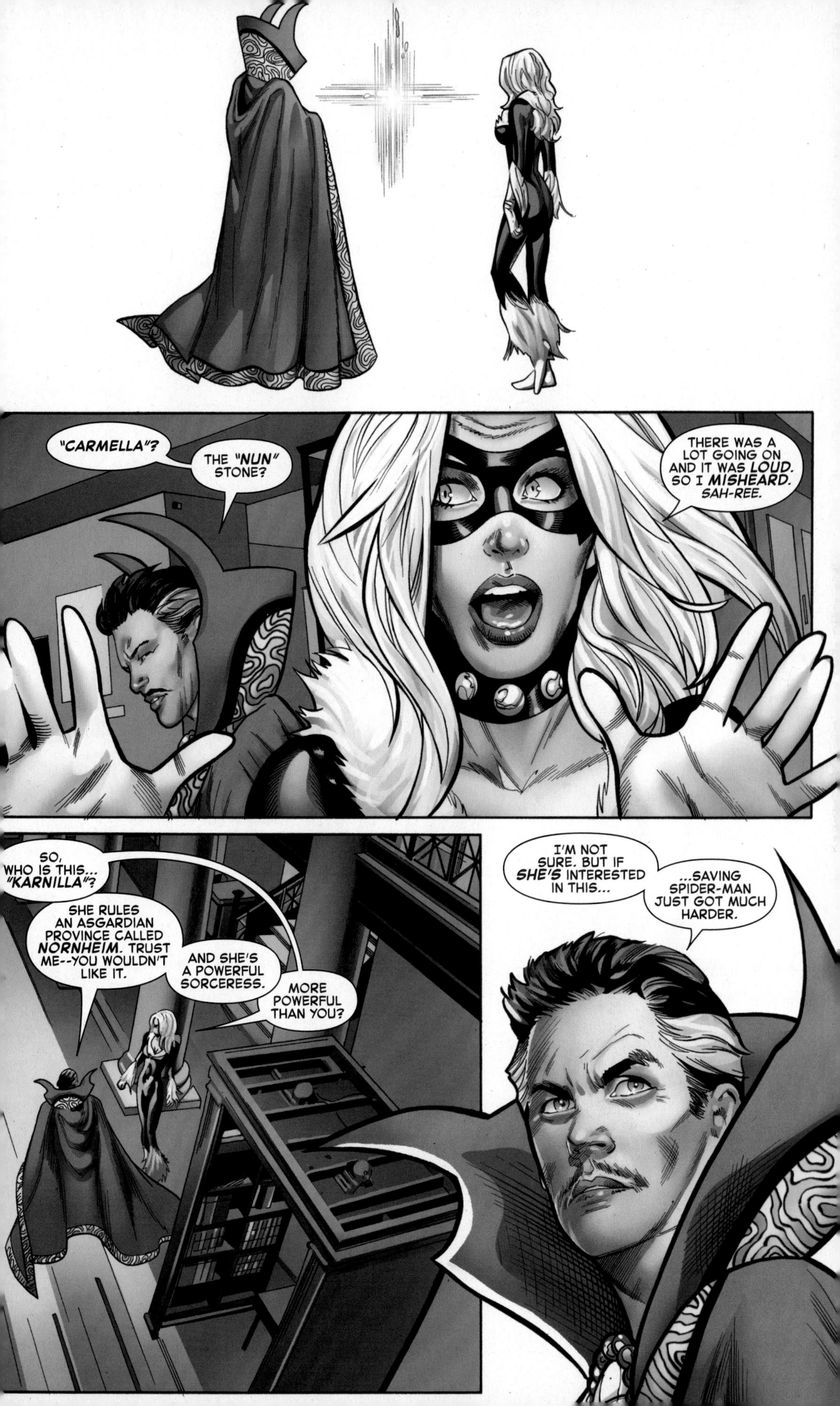
"CARMELLA"?
THE "NUN" STONE?
THERE WAS A LOT GOING ON AND IT WAS LOUD. SO I MISHEARD. SAH-REE.
SO, WHO IS THIS... "KARNILLA"?
SHE RULES AN ASGARDIAN PROVINCE CALLED NORNHEIM. TRUST ME--YOU WOULDN'T LIKE IT.
AND SHE'S A POWERFUL SORCERESS.
MORE POWERFUL THAN YOU?
I'M NOT SURE. BUT IF SHE'S INTERESTED IN THIS...
...SAVING SPIDER-MAN JUST GOT MUCH HARDER.

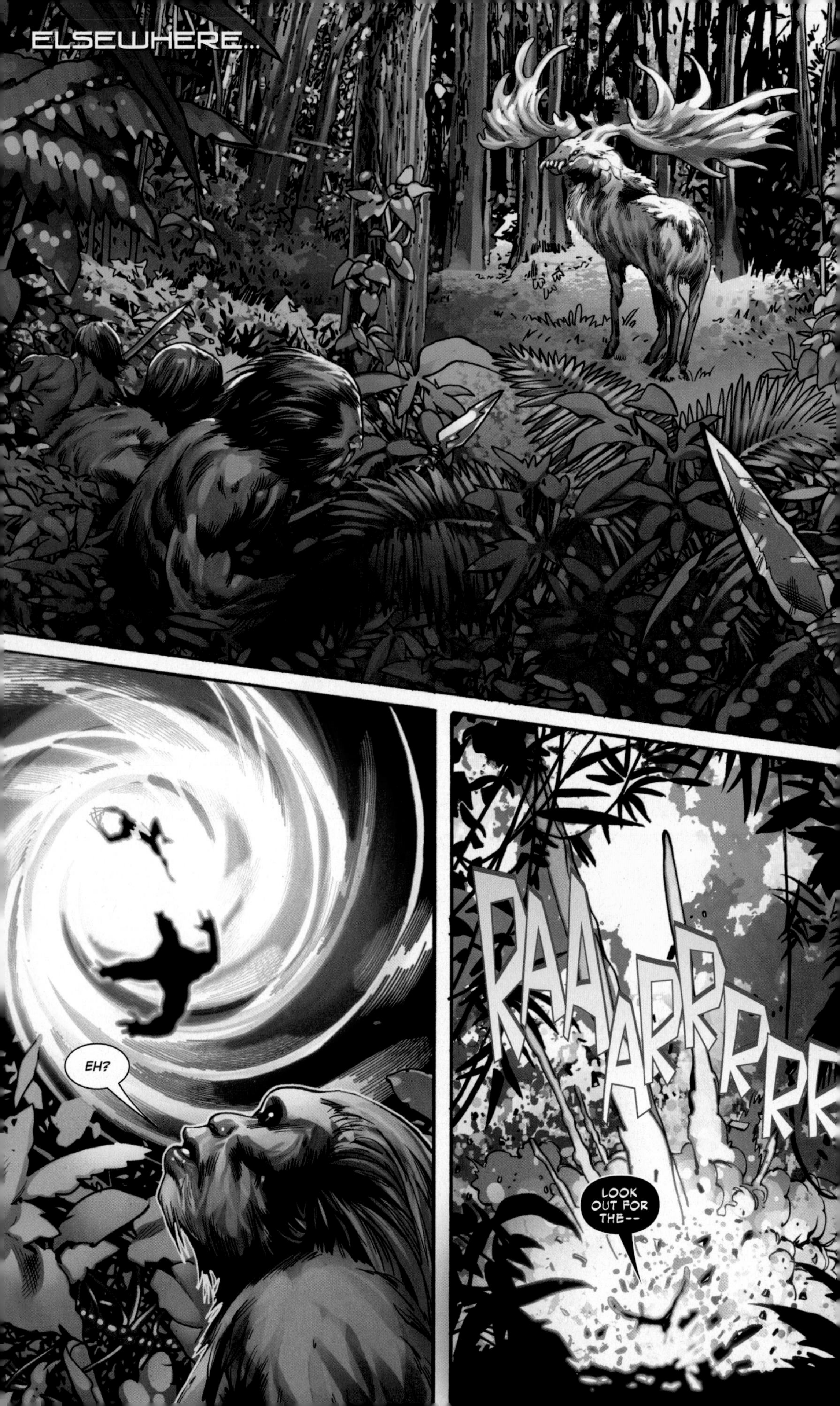
ELSEWHERE...
EH?
RAAAARRRRR
LOOK OUT FOR THE--

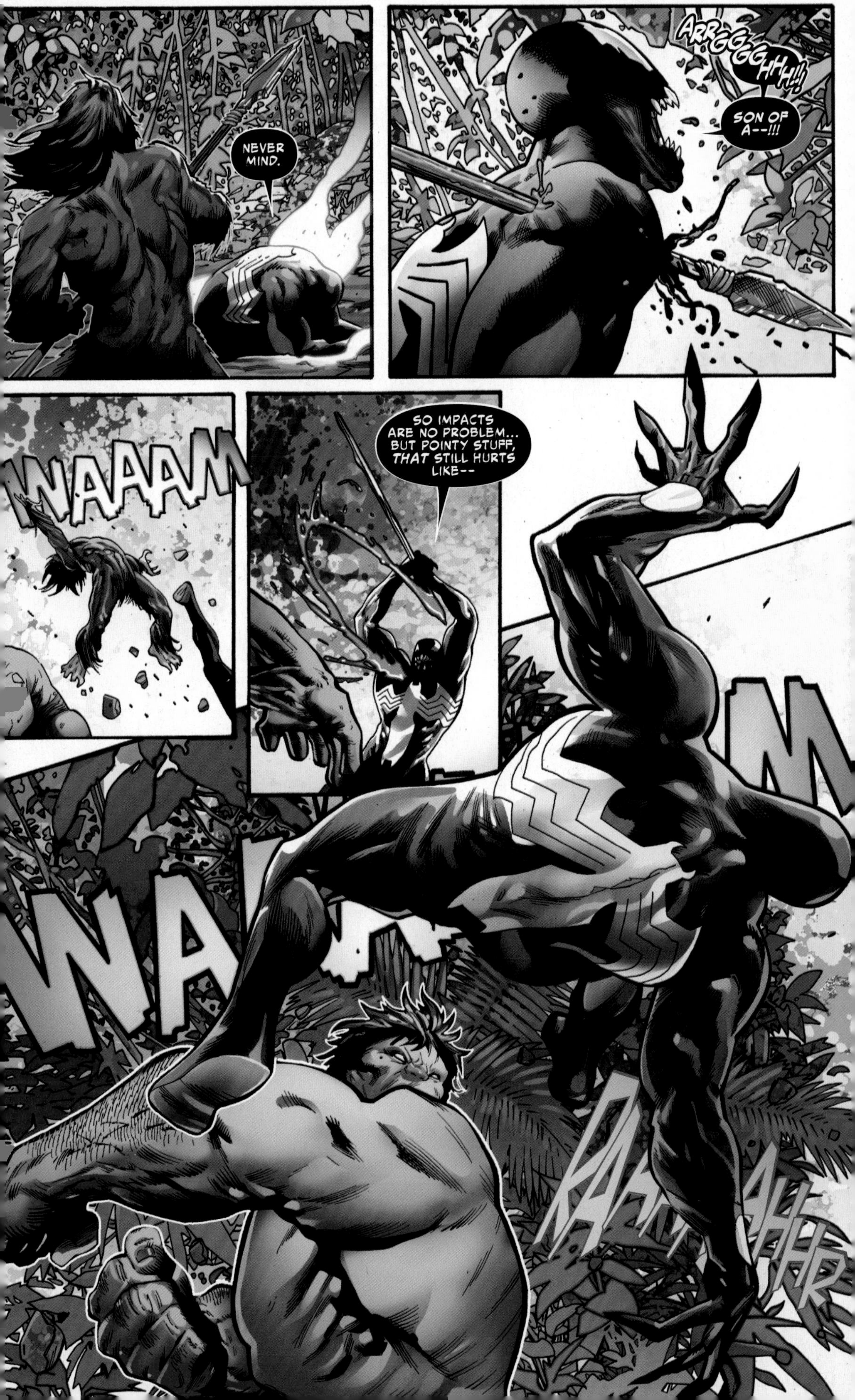
NEVER MIND.
ARRGGGGHHH!!!
SON OF A--!!!
WAAAM
SO IMPACTS ARE NO PROBLEM... BUT POINTY STUFF, THAT STILL HURTS LIKE--

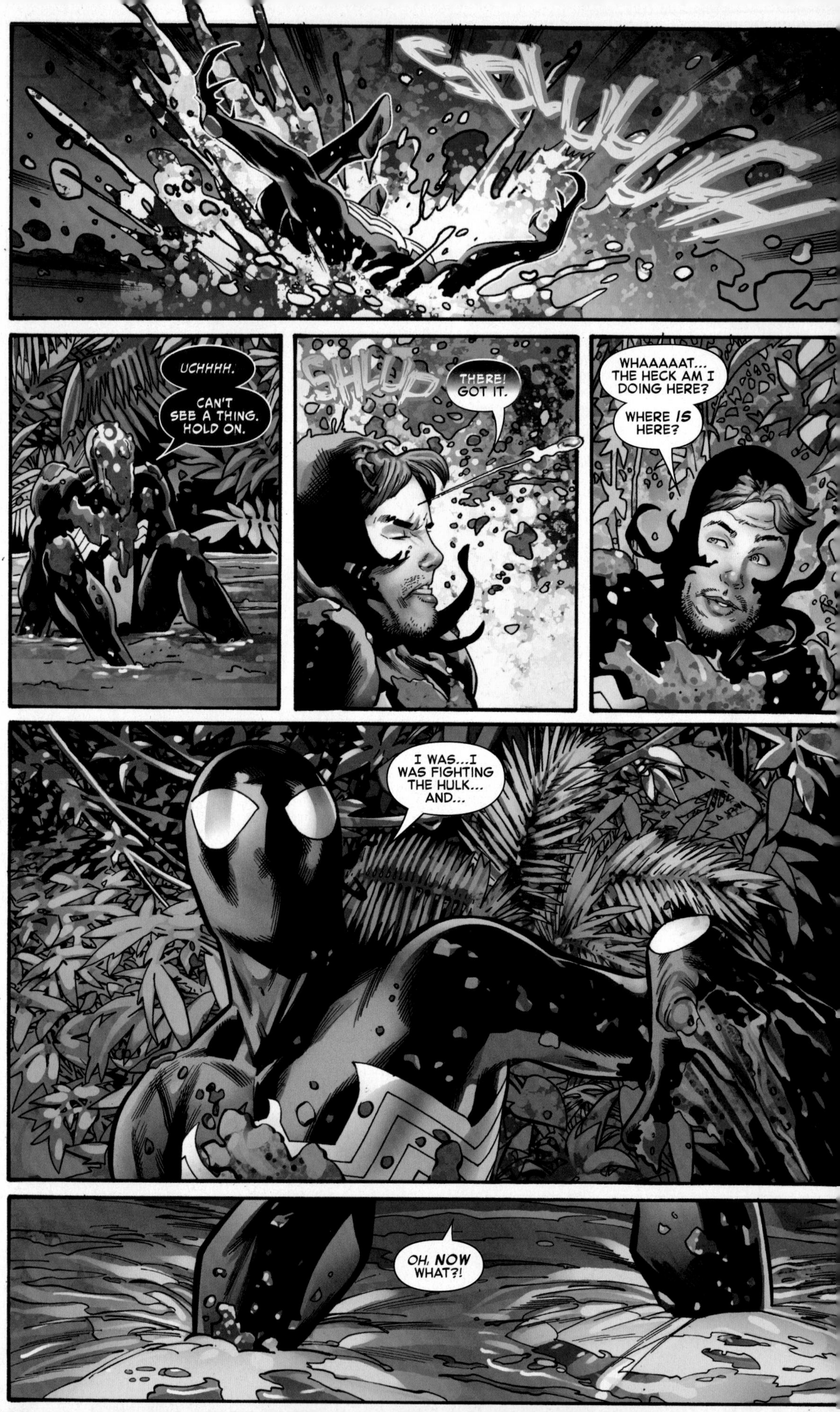
SPLUUUSH
UCHHHH.
CAN'T SEE A THING. HOLD ON.
SHLUP
THERE! GOT IT.
WHAAAAAT... THE HECK AM I DOING HERE?
WHERE IS HERE?
I WAS...I WAS FIGHTING THE HULK... AND...
OH, NOW WHAT?!

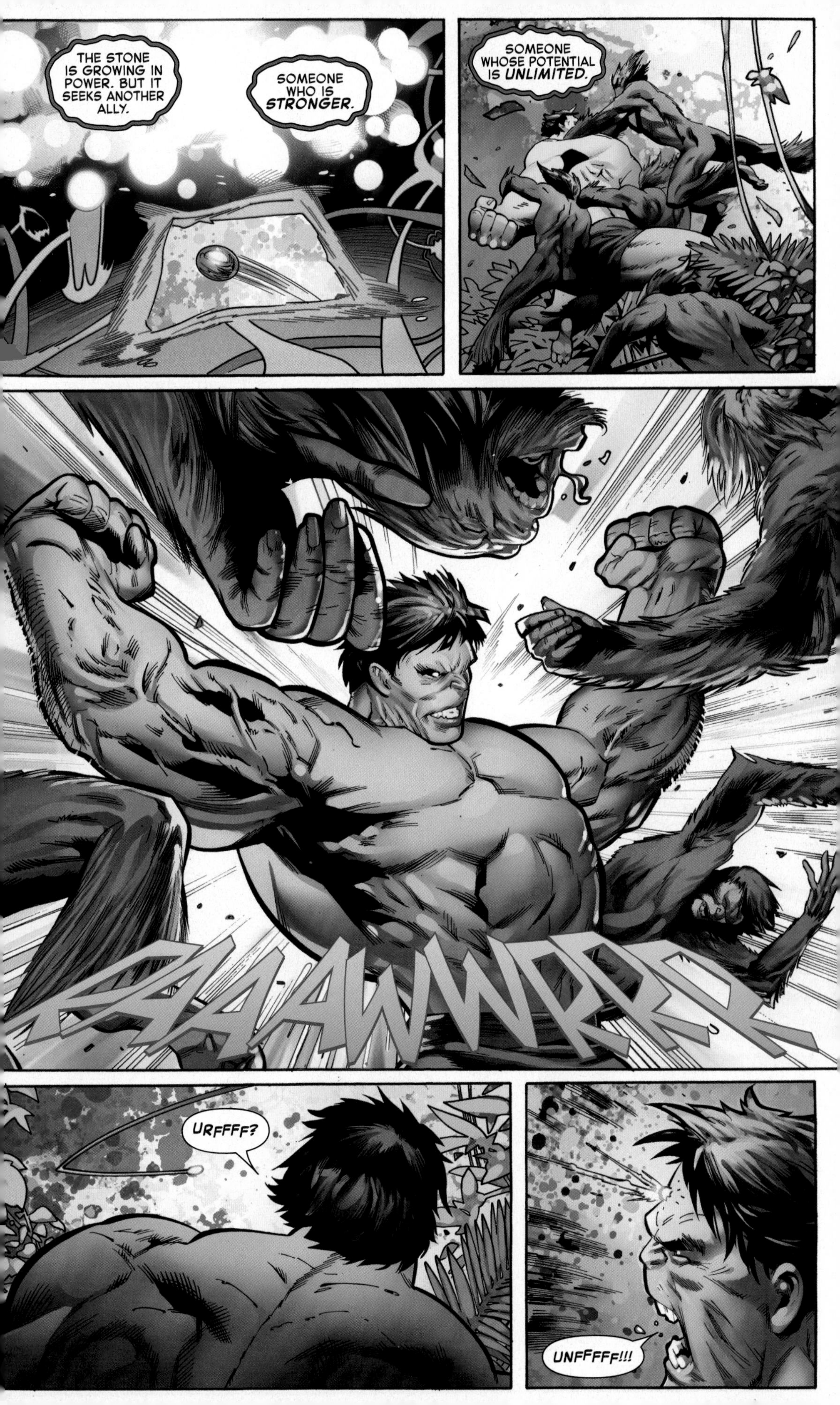
THE STONE IS GROWING IN POWER. BUT IT SEEKS ANOTHER ALLY.
SOMEONE WHO IS STRONGER.
SOMEONE WHOSE POTENTIAL IS UNLIMITED.
RAAAWRRR
URFFFF?
UNFFFFF!!!

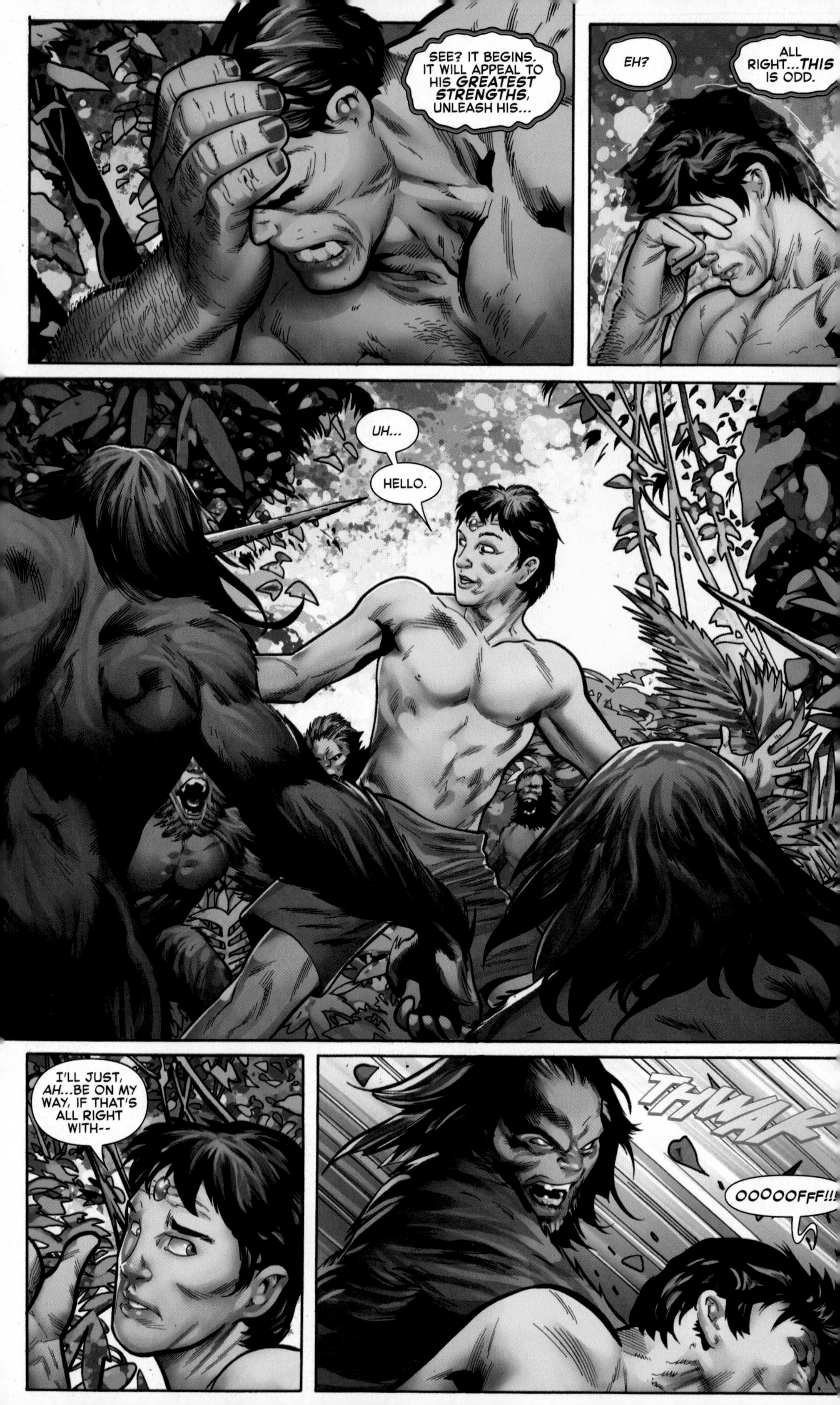
SEE? IT BEGINS. IT WILL APPEAL TO HIS GREATEST STRENGTHS, UNLEASH HIS...
EH?
ALL RIGHT...THIS IS ODD.
UH...
HELLO.
I'LL JUST, AH...BE ON MY WAY, IF THAT'S ALL RIGHT WITH--
THWAK
OOOOOFFF!!!

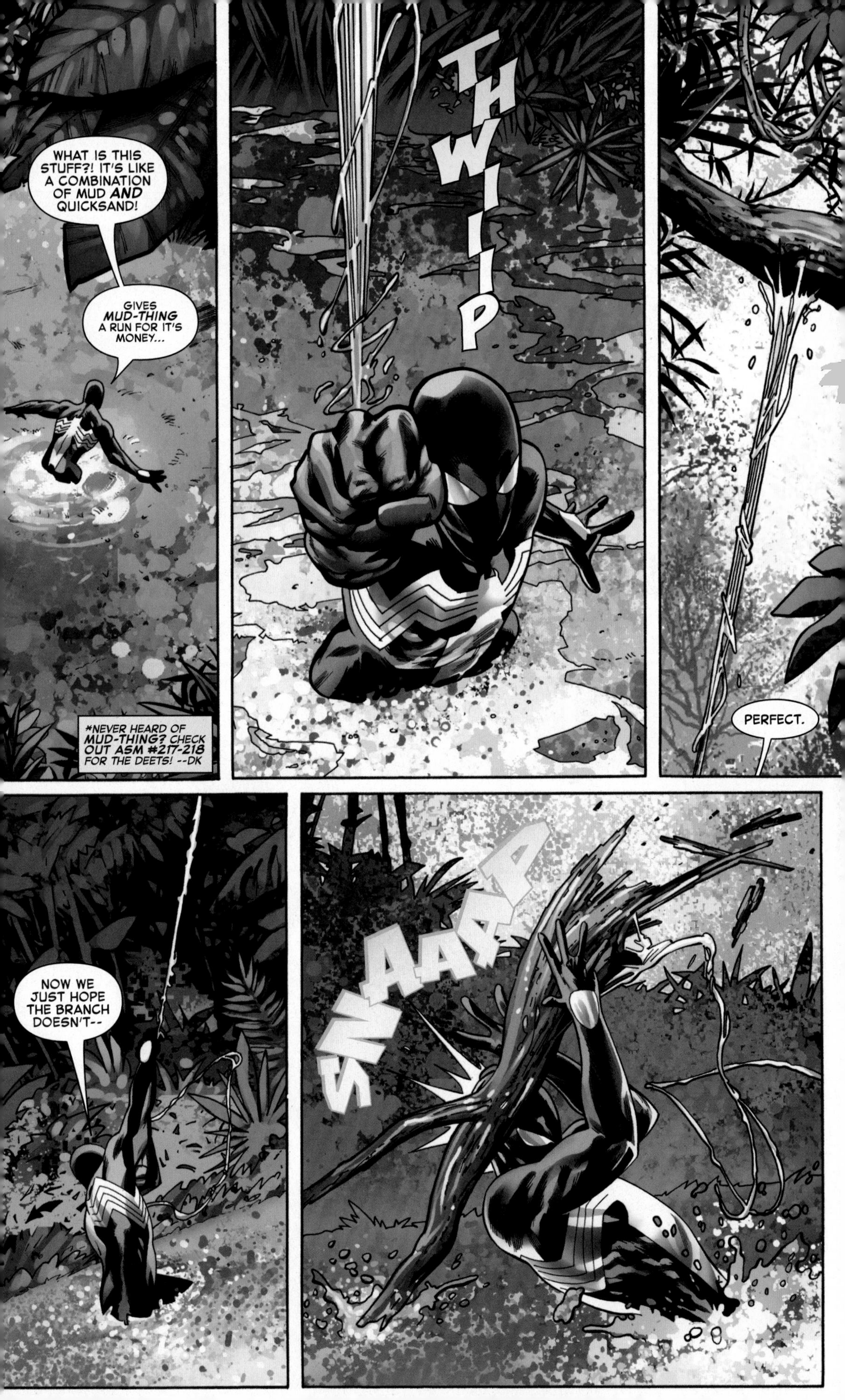
WHAT IS THIS STUFF?! IT'S LIKE A COMBINATION OF MUD AND QUICKSAND!
GIVES MUD-THING A RUN FOR IT'S MONEY...
*NEVER HEARD OF MUD-THING? CHECK OUT ASM #217-218 FOR THE DEETS! --DK
THWIIP
PERFECT.
NOW WE JUST HOPE THE BRANCH DOESN'T--
SNAAAAA

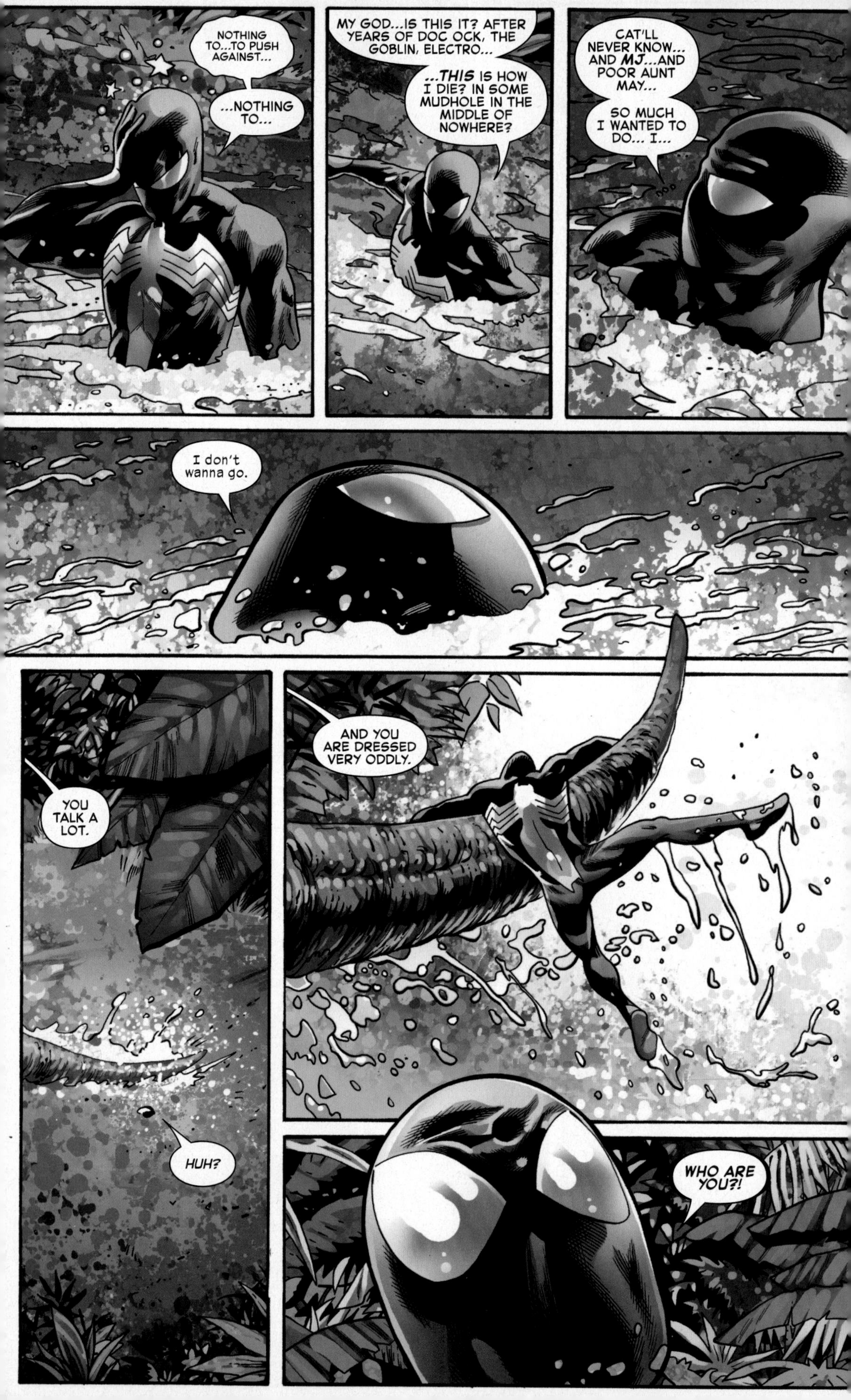
NOTHING TO...TO PUSH AGAINST...
...NOTHING TO...
MY GOD...IS THIS IT? AFTER YEARS OF DOC OCK, THE GOBLIN, ELECTRO...
...THIS IS HOW I DIE? IN SOME MUDHOLE IN THE MIDDLE OF NOWHERE?
CAT'LL NEVER KNOW... AND MJ...AND POOR AUNT MAY...
SO MUCH I WANTED TO DO... I...
I don't wanna go.
YOU TALK A LOT.
AND YOU ARE DRESSED VERY ODDLY.
HUH?
WHO ARE YOU?!

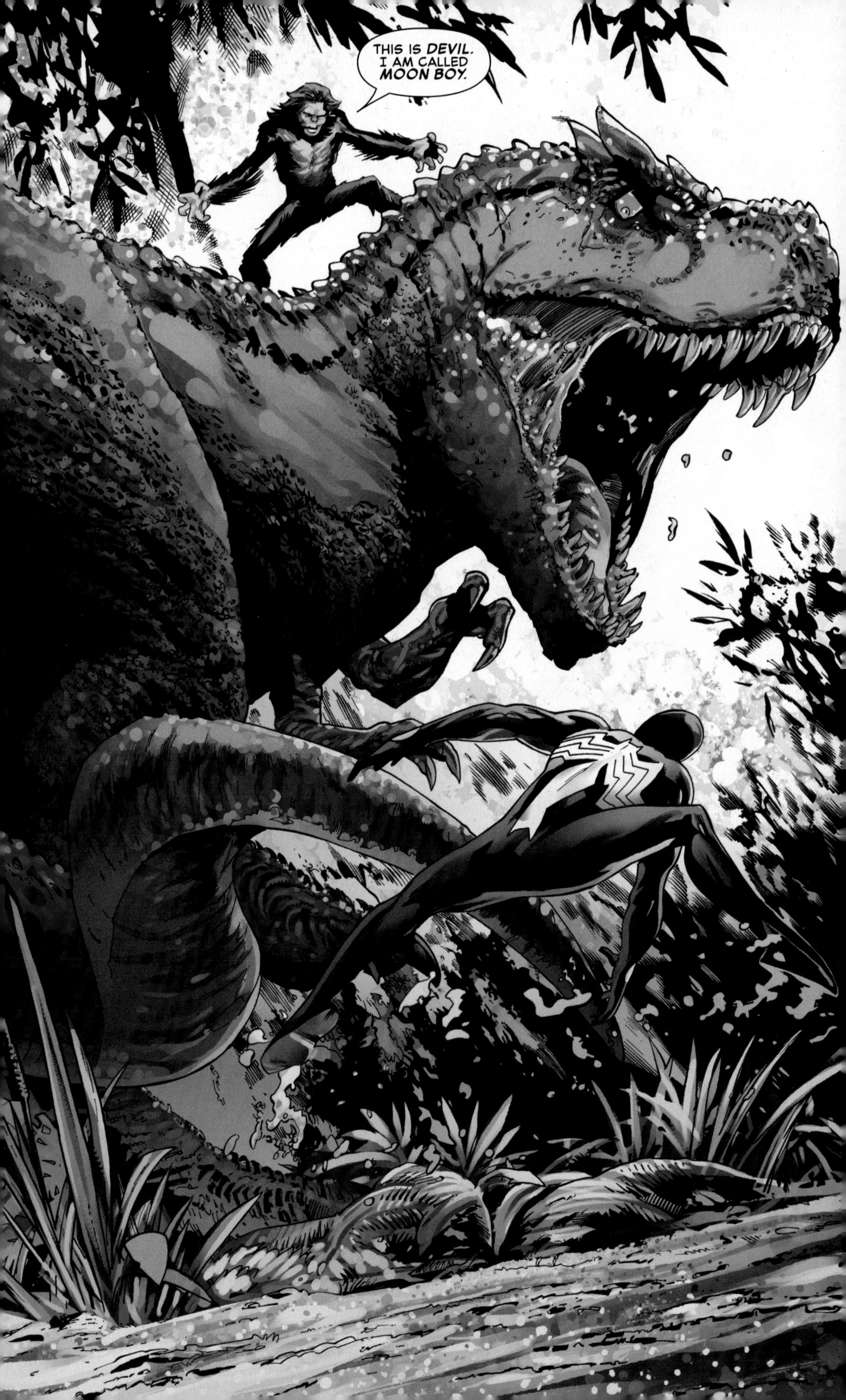
THIS IS DEVIL. I AM CALLED MOON BOY.

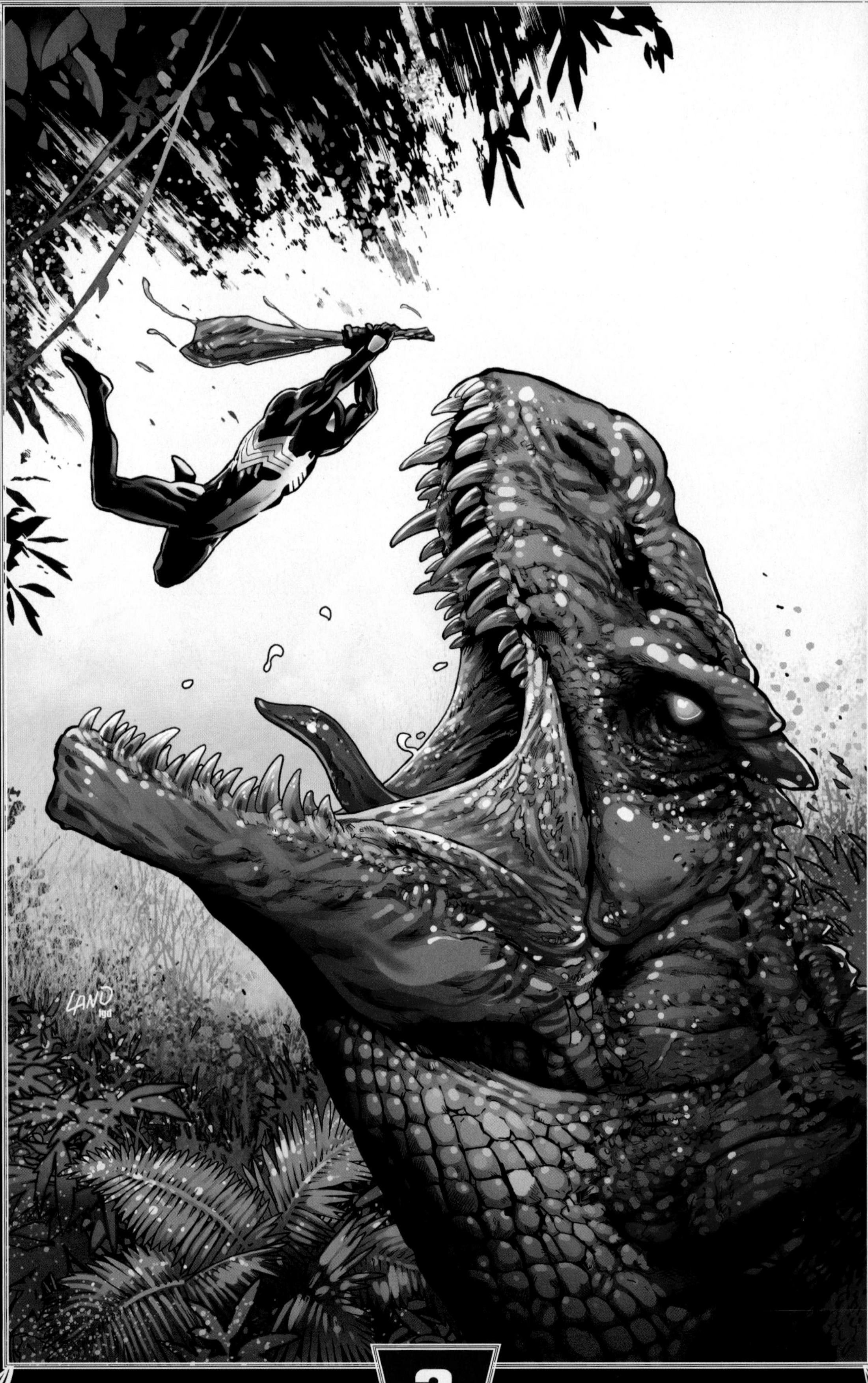
LAND

3

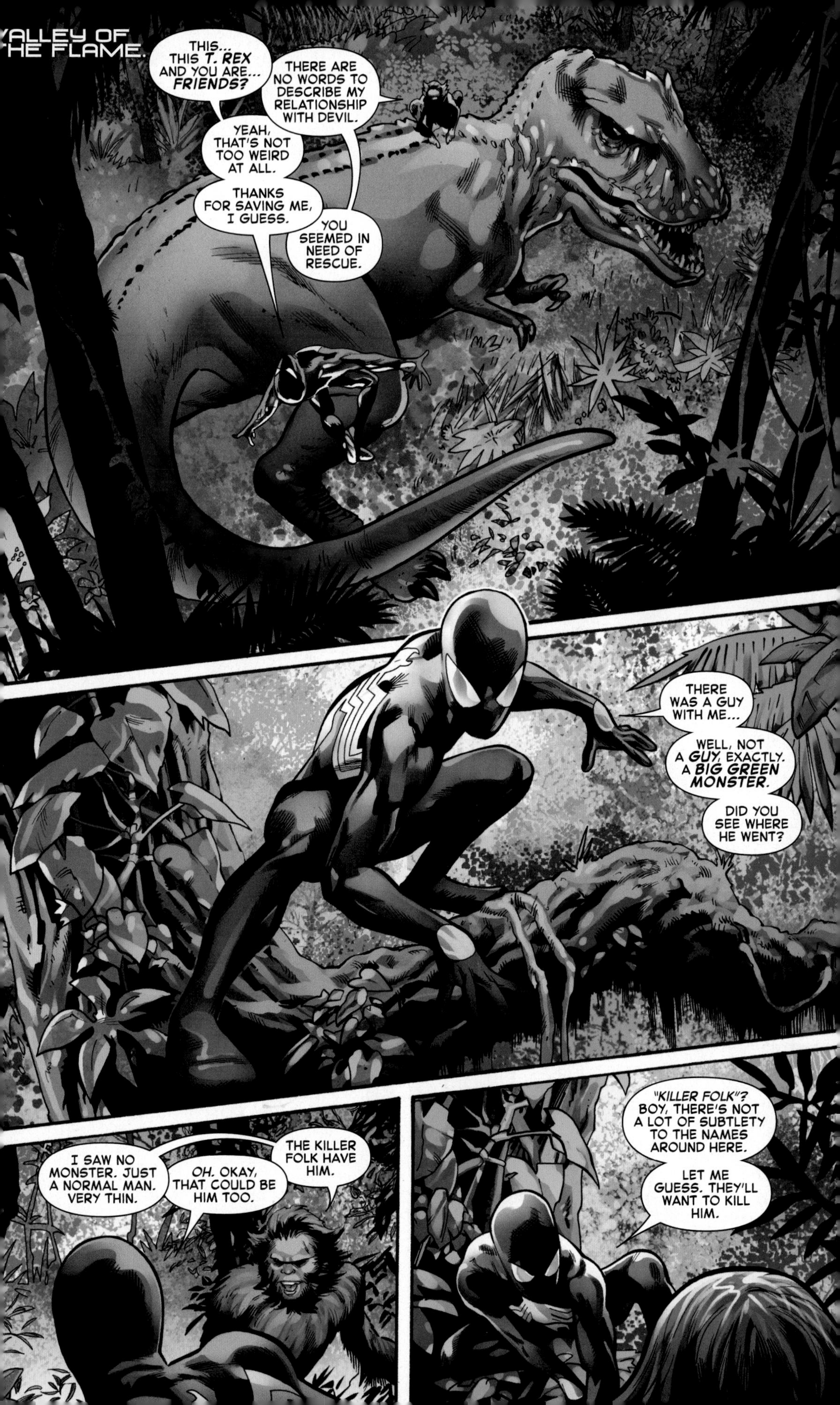
VALLEY OF THE FLAME.
THIS... THIS T. REX AND YOU ARE... FRIENDS?
THERE ARE NO WORDS TO DESCRIBE MY RELATIONSHIP WITH DEVIL.
YEAH, THAT'S NOT TOO WEIRD AT ALL.
THANKS FOR SAVING ME, I GUESS.
YOU SEEMED IN NEED OF RESCUE.
THERE WAS A GUY WITH ME...
WELL, NOT A GUY, EXACTLY. A BIG GREEN MONSTER.
DID YOU SEE WHERE HE WENT?
I SAW NO MONSTER. JUST A NORMAL MAN. VERY THIN.
OH. OKAY, THAT COULD BE HIM TOO.
THE KILLER FOLK HAVE HIM.
"KILLER FOLK"? BOY, THERE'S NOT A LOT OF SUBTLETY TO THE NAMES AROUND HERE.
LET ME GUESS. THEY'LL WANT TO KILL HIM.

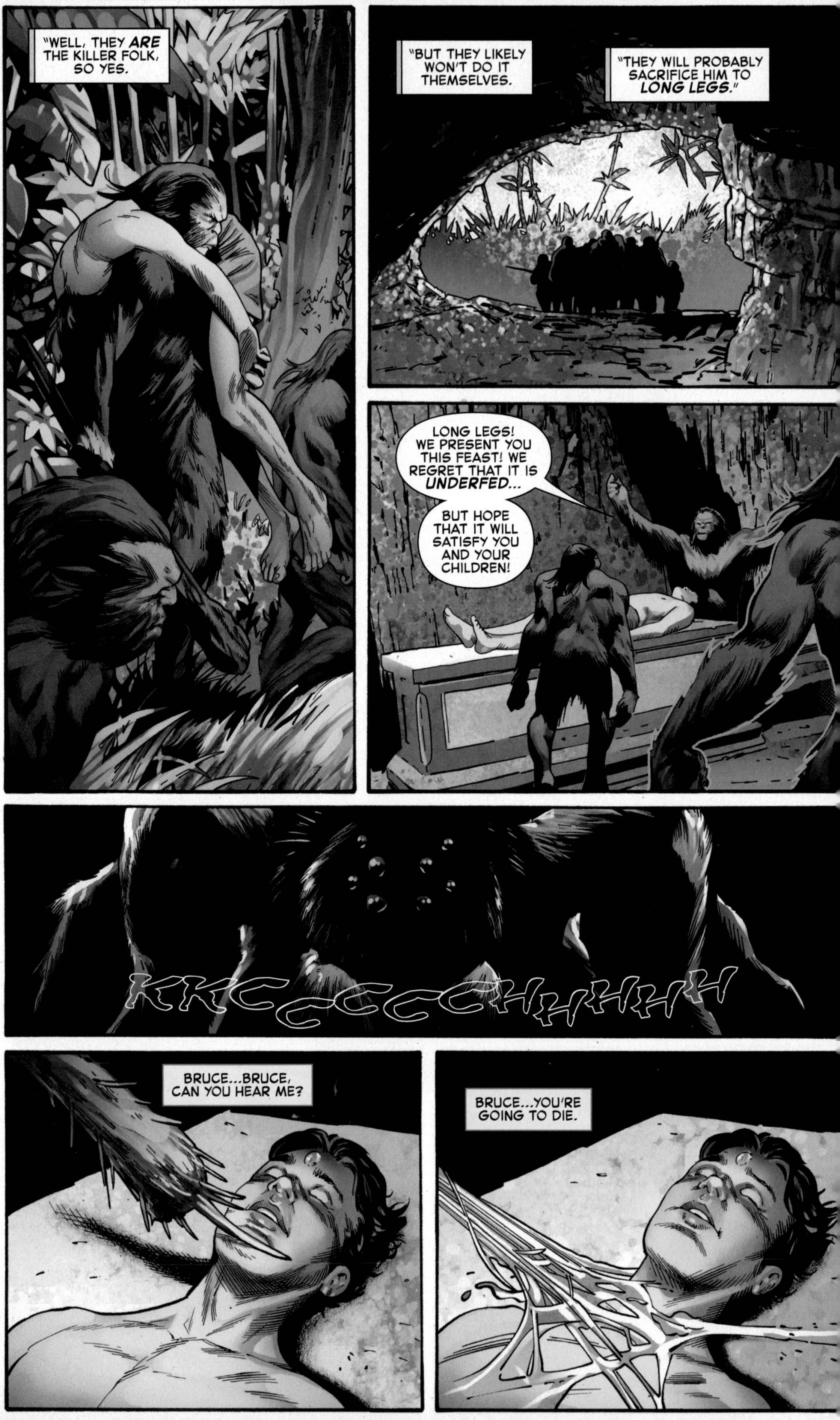
"WELL, THEY ARE THE KILLER FOLK, SO YES.
"BUT THEY LIKELY WON'T DO IT THEMSELVES.
"THEY WILL PROBABLY SACRIFICE HIM TO LONG LEGS."
LONG LEGS! WE PRESENT YOU THIS FEAST! WE REGRET THAT IT IS UNDERFED...
BUT HOPE THAT IT WILL SATISFY YOU AND YOUR CHILDREN!
KKCCCCCHHHHHH
BRUCE...BRUCE, CAN YOU HEAR ME?
BRUCE...YOU'RE GOING TO DIE.

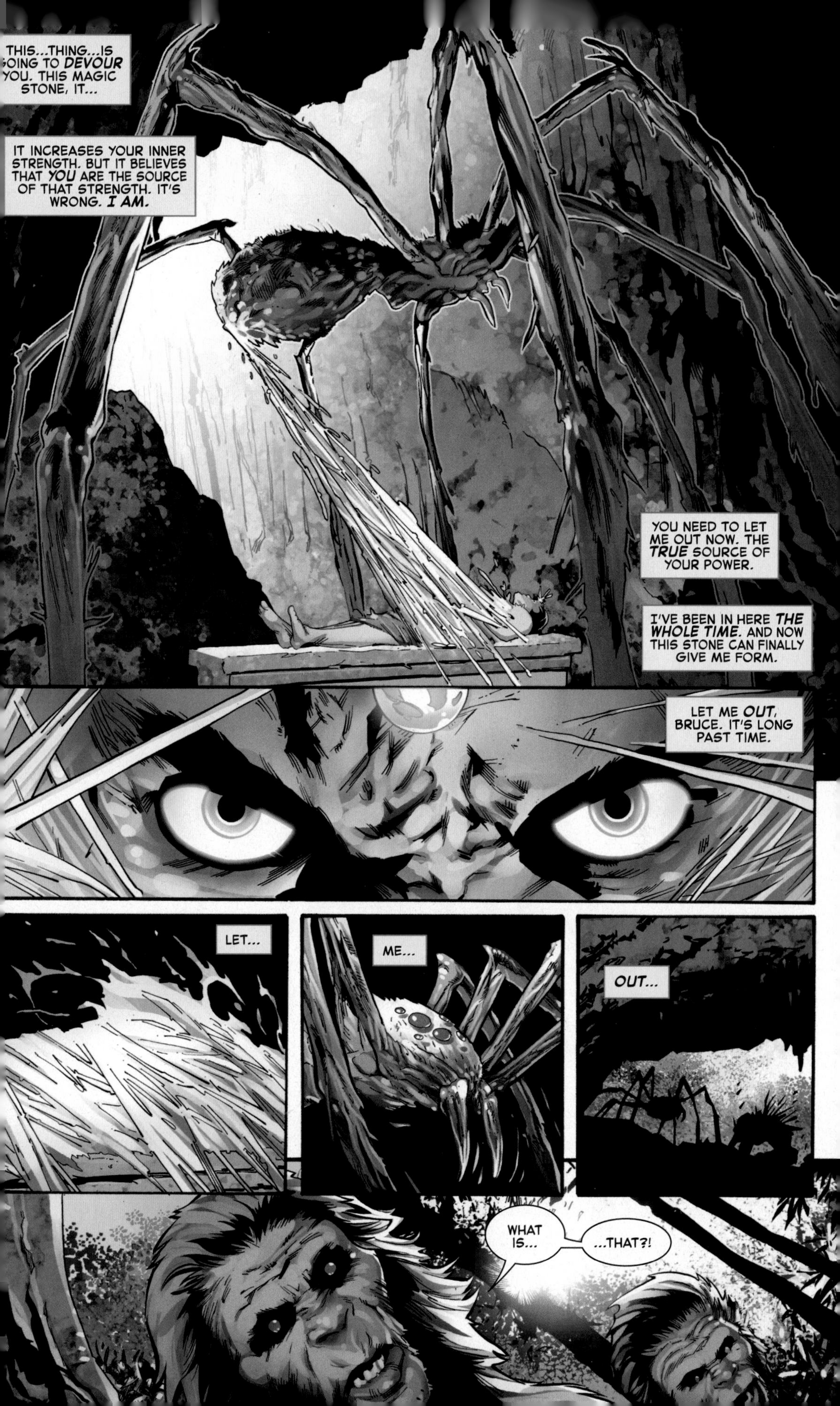
THIS...THING...IS GOING TO DEVOUR YOU. THIS MAGIC STONE, IT...
IT INCREASES YOUR INNER STRENGTH. BUT IT BELIEVES THAT YOU ARE THE SOURCE OF THAT STRENGTH. IT'S WRONG. I AM.
YOU NEED TO LET ME OUT NOW. THE TRUE SOURCE OF YOUR POWER.
I'VE BEEN IN HERE THE WHOLE TIME. AND NOW THIS STONE CAN FINALLY GIVE ME FORM.
LET ME OUT, BRUCE. IT'S LONG PAST TIME.
LET...
ME...
OUT...
WHAT IS...
...THAT?!

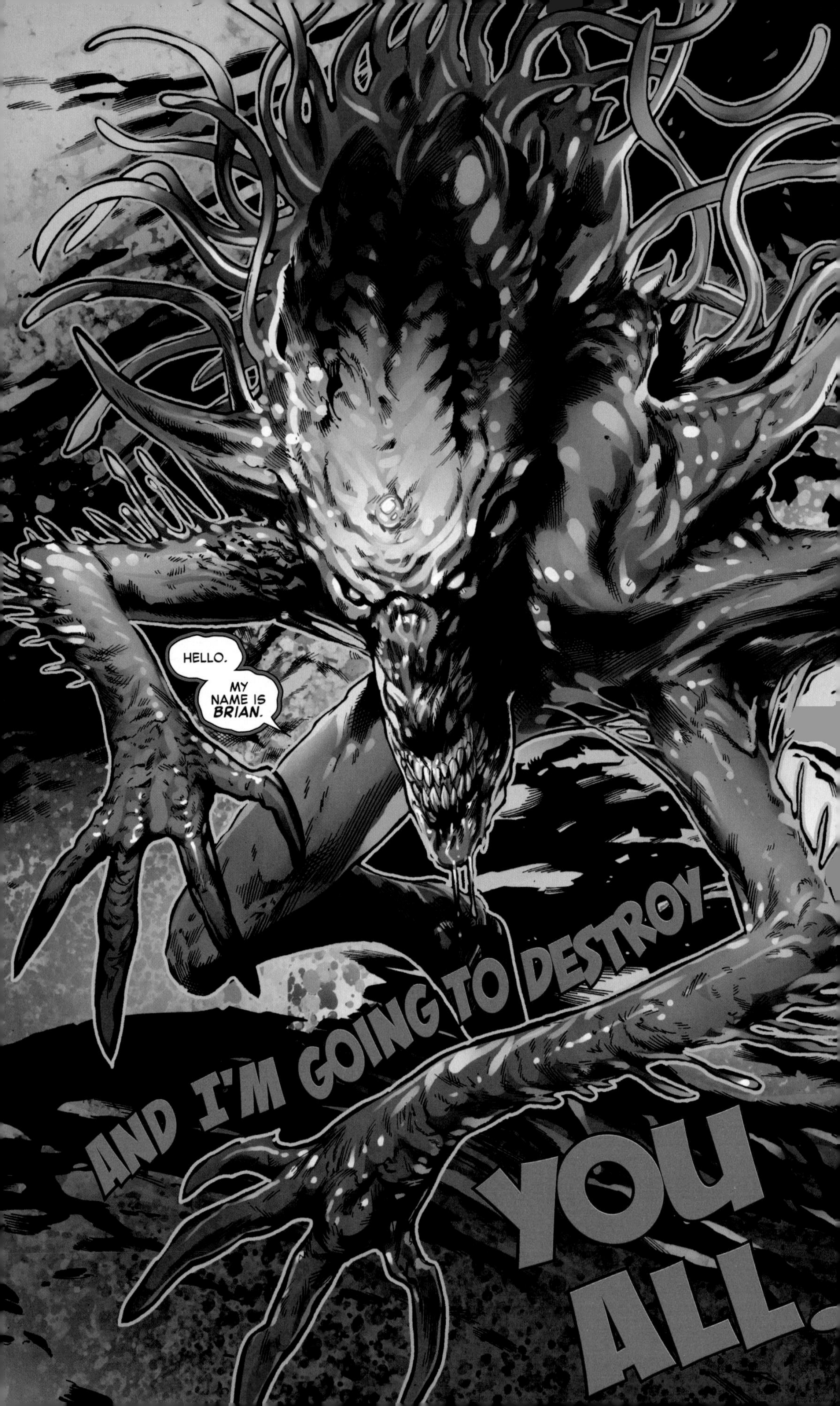
HELLO.
MY NAME IS BRIAN.
AND I'M GOING TO DESTROY
YOU ALL.

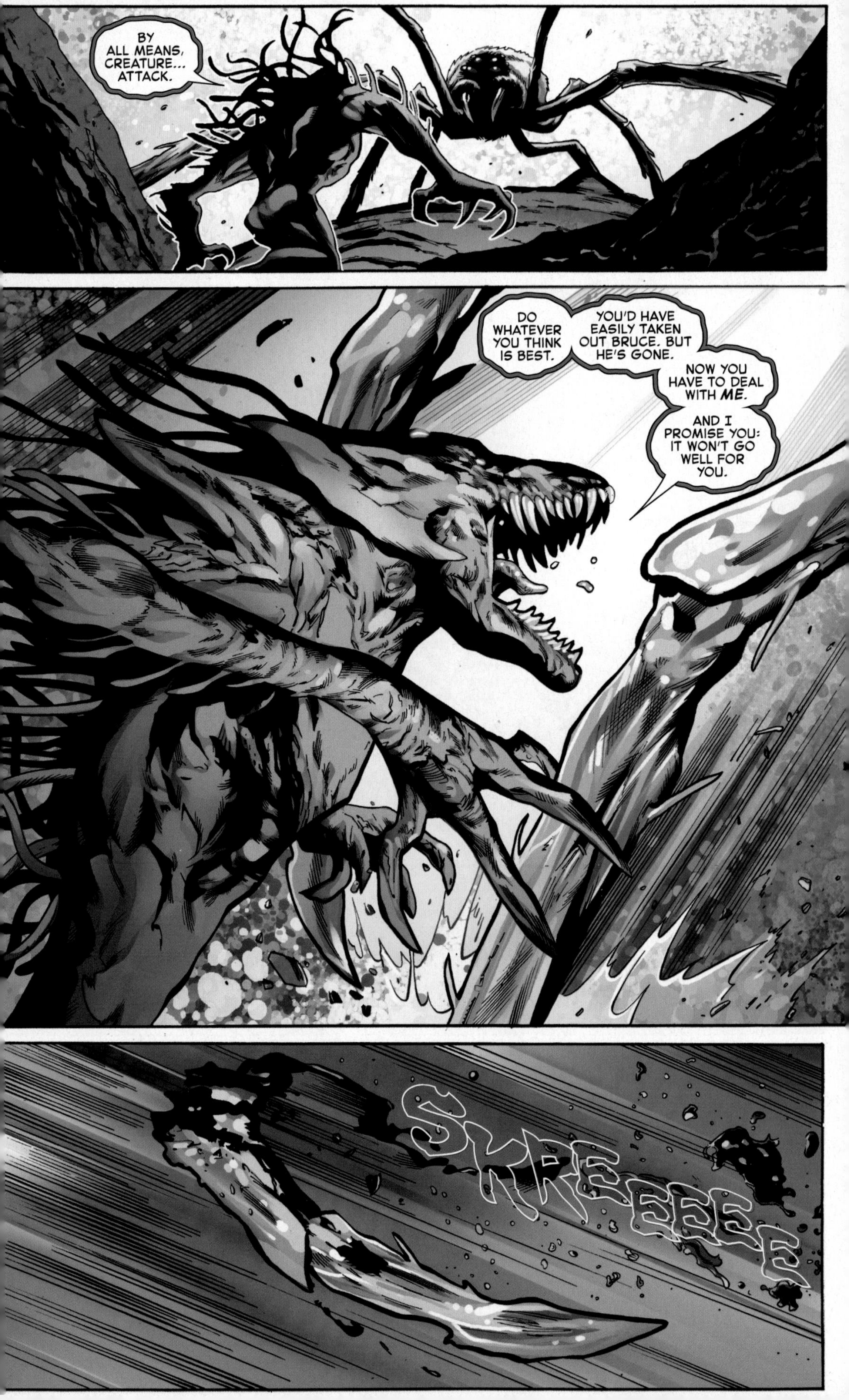
BY ALL MEANS, CREATURE... ATTACK.
DO WHATEVER YOU THINK IS BEST.
YOU'D HAVE EASILY TAKEN OUT BRUCE. BUT HE'S GONE.
NOW YOU HAVE TO DEAL WITH *ME*.
AND I PROMISE YOU: IT WON'T GO WELL FOR YOU.
SKREEEEE

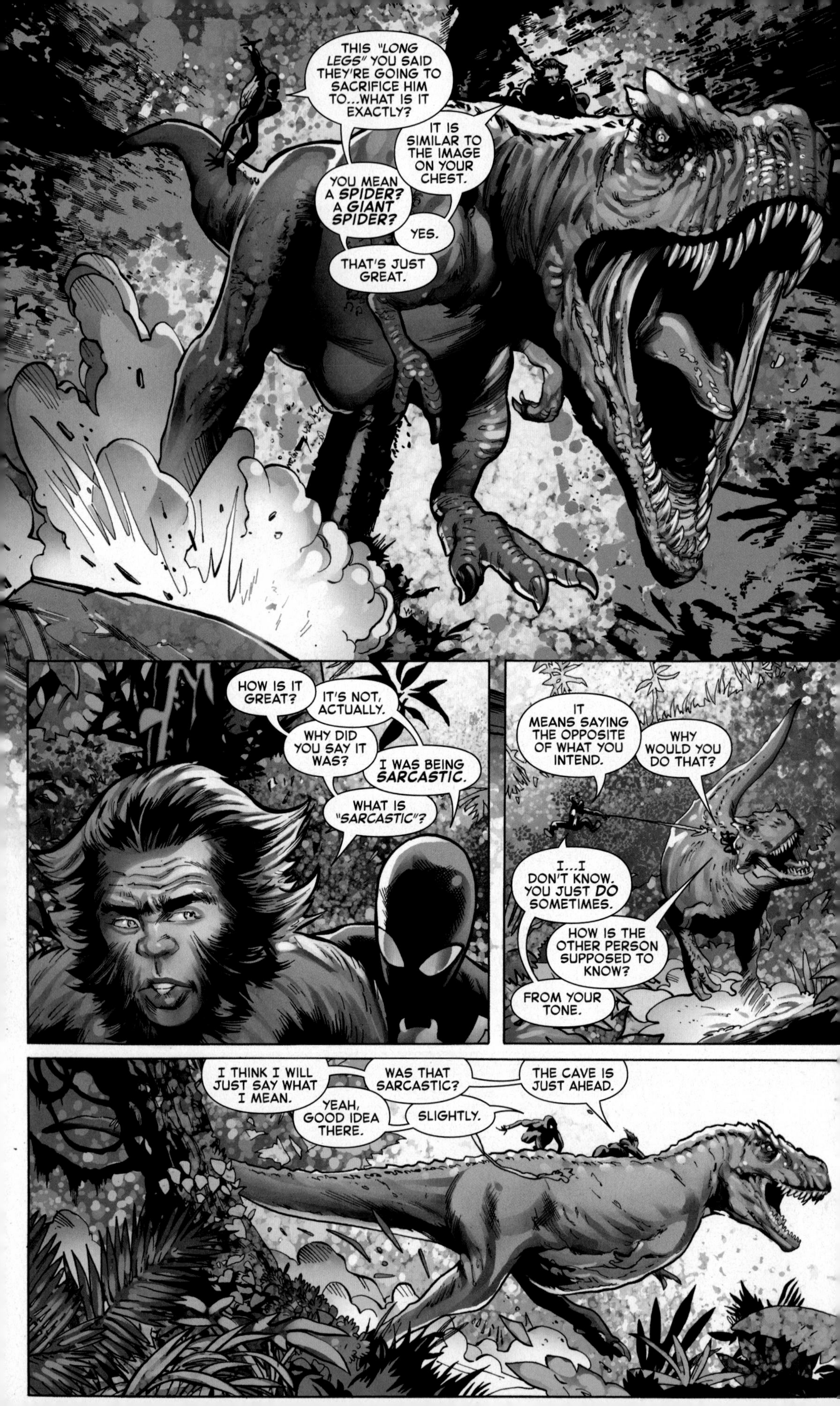
THIS "LONG LEGS" YOU SAID THEY'RE GOING TO SACRIFICE HIM TO...WHAT IS IT EXACTLY?
IT IS SIMILAR TO THE IMAGE ON YOUR CHEST.
YOU MEAN A SPIDER? A GIANT SPIDER?
YES.
THAT'S JUST GREAT.
HOW IS IT GREAT?
IT'S NOT, ACTUALLY.
WHY DID YOU SAY IT WAS?
I WAS BEING SARCASTIC.
WHAT IS "SARCASTIC"?
IT MEANS SAYING THE OPPOSITE OF WHAT YOU INTEND.
WHY WOULD YOU DO THAT?
I...I DON'T KNOW. YOU JUST DO SOMETIMES.
HOW IS THE OTHER PERSON SUPPOSED TO KNOW?
FROM YOUR TONE.
I THINK I WILL JUST SAY WHAT I MEAN.
YEAH, GOOD IDEA THERE.
WAS THAT SARCASTIC?
SLIGHTLY.
THE CAVE IS JUST AHEAD.

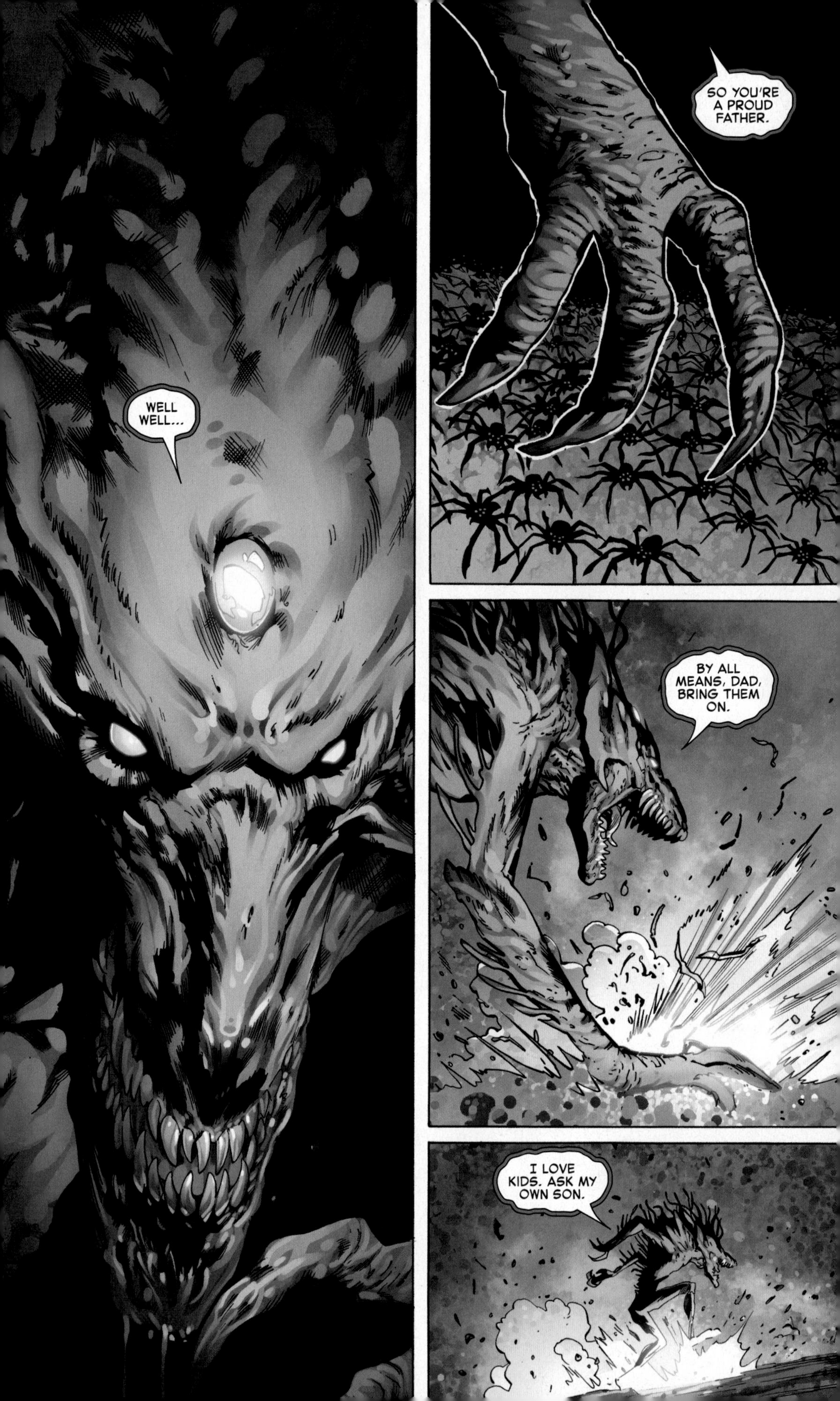

WELL WELL...
SO YOU'RE A PROUD FATHER.
BY ALL MEANS, DAD, BRING THEM ON.
I LOVE KIDS. ASK MY OWN SON.

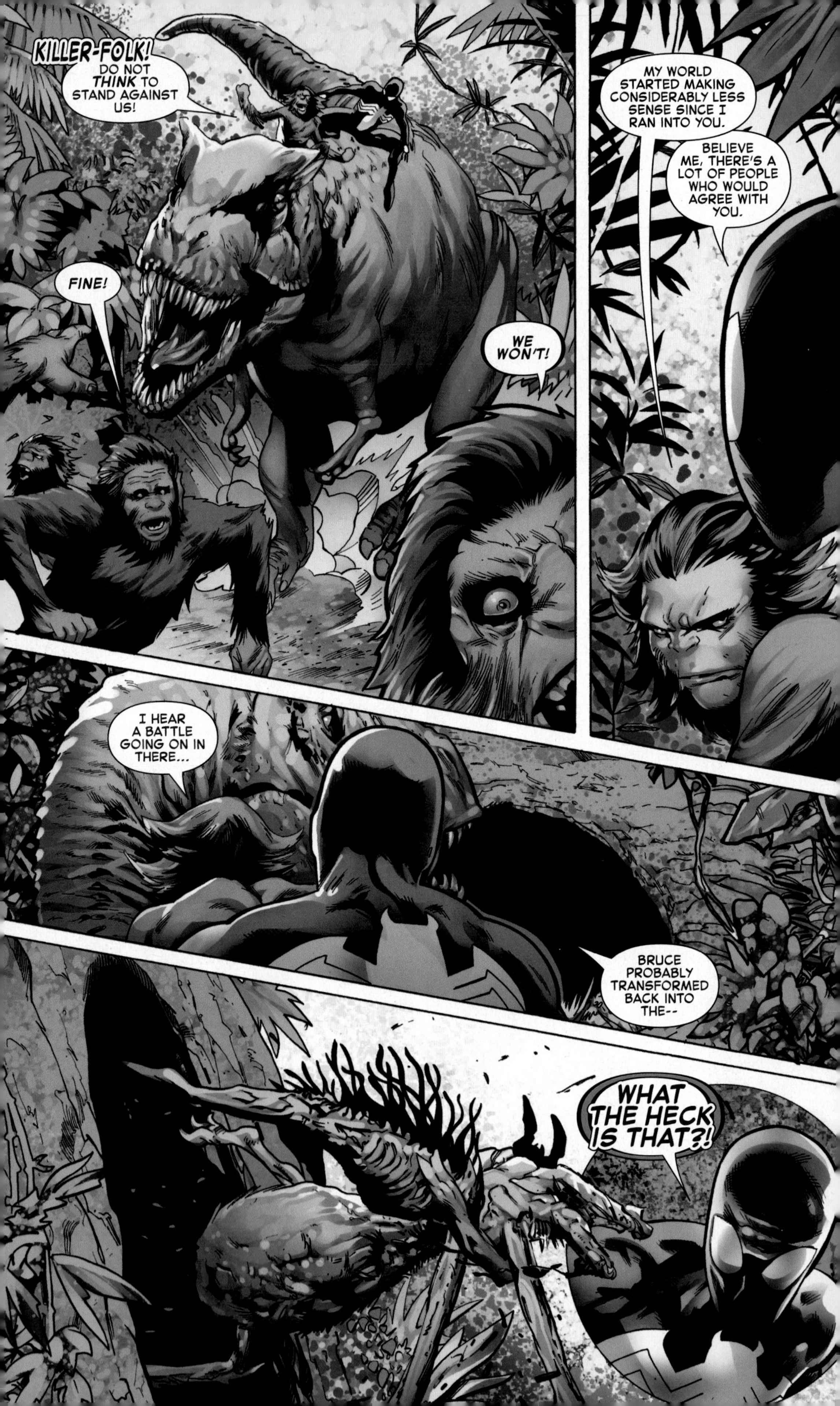
KILLER-FOLK!
DO NOT THINK TO STAND AGAINST US!
FINE!
WE WON'T!
MY WORLD STARTED MAKING CONSIDERABLY LESS SENSE SINCE I RAN INTO YOU.
BELIEVE ME, THERE'S A LOT OF PEOPLE WHO WOULD AGREE WITH YOU.
I HEAR A BATTLE GOING ON IN THERE...
BRUCE PROBABLY TRANSFORMED BACK INTO THE--
WHAT THE HECK IS THAT?!

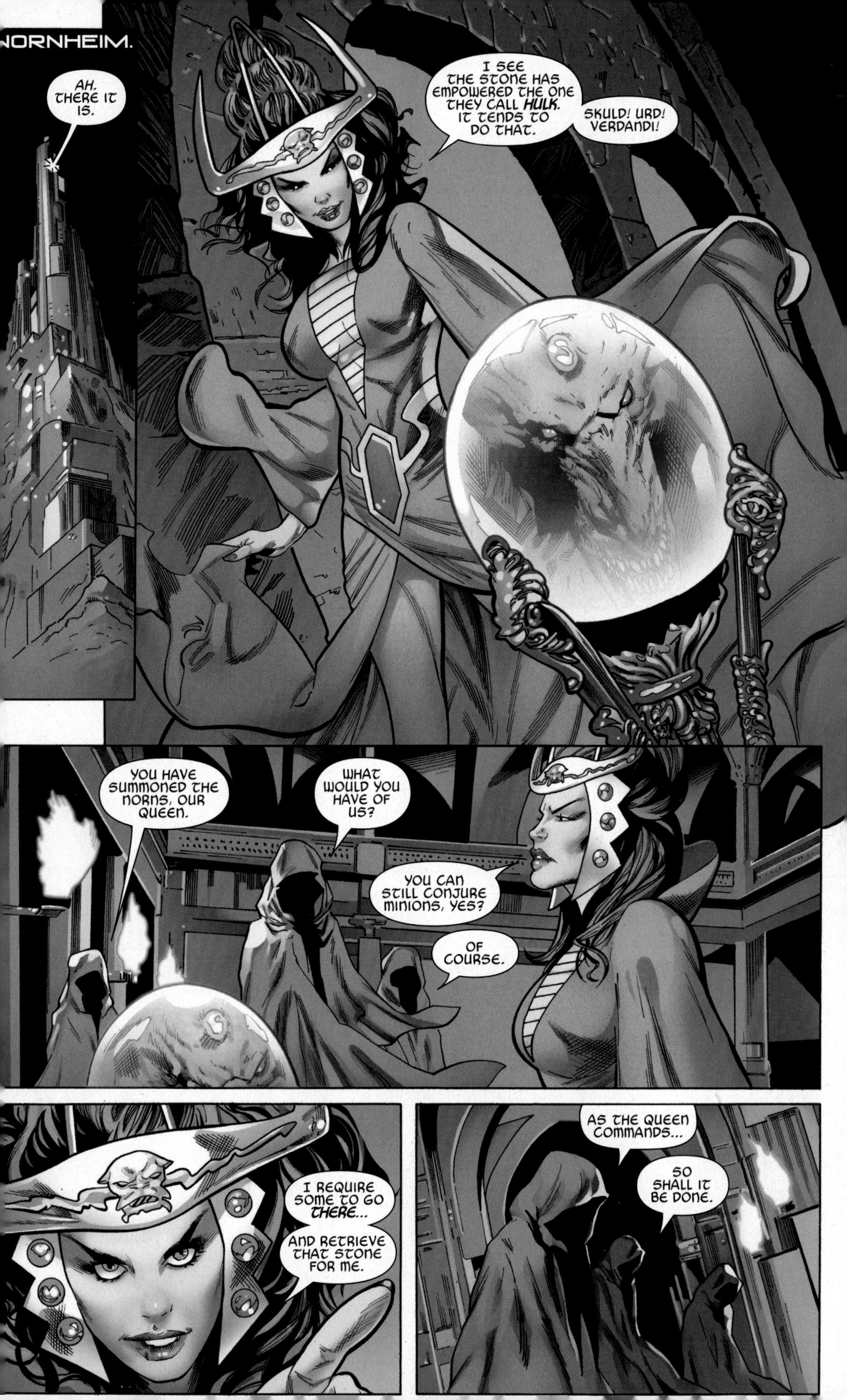
NORNHEIM.
AH. THERE IT IS.
I SEE THE STONE HAS EMPOWERED THE ONE THEY CALL HULK. IT TENDS TO DO THAT.
SKULD! URD! VERDANDI!
YOU HAVE SUMMONED THE NORNS, OUR QUEEN.
WHAT WOULD YOU HAVE OF US?
YOU CAN STILL CONJURE MINIONS, YES?
OF COURSE.
I REQUIRE SOME TO GO THERE...
AND RETRIEVE THAT STONE FOR ME.
AS THE QUEEN COMMANDS...
SO SHALL IT BE DONE.

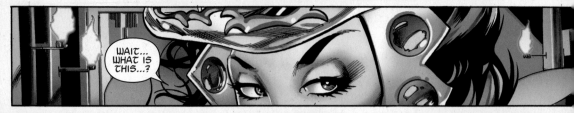

WAIT... WHAT IS THIS...?

SOMEONE ELSE IS WATCHING AS WELL!

WHO?

I ENCOUNTERED A MORTAL MAGICIAN A BIT EARLIER...

IT MIGHT BE HIM.

A MORTAL? CERTAINLY A MORTAL PRESENTS NO THREAT TO YOU, MISTRESS.

I DON'T KNOW ABOUT THAT...

SOME OF THEM CAN PROVE TO BE...

PROBLEMATIC.

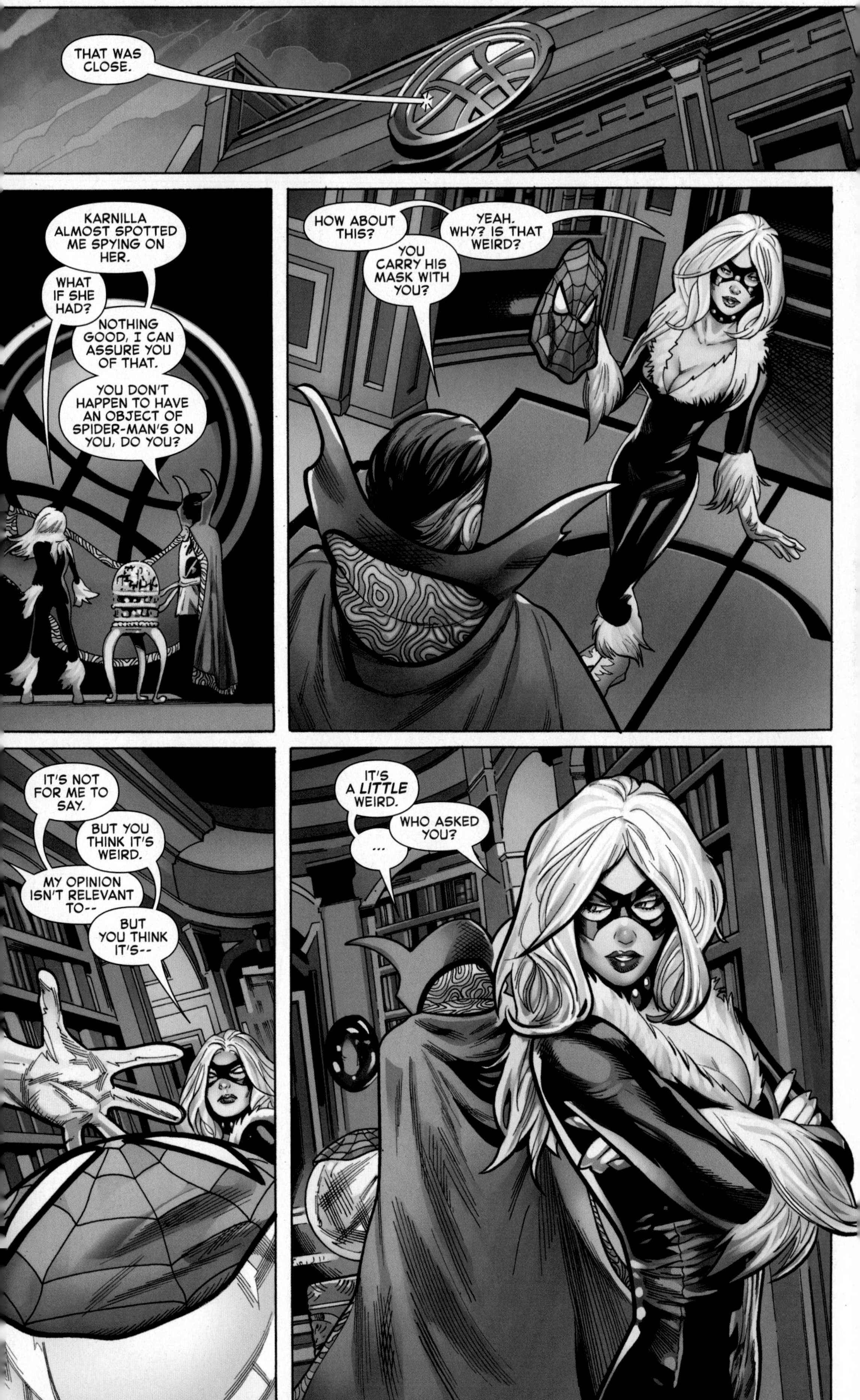
THAT WAS CLOSE.
KARNILLA ALMOST SPOTTED ME SPYING ON HER.
WHAT IF SHE HAD?
NOTHING GOOD, I CAN ASSURE YOU OF THAT.
YOU DON'T HAPPEN TO HAVE AN OBJECT OF SPIDER-MAN'S ON YOU, DO YOU?
HOW ABOUT THIS?
YOU CARRY HIS MASK WITH YOU?
YEAH. WHY? IS THAT WEIRD?
IT'S NOT FOR ME TO SAY.
BUT YOU THINK IT'S WEIRD.
MY OPINION ISN'T RELEVANT TO--
BUT YOU THINK IT'S--
IT'S A LITTLE WEIRD.
...
WHO ASKED YOU?

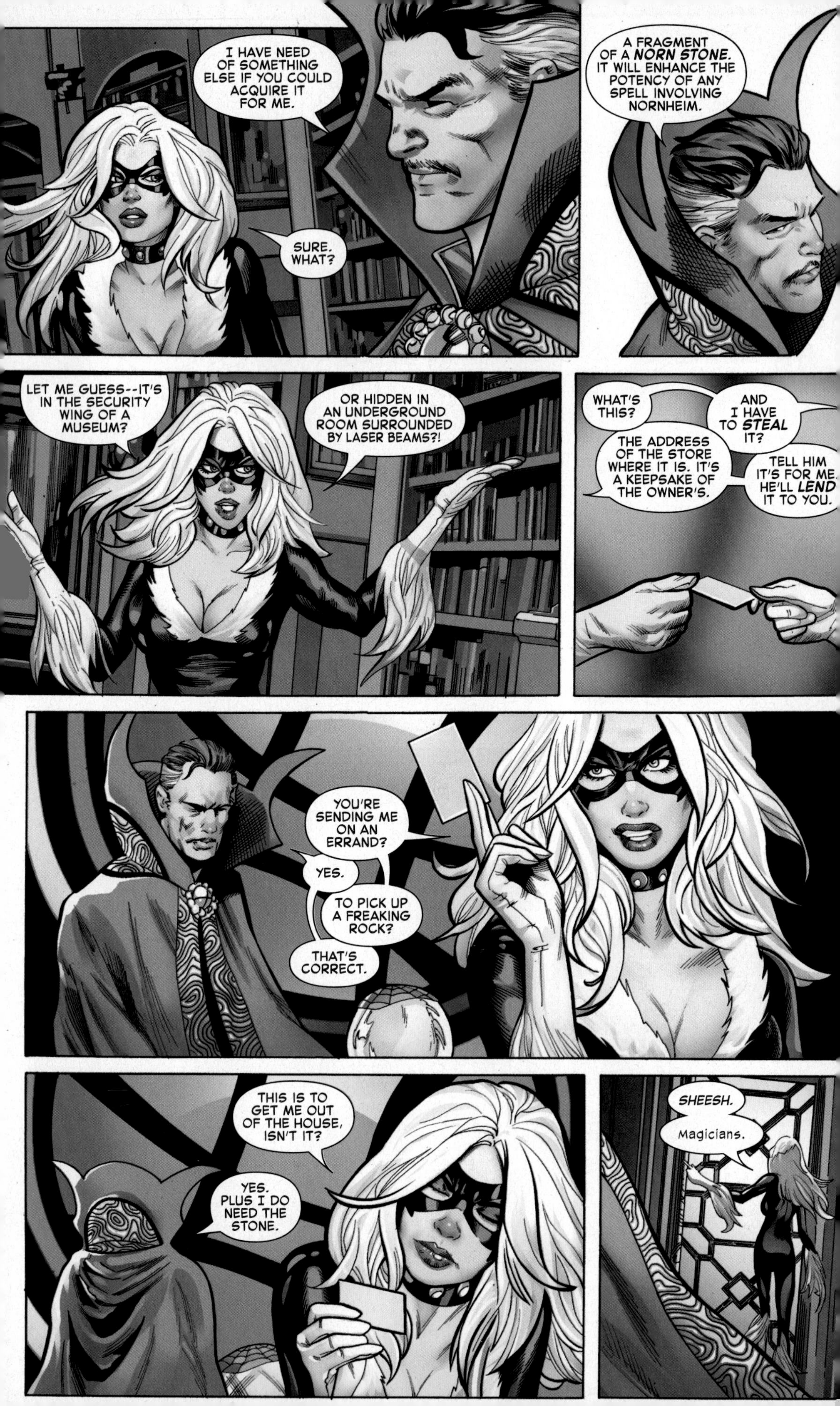
I HAVE NEED OF SOMETHING ELSE IF YOU COULD ACQUIRE IT FOR ME.
SURE. WHAT?
A FRAGMENT OF A NORN STONE. IT WILL ENHANCE THE POTENCY OF ANY SPELL INVOLVING NORNHEIM.
LET ME GUESS--IT'S IN THE SECURITY WING OF A MUSEUM?
OR HIDDEN IN AN UNDERGROUND ROOM SURROUNDED BY LASER BEAMS?!
WHAT'S THIS?
THE ADDRESS OF THE STORE WHERE IT IS. IT'S A KEEPSAKE OF THE OWNER'S.
AND I HAVE TO STEAL IT?
TELL HIM IT'S FOR ME. HE'LL LEND IT TO YOU.
YOU'RE SENDING ME ON AN ERRAND?
YES.
TO PICK UP A FREAKING ROCK?
THAT'S CORRECT.
THIS IS TO GET ME OUT OF THE HOUSE, ISN'T IT?
YES. PLUS I DO NEED THE STONE.
SHEESH.
Magicians.

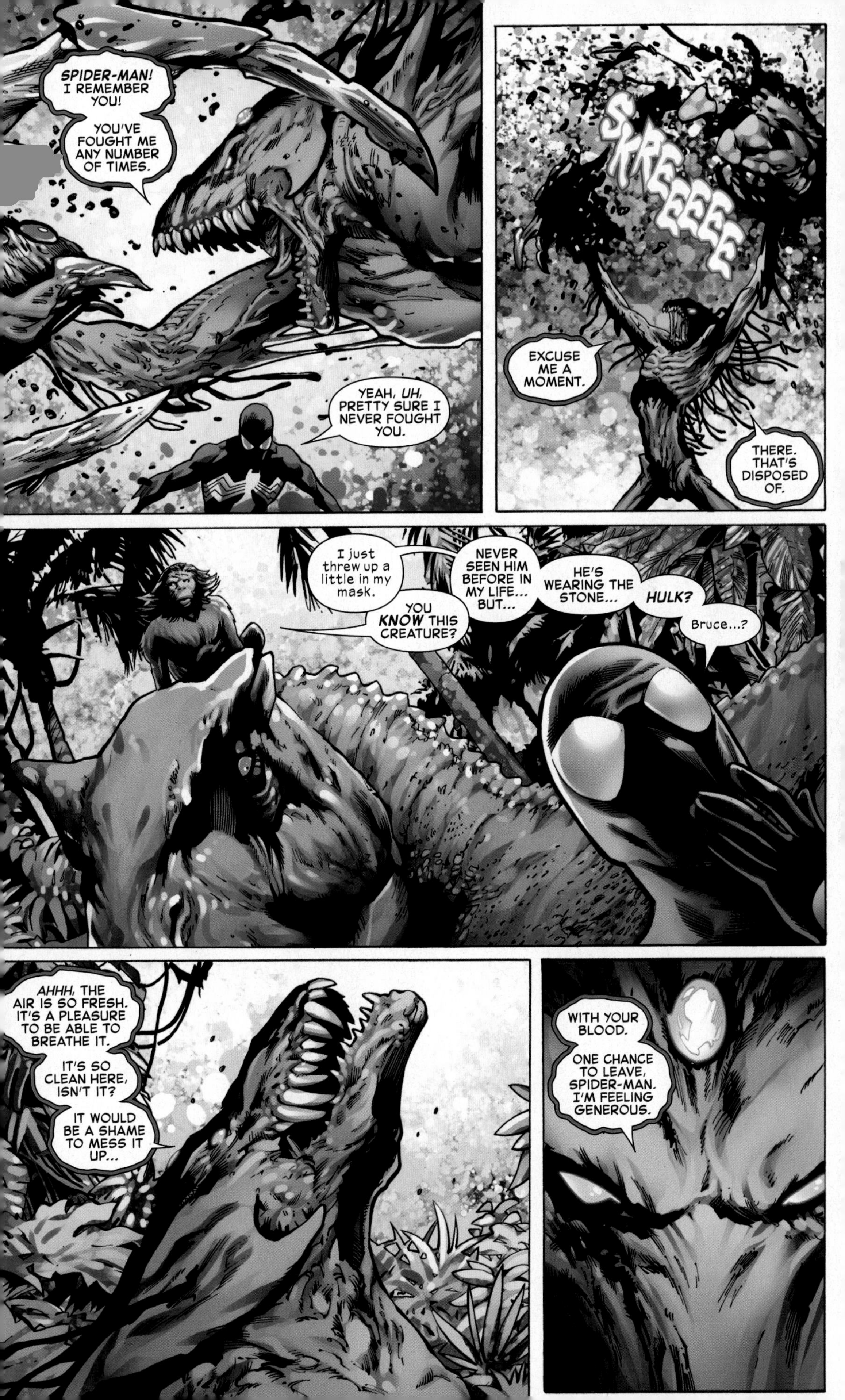
SPIDER-MAN! I REMEMBER YOU!
YOU'VE FOUGHT ME ANY NUMBER OF TIMES.
YEAH, UH, PRETTY SURE I NEVER FOUGHT YOU.
SKREEEEEE
EXCUSE ME A MOMENT.
THERE. THAT'S DISPOSED OF.
I just threw up a little in my mask.
YOU KNOW THIS CREATURE?
NEVER SEEN HIM BEFORE IN MY LIFE... BUT...
HE'S WEARING THE STONE...
HULK?
Bruce...?
AHHH, THE AIR IS SO FRESH. IT'S A PLEASURE TO BE ABLE TO BREATHE IT.
IT'S SO CLEAN HERE, ISN'T IT?
IT WOULD BE A SHAME TO MESS IT UP...
WITH YOUR BLOOD.
ONE CHANCE TO LEAVE, SPIDER-MAN. I'M FEELING GENEROUS.

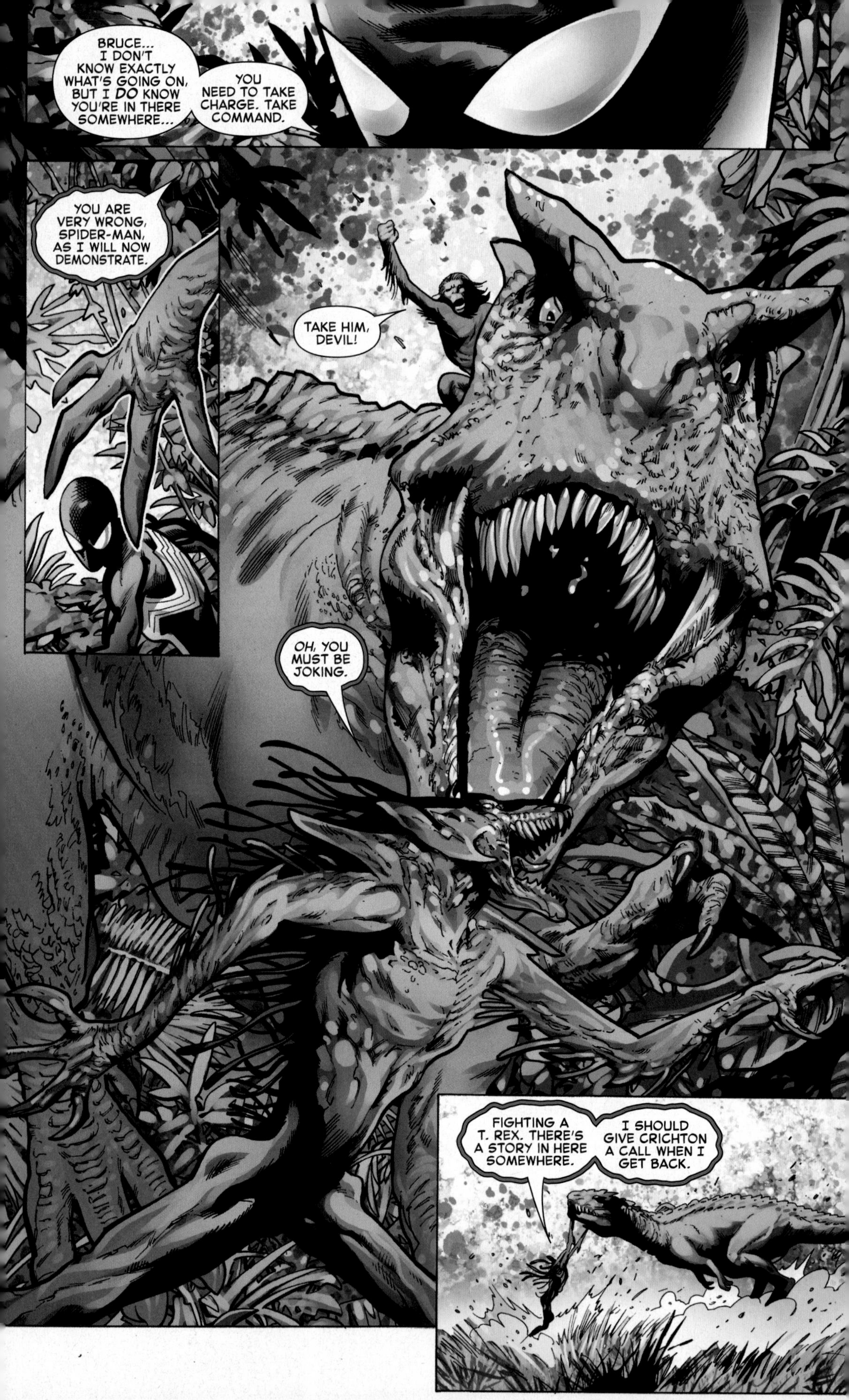
BRUCE... I DON'T KNOW EXACTLY WHAT'S GOING ON, BUT I DO KNOW YOU'RE IN THERE SOMEWHERE...
YOU NEED TO TAKE CHARGE. TAKE COMMAND.
YOU ARE VERY WRONG, SPIDER-MAN, AS I WILL NOW DEMONSTRATE.
TAKE HIM, DEVIL!
OH, YOU MUST BE JOKING.
FIGHTING A T. REX. THERE'S A STORY IN HERE SOMEWHERE.
I SHOULD GIVE CRICHTON A CALL WHEN I GET BACK.

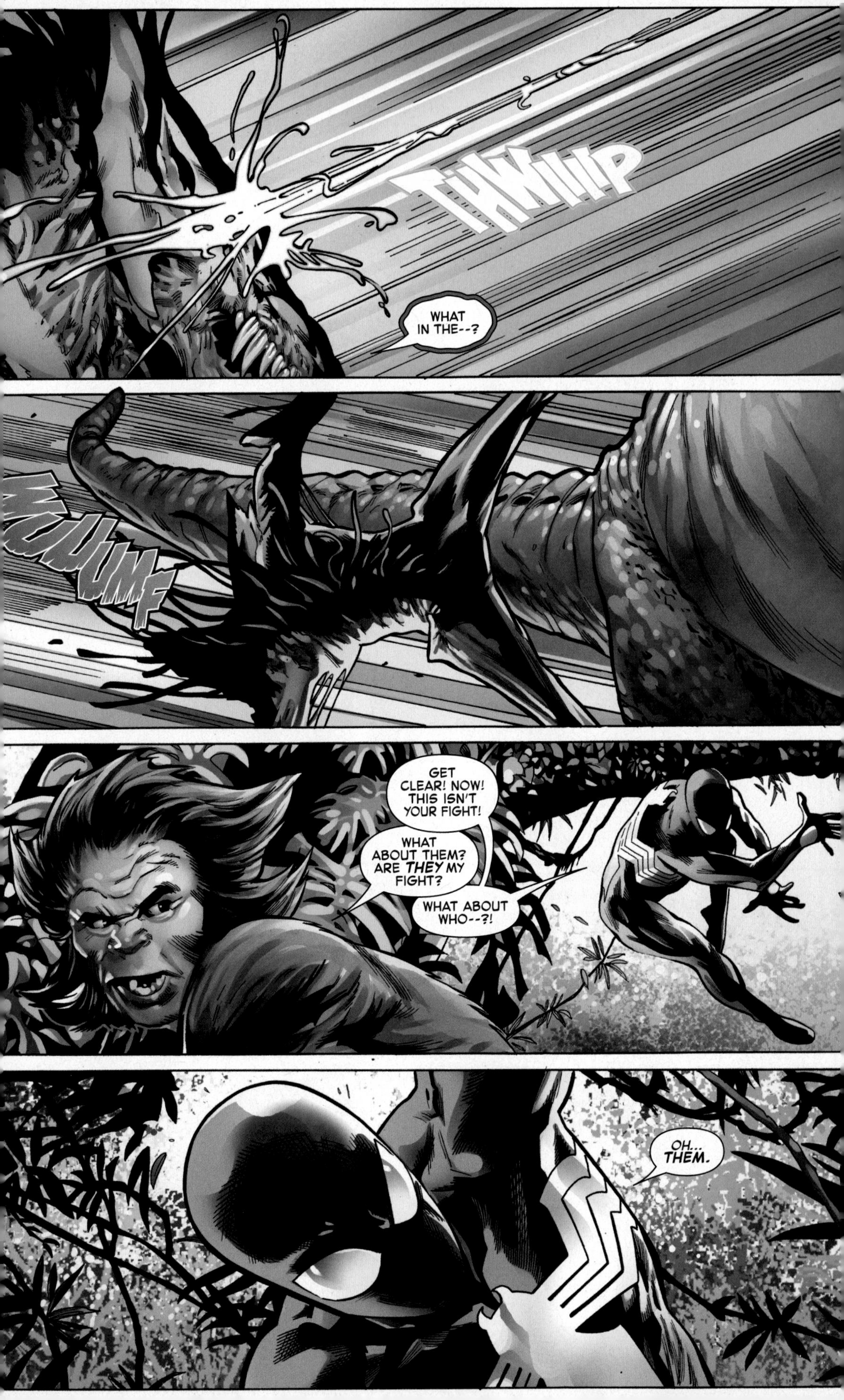
THWIIP
WHAT IN THE--?
WHUUMF
GET CLEAR! NOW! THIS ISN'T YOUR FIGHT!
WHAT ABOUT THEM? ARE THEY MY FIGHT?
WHAT ABOUT WHO--?!
OH... THEM.

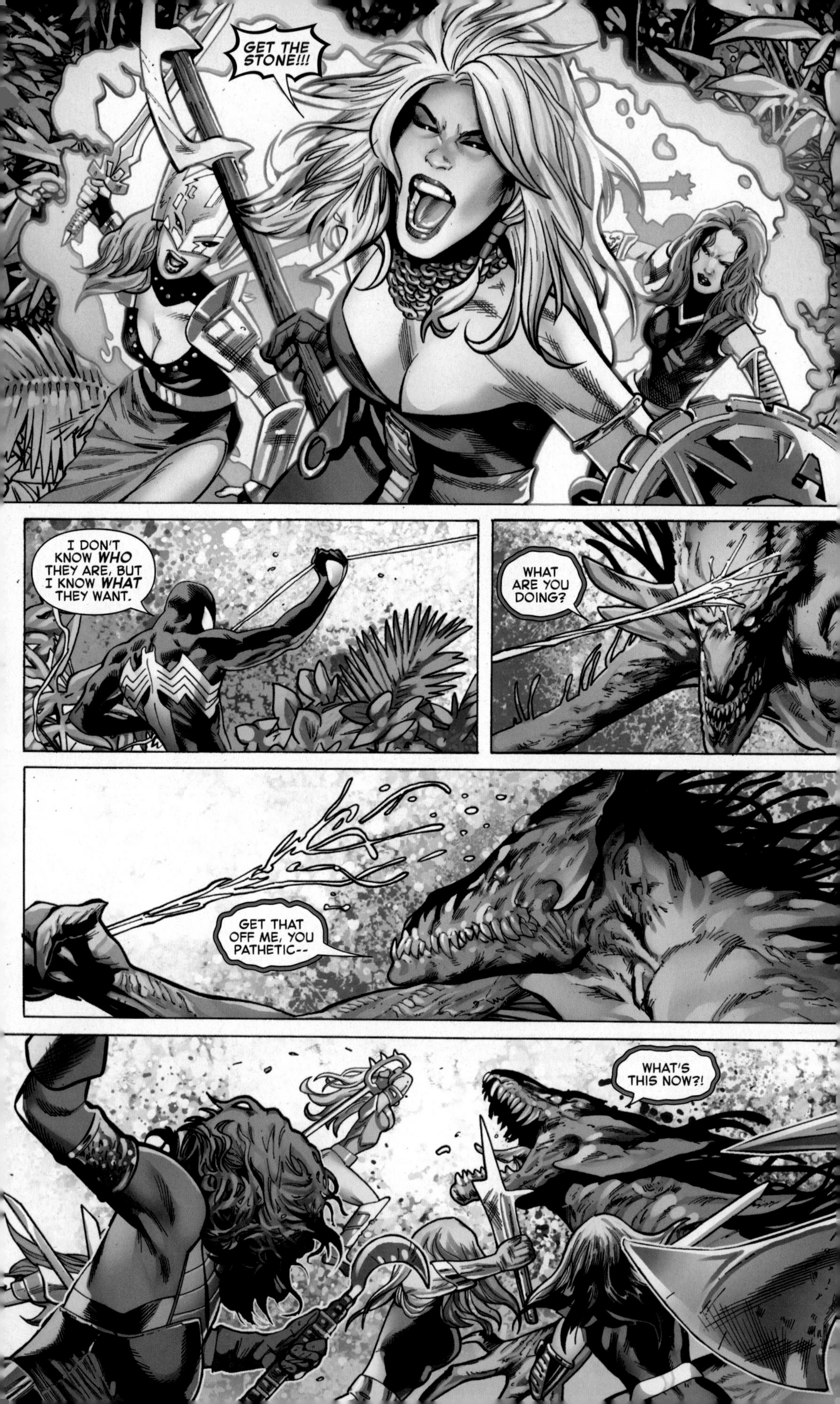
GET THE STONE!!!
I DON'T KNOW WHO THEY ARE, BUT I KNOW WHAT THEY WANT.
WHAT ARE YOU DOING?
GET THAT OFF ME, YOU PATHETIC--
WHAT'S THIS NOW?!

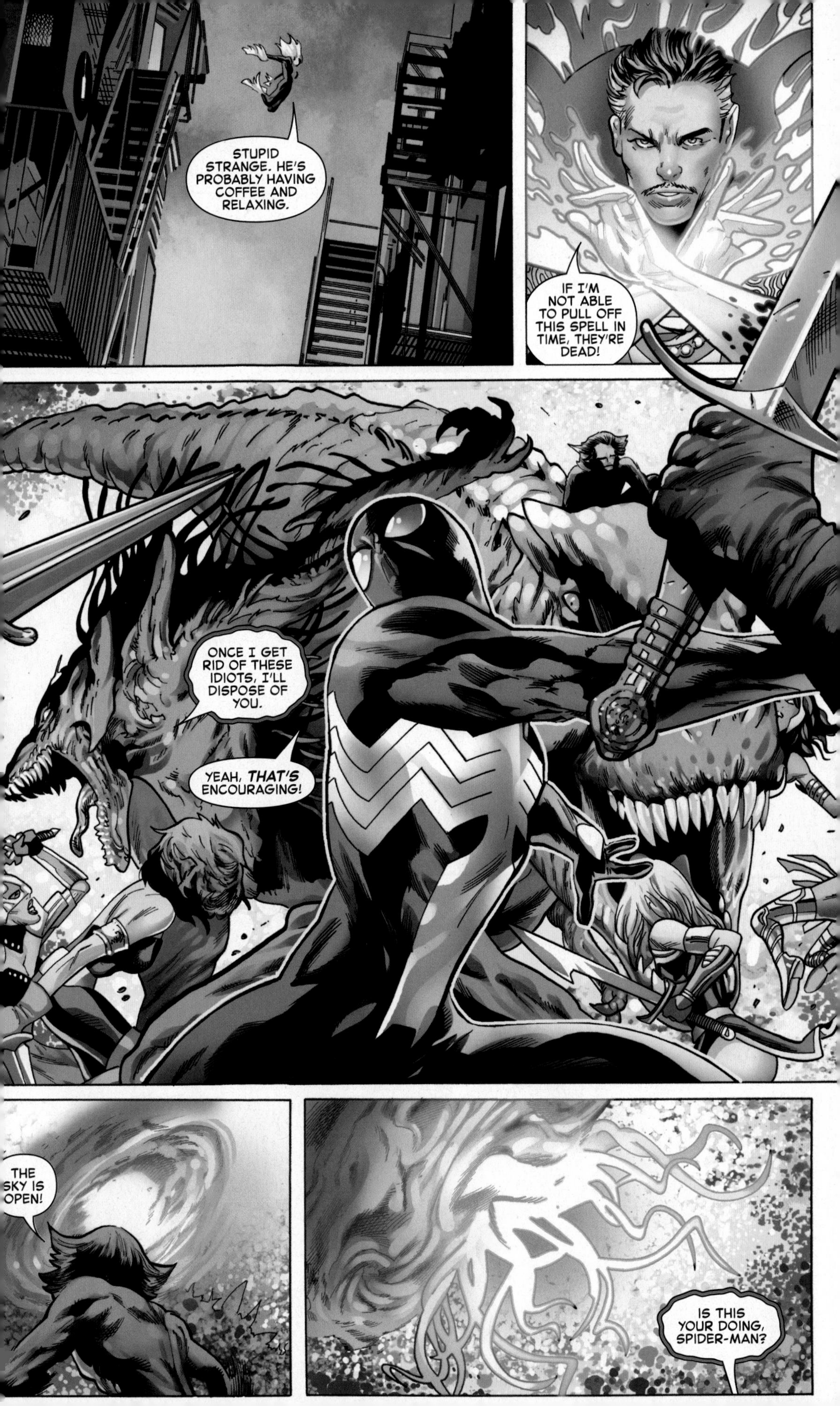
STUPID STRANGE. HE'S PROBABLY HAVING COFFEE AND RELAXING.
IF I'M NOT ABLE TO PULL OFF THIS SPELL IN TIME, THEY'RE DEAD!
ONCE I GET RID OF THESE IDIOTS, I'LL DISPOSE OF YOU.
YEAH, THAT'S ENCOURAGING!
THE SKY IS OPEN!
IS THIS YOUR DOING, SPIDER-MAN?

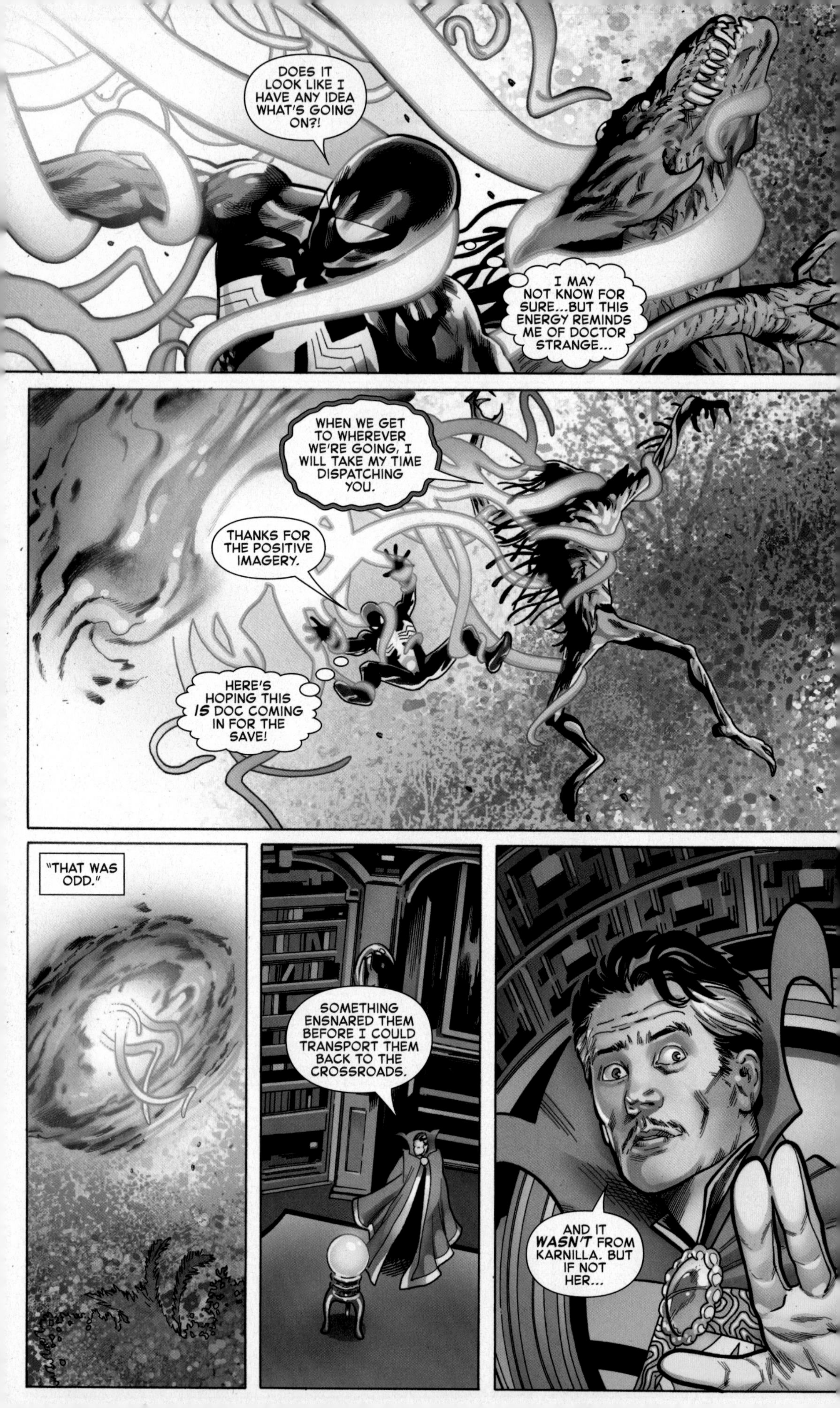
DOES IT LOOK LIKE I HAVE ANY IDEA WHAT'S GOING ON?!
I MAY NOT KNOW FOR SURE...BUT THIS ENERGY REMINDS ME OF DOCTOR STRANGE...
WHEN WE GET TO WHEREVER WE'RE GOING, I WILL TAKE MY TIME DISPATCHING YOU.
THANKS FOR THE POSITIVE IMAGERY.
HERE'S HOPING THIS *IS* DOC COMING IN FOR THE SAVE!
"THAT WAS ODD."
SOMETHING ENSNARED THEM BEFORE I COULD TRANSPORT THEM BACK TO THE CROSSROADS.
AND IT *WASN'T* FROM KARNILLA. BUT IF NOT HER...

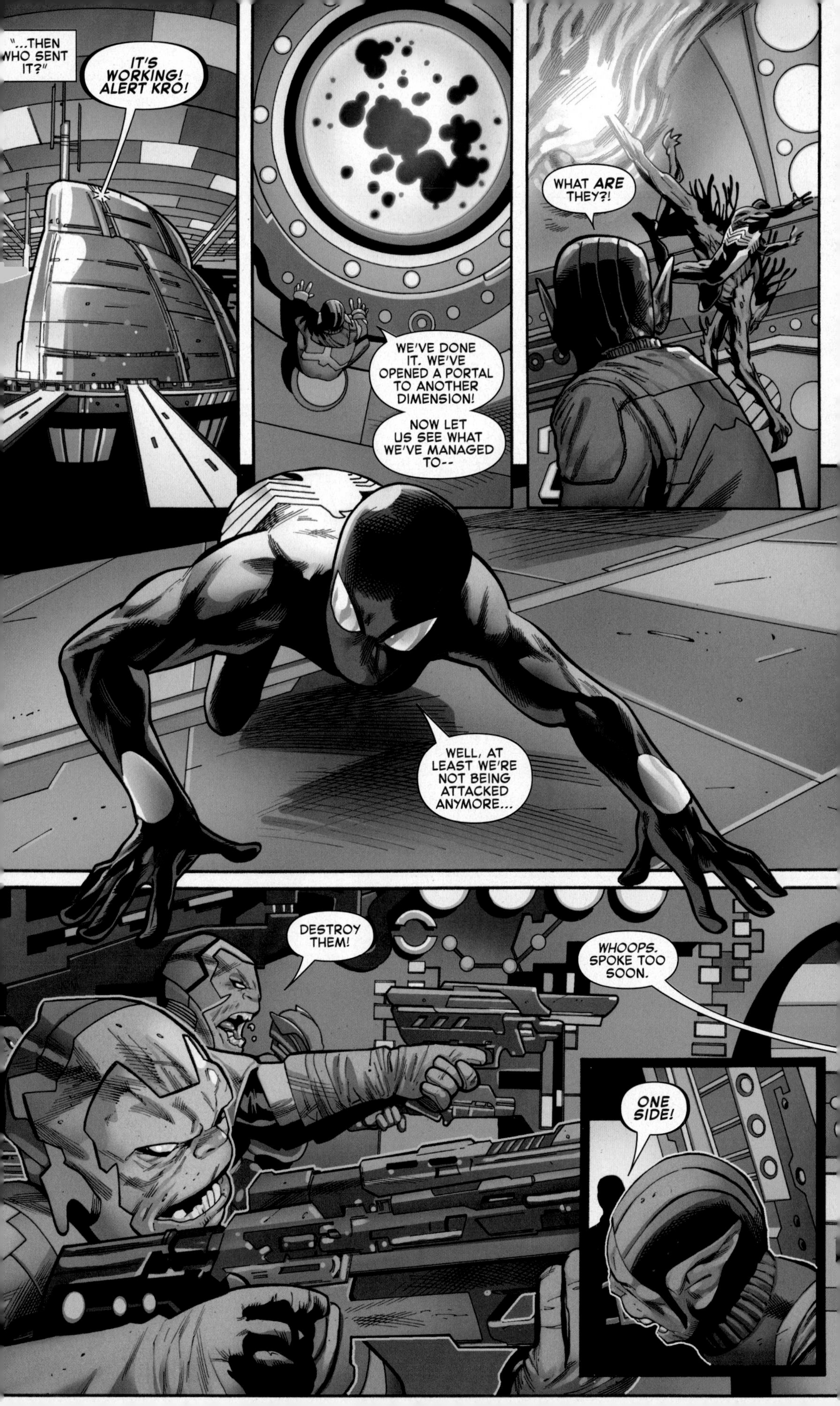
"...THEN WHO SENT IT?"
IT'S WORKING! ALERT KRO!
WE'VE DONE IT. WE'VE OPENED A PORTAL TO ANOTHER DIMENSION!
NOW LET US SEE WHAT WE'VE MANAGED TO--
WHAT ARE THEY?!
WELL, AT LEAST WE'RE NOT BEING ATTACKED ANYMORE...
DESTROY THEM!
WHOOPS. SPOKE TOO SOON.
ONE SIDE!

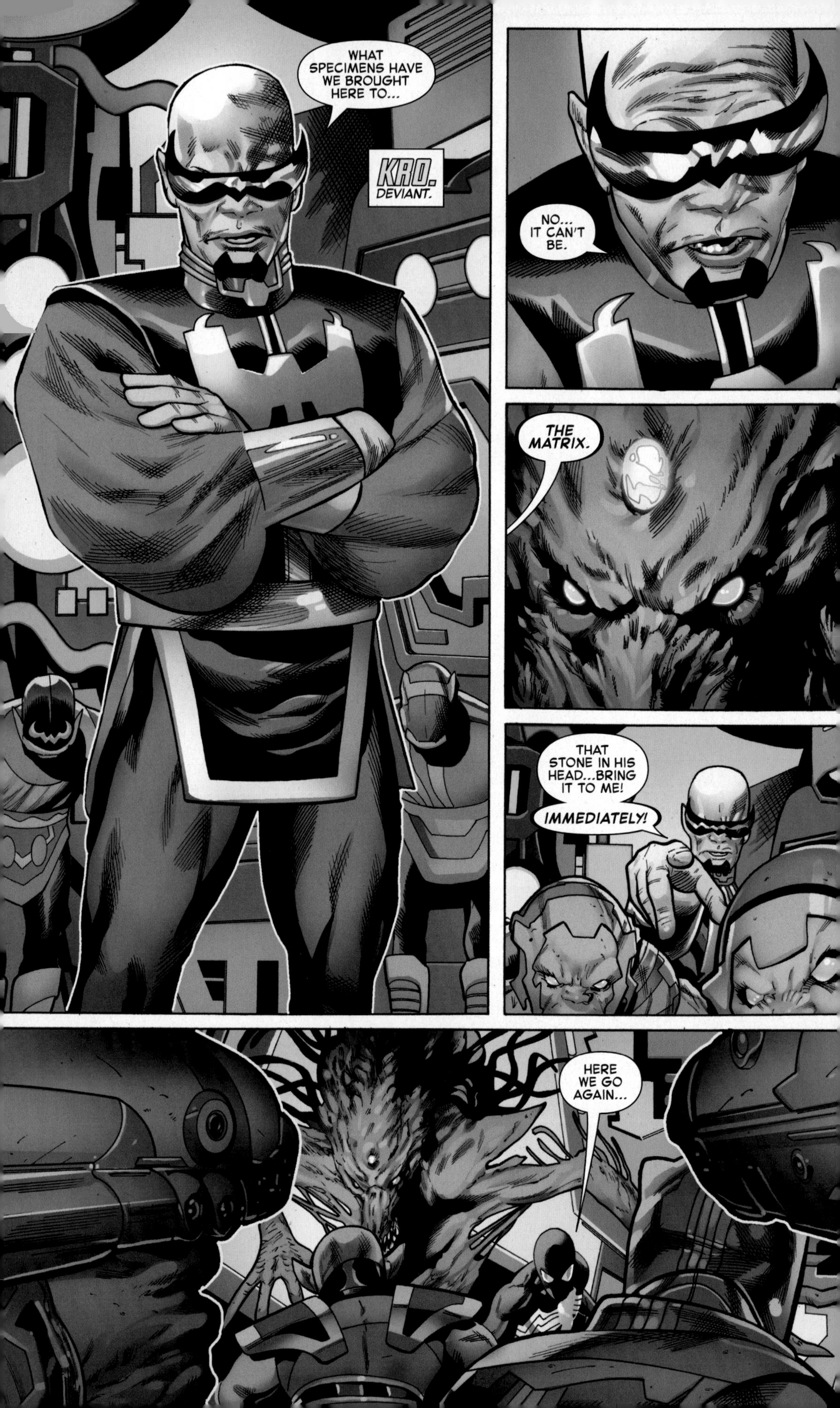
WHAT SPECIMENS HAVE WE BROUGHT HERE TO...
KRO. DEVIANT.
NO... IT CAN'T BE.
THE MATRIX.
THAT STONE IN HIS HEAD...BRING IT TO ME!
IMMEDIATELY!
HERE WE GO AGAIN...

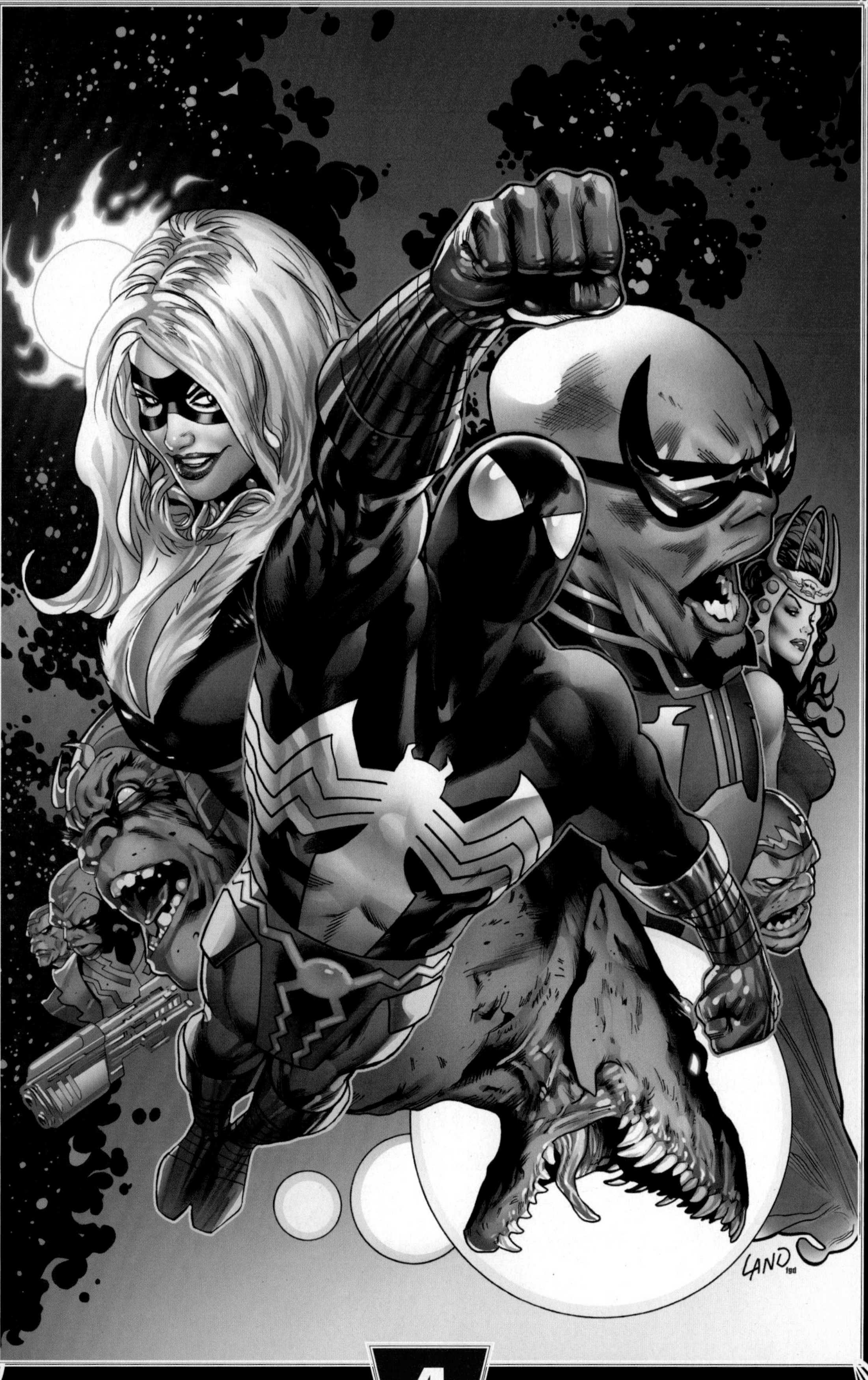

4

YOU ARE CERTAIN OF THIS, ZURAS?

DOMO WAS MOST CERTAIN. I TEND TO TRUST HIM WHEN HE PROVIDES US WITH INFORMATION.

HE IS OUR HEAD TECHNOLOGIST, AFTER ALL.

WITH RESPECT, ZURAS, I KNOW WHO HE IS.

BUT THE STONE? AFTER ALL THIS TIME?

SIMPLY REAPPEARING WITH NO WARNING?

THINGS DON'T ALWAYS ANNOUNCE THEMSELVES, IKARIS.

WHERE ELSE DO SURPRISES COME FROM, AFTER ALL?

I SEE WE'RE ALL STATING THE OBVIOUS TODAY.

THEN LET US STATE THE MOST OBVIOUS THING OF ALL--

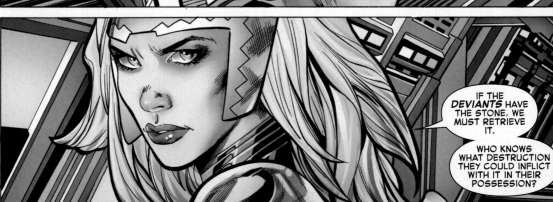

IF THE DEVIANTS HAVE THE STONE, WE MUST RETRIEVE IT.

WHO KNOWS WHAT DESTRUCTION THEY COULD INFLICT WITH IT IN THEIR POSSESSION?

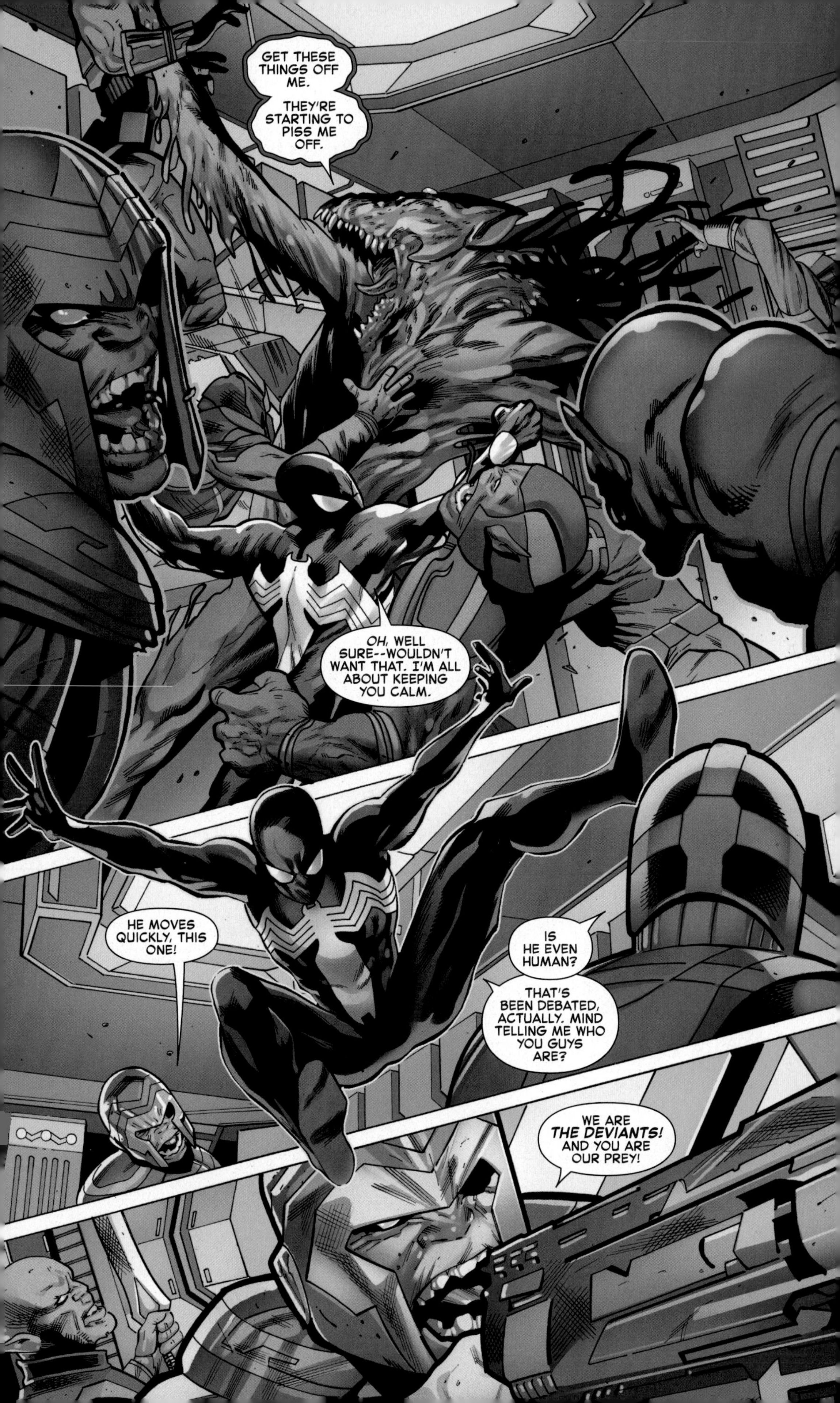

GET THESE THINGS OFF ME.
THEY'RE STARTING TO PISS ME OFF.
OH, WELL SURE--WOULDN'T WANT THAT. I'M ALL ABOUT KEEPING YOU CALM.
HE MOVES QUICKLY, THIS ONE!
IS HE EVEN HUMAN?
THAT'S BEEN DEBATED, ACTUALLY. MIND TELLING ME WHO YOU GUYS ARE?
WE ARE THE DEVIANTS! AND YOU ARE OUR PREY!

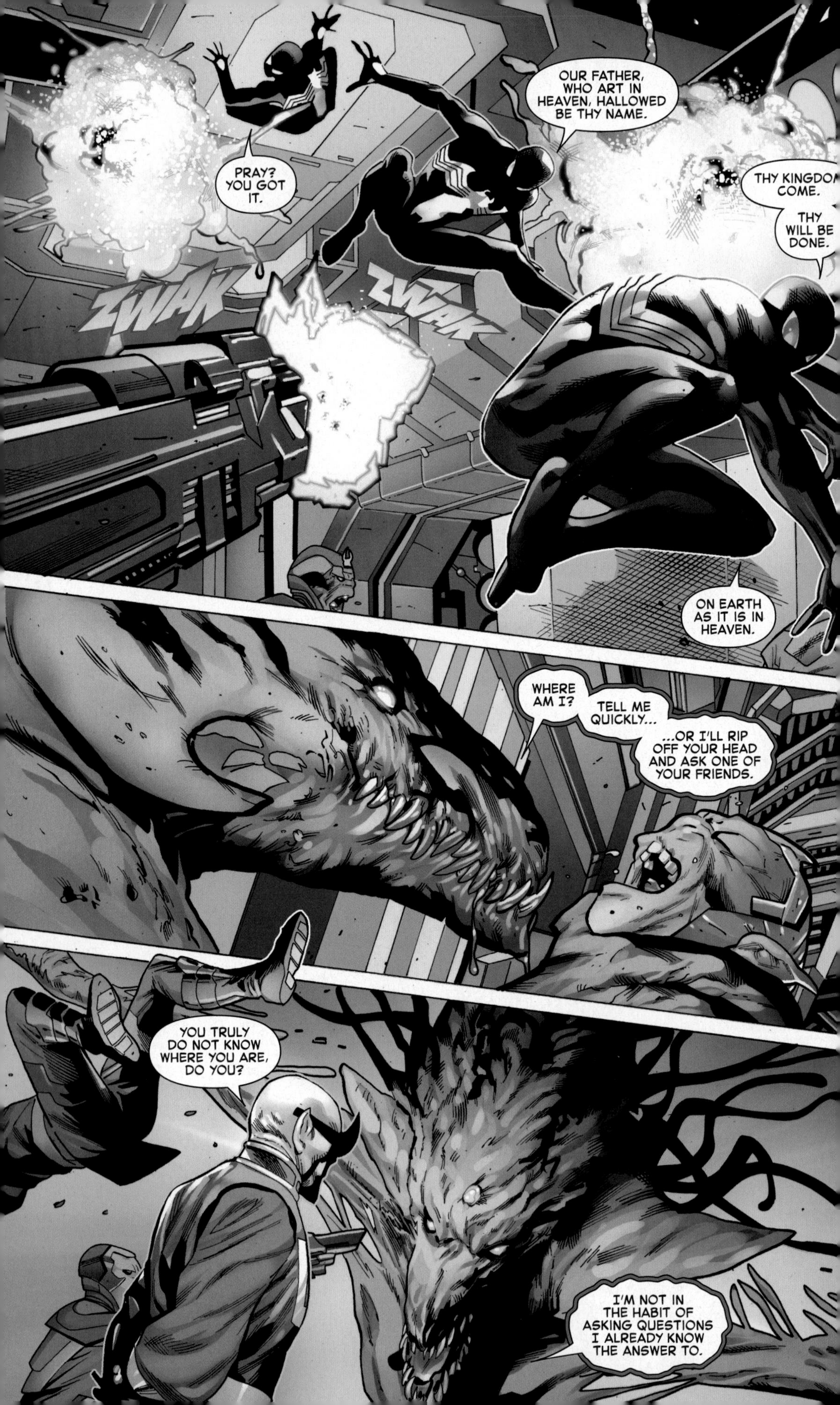
PRAY? YOU GOT IT.
OUR FATHER, WHO ART IN HEAVEN, HALLOWED BE THY NAME.
THY KINGDOM COME.
THY WILL BE DONE.
ZWAK
ZWAK
ON EARTH AS IT IS IN HEAVEN.
WHERE AM I?
TELL ME QUICKLY...
...OR I'LL RIP OFF YOUR HEAD AND ASK ONE OF YOUR FRIENDS.
YOU TRULY DO NOT KNOW WHERE YOU ARE, DO YOU?
I'M NOT IN THE HABIT OF ASKING QUESTIONS I ALREADY KNOW THE ANSWER TO.

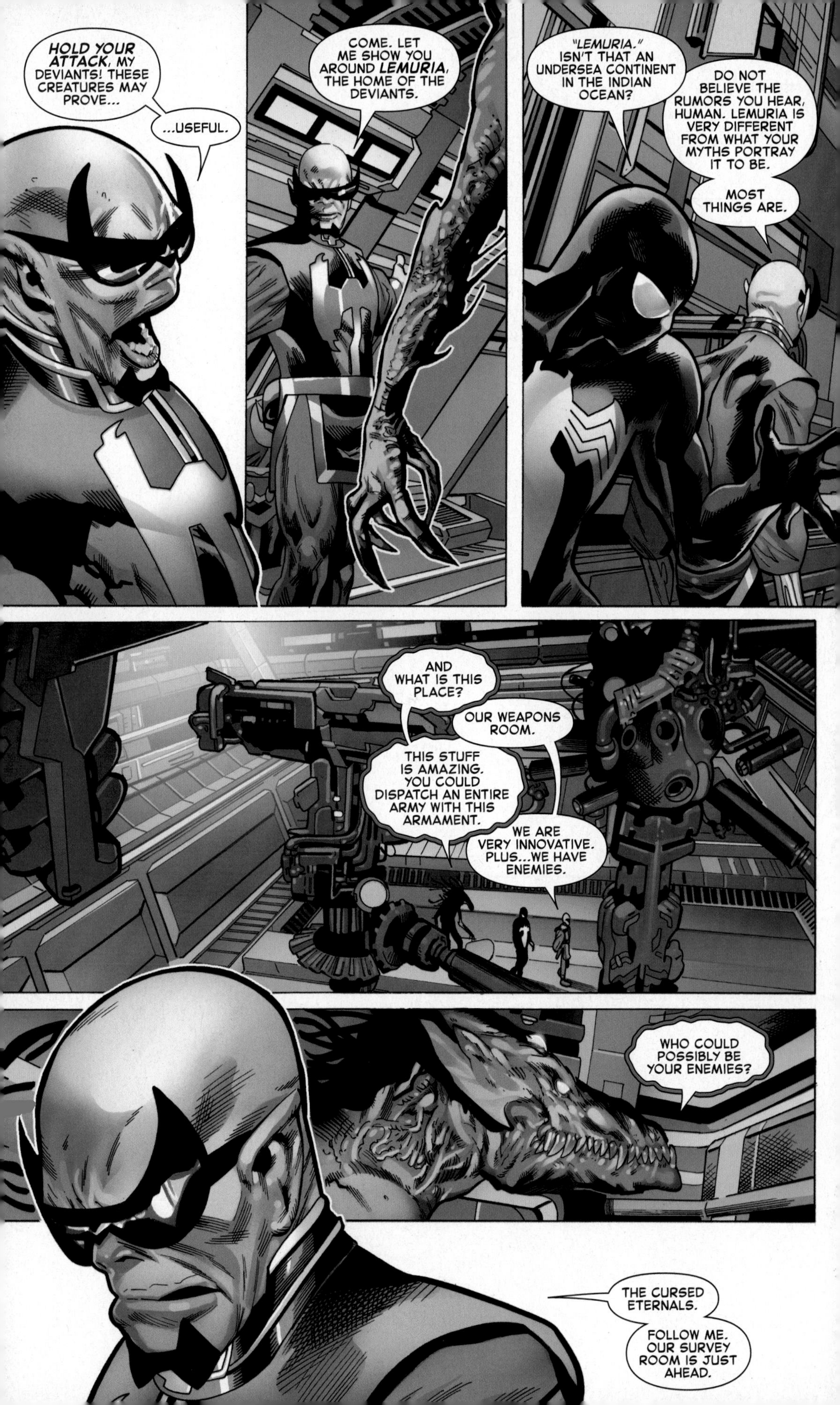
HOLD YOUR ATTACK, MY DEVIANTS! THESE CREATURES MAY PROVE...
...USEFUL.
COME. LET ME SHOW YOU AROUND LEMURIA, THE HOME OF THE DEVIANTS.
"LEMURIA." ISN'T THAT AN UNDERSEA CONTINENT IN THE INDIAN OCEAN?
DO NOT BELIEVE THE RUMORS YOU HEAR, HUMAN. LEMURIA IS VERY DIFFERENT FROM WHAT YOUR MYTHS PORTRAY IT TO BE.
MOST THINGS ARE.
AND WHAT IS THIS PLACE?
OUR WEAPONS ROOM.
THIS STUFF IS AMAZING. YOU COULD DISPATCH AN ENTIRE ARMY WITH THIS ARMAMENT.
WE ARE VERY INNOVATIVE. PLUS...WE HAVE ENEMIES.
WHO COULD POSSIBLY BE YOUR ENEMIES?
THE CURSED ETERNALS.
FOLLOW ME. OUR SURVEY ROOM IS JUST AHEAD.

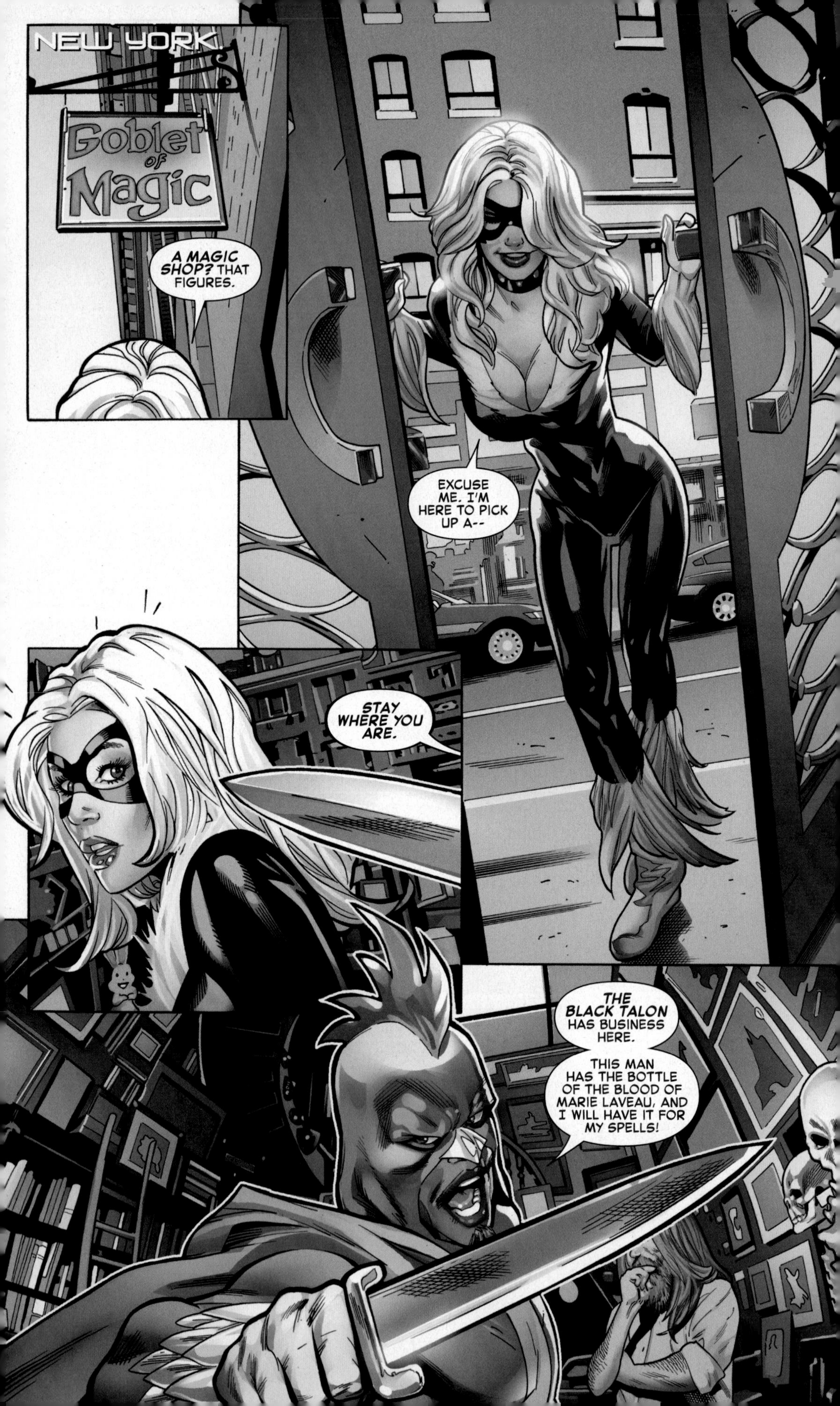
NEW YORK.
Goblet of Magic
A MAGIC SHOP? THAT FIGURES.
EXCUSE ME. I'M HERE TO PICK UP A--
STAY WHERE YOU ARE.
THE BLACK TALON HAS BUSINESS HERE.
THIS MAN HAS THE BOTTLE OF THE BLOOD OF MARIE LAVEAU, AND I WILL HAVE IT FOR MY SPELLS!

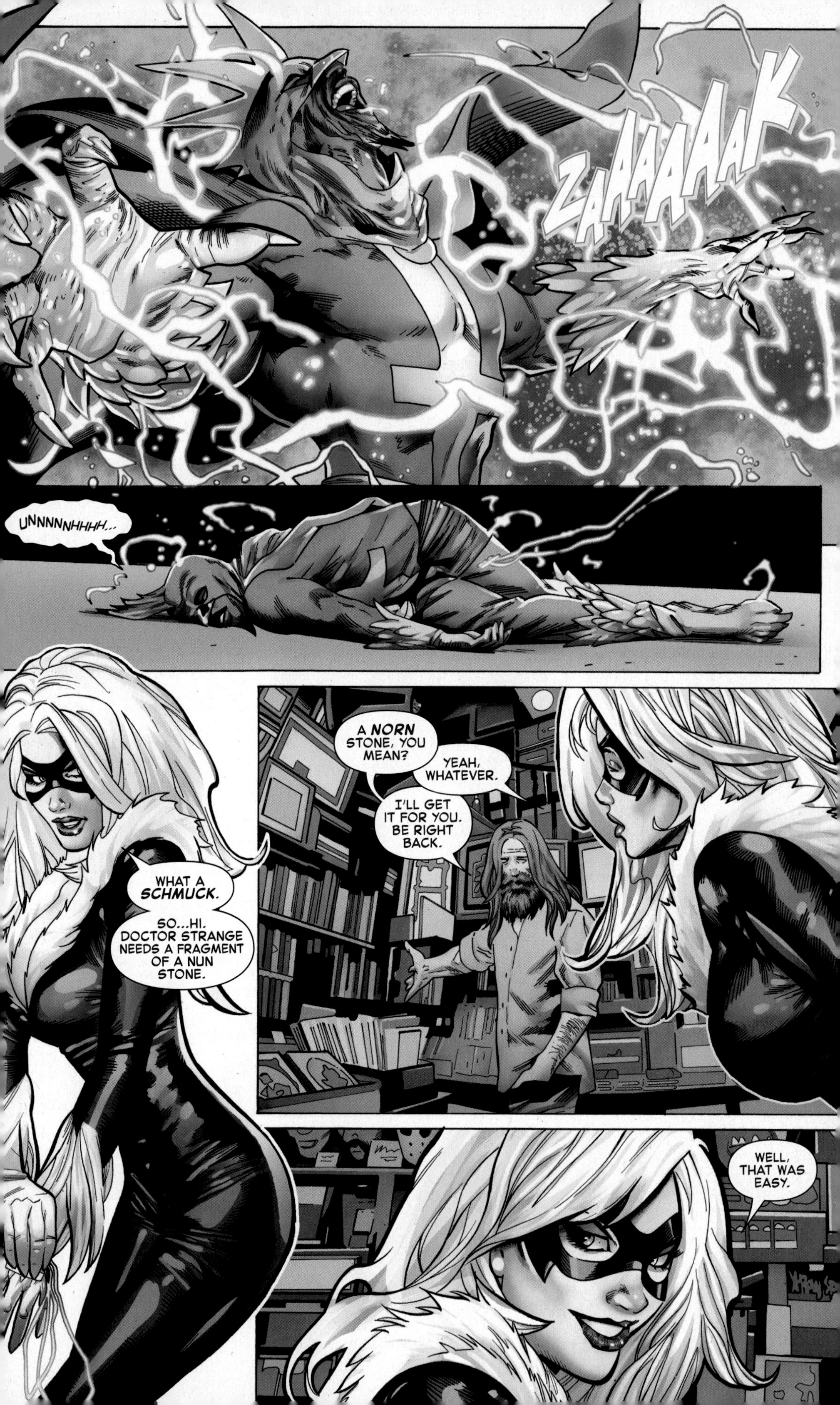
ZAAAAAAK
UNNNNNHHHH...
WHAT A SCHMUCK.
SO...HI. DOCTOR STRANGE NEEDS A FRAGMENT OF A NUN STONE.
A NORN STONE, YOU MEAN?
YEAH, WHATEVER.
I'LL GET IT FOR YOU. BE RIGHT BACK.
WELL, THAT WAS EASY.

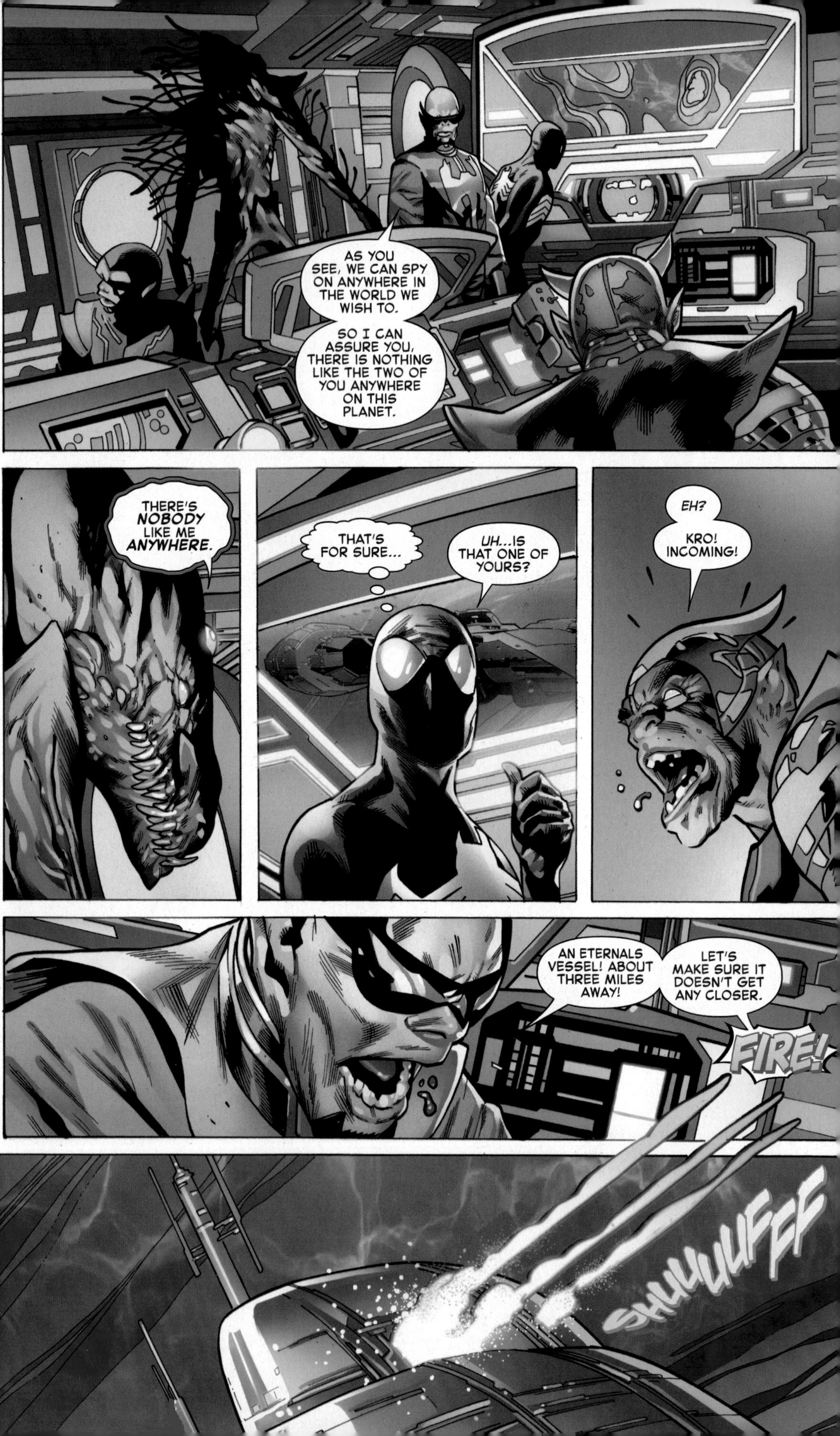
AS YOU SEE, WE CAN SPY ON ANYWHERE IN THE WORLD WE WISH TO.
SO I CAN ASSURE YOU, THERE IS NOTHING LIKE THE TWO OF YOU ANYWHERE ON THIS PLANET.
THERE'S *NOBODY* LIKE ME *ANYWHERE*.
THAT'S FOR SURE...
UH...IS THAT ONE OF YOURS?
EH?
KRO! INCOMING!
AN ETERNALS VESSEL! ABOUT THREE MILES AWAY!
LET'S MAKE SURE IT DOESN'T GET ANY CLOSER.
FIRE!
SHHUUUFFF

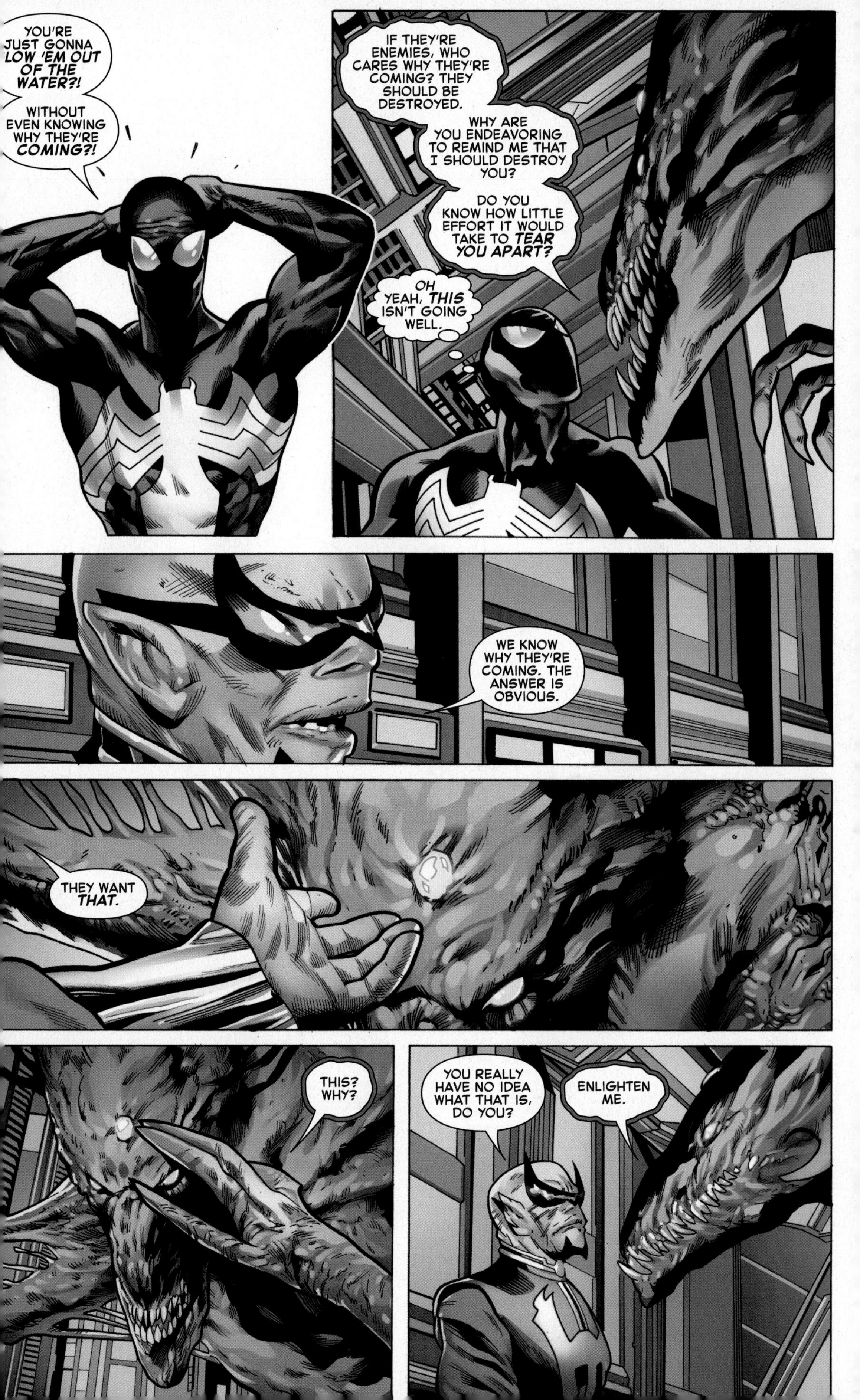
YOU'RE JUST GONNA LOW 'EM OUT OF THE WATER?!
WITHOUT EVEN KNOWING WHY THEY'RE COMING?!
IF THEY'RE ENEMIES, WHO CARES WHY THEY'RE COMING? THEY SHOULD BE DESTROYED.
WHY ARE YOU ENDEAVORING TO REMIND ME THAT I SHOULD DESTROY YOU?
DO YOU KNOW HOW LITTLE EFFORT IT WOULD TAKE TO TEAR YOU APART?
OH YEAH, THIS ISN'T GOING WELL.
WE KNOW WHY THEY'RE COMING. THE ANSWER IS OBVIOUS.
THEY WANT THAT.
THIS? WHY?
YOU REALLY HAVE NO IDEA WHAT THAT IS, DO YOU?
ENLIGHTEN ME.

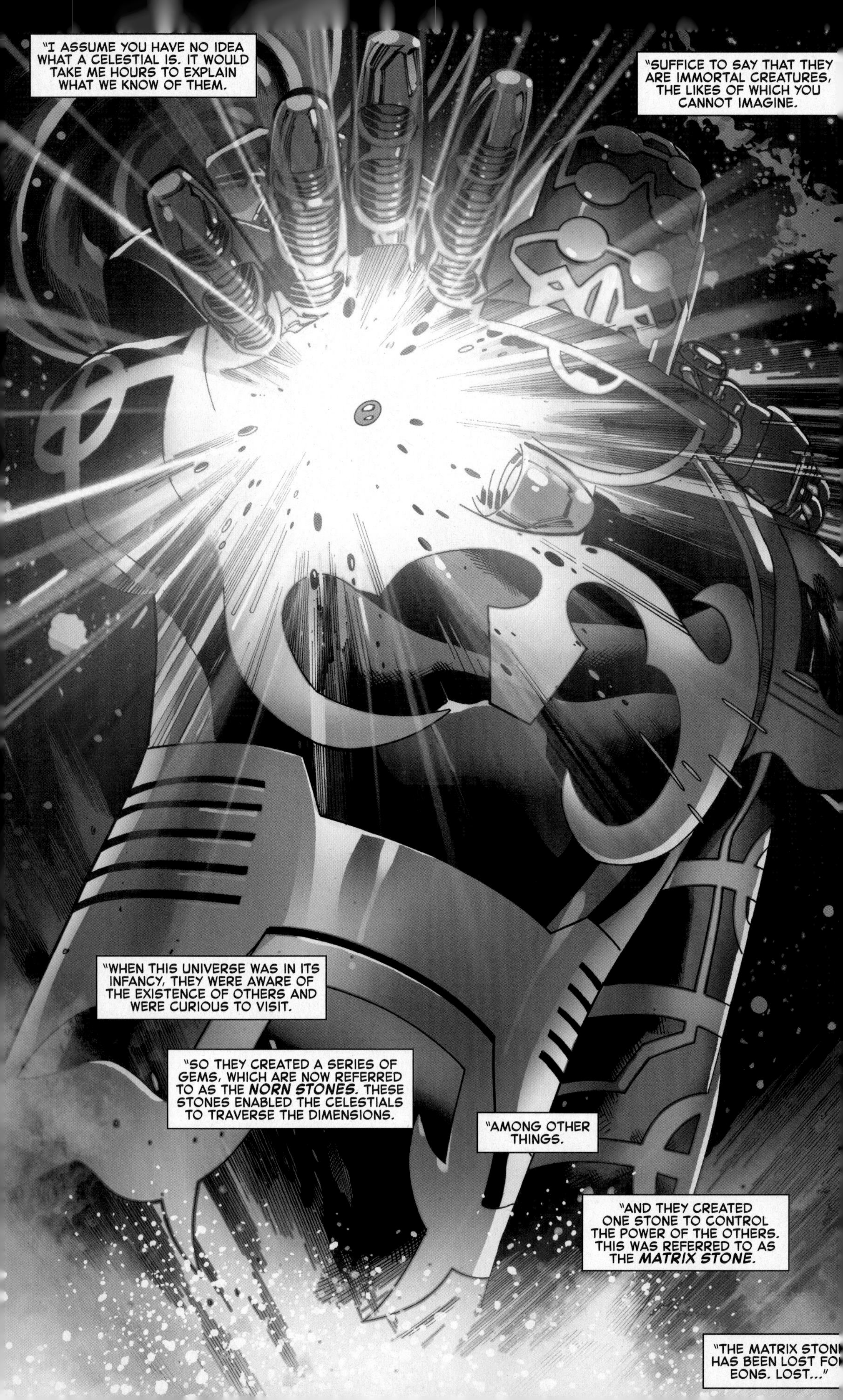
"I ASSUME YOU HAVE NO IDEA WHAT A CELESTIAL IS. IT WOULD TAKE ME HOURS TO EXPLAIN WHAT WE KNOW OF THEM.
"SUFFICE TO SAY THAT THEY ARE IMMORTAL CREATURES, THE LIKES OF WHICH YOU CANNOT IMAGINE.
"WHEN THIS UNIVERSE WAS IN ITS INFANCY, THEY WERE AWARE OF THE EXISTENCE OF OTHERS AND WERE CURIOUS TO VISIT.
"SO THEY CREATED A SERIES OF GEMS, WHICH ARE NOW REFERRED TO AS THE NORN STONES. THESE STONES ENABLED THE CELESTIALS TO TRAVERSE THE DIMENSIONS.
"AMONG OTHER THINGS.
"AND THEY CREATED ONE STONE TO CONTROL THE POWER OF THE OTHERS. THIS WAS REFERRED TO AS THE MATRIX STONE.
"THE MATRIX STON HAS BEEN LOST FO EONS. LOST..."

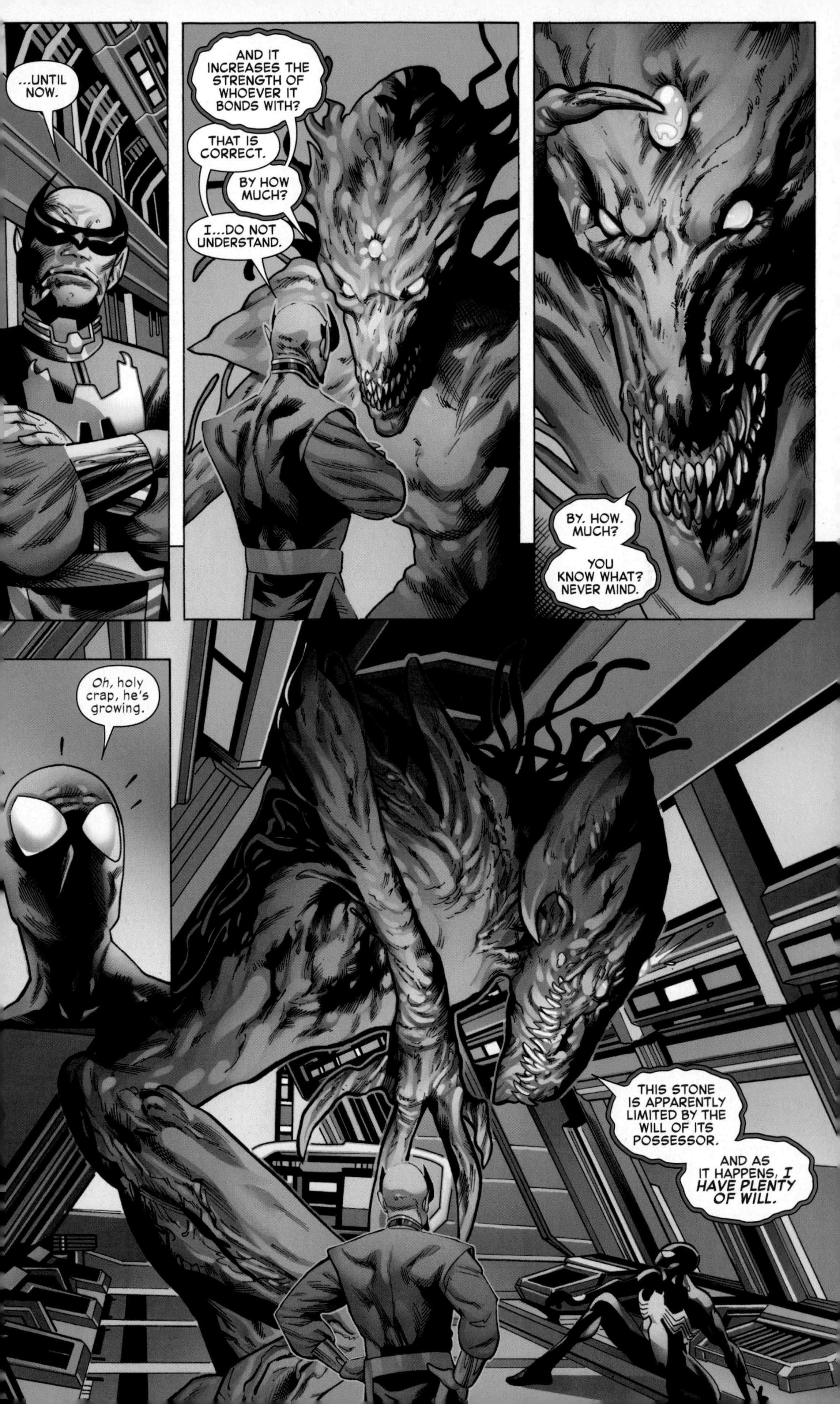
...UNTIL NOW.
AND IT INCREASES THE STRENGTH OF WHOEVER IT BONDS WITH?
THAT IS CORRECT.
BY HOW MUCH?
I...DO NOT UNDERSTAND.
BY. HOW. MUCH?
YOU KNOW WHAT? NEVER MIND.
Oh, holy crap, he's growing.
THIS STONE IS APPARENTLY LIMITED BY THE WILL OF ITS POSSESSOR.
AND AS IT HAPPENS, I HAVE PLENTY OF WILL.

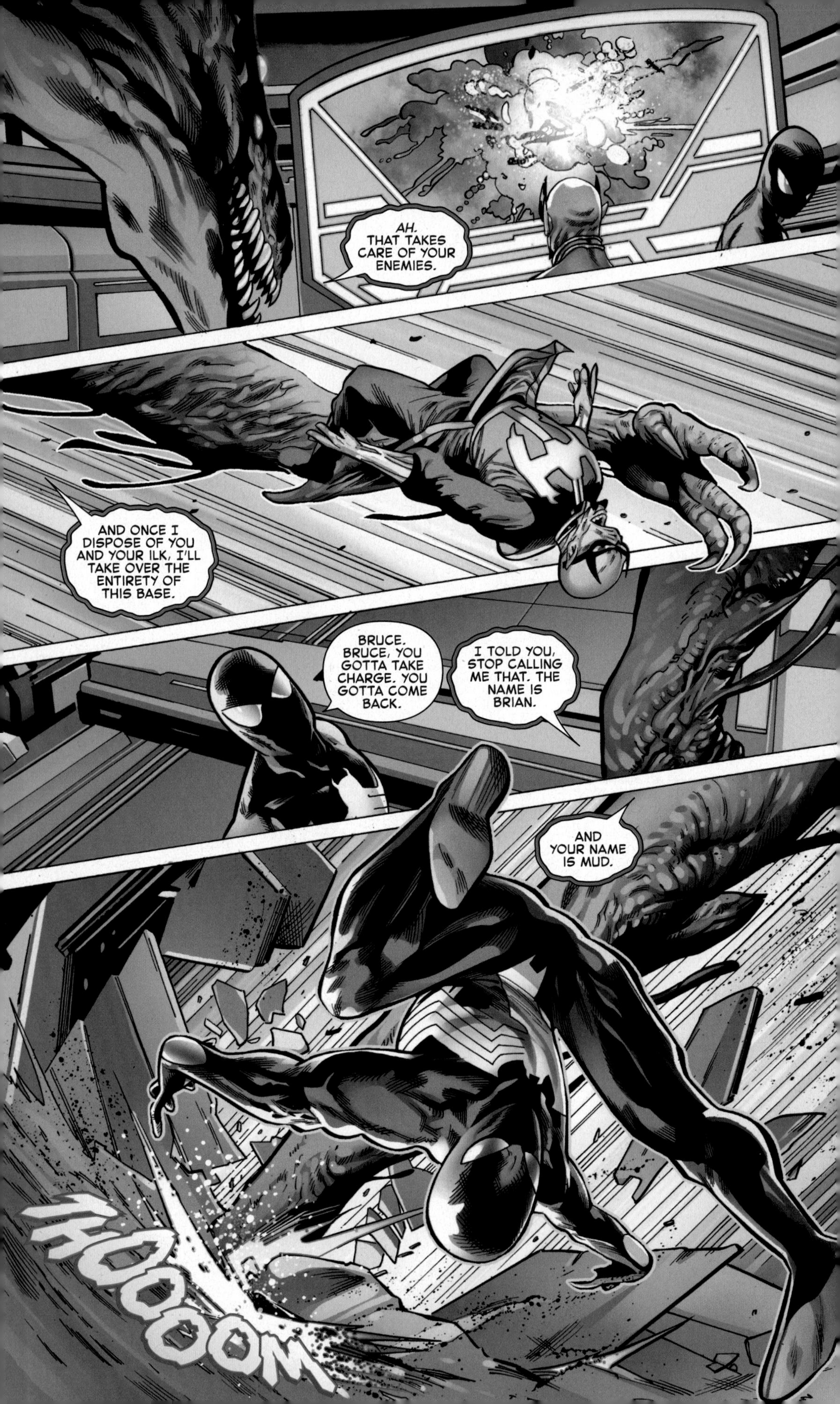
AH. THAT TAKES CARE OF YOUR ENEMIES.
AND ONCE I DISPOSE OF YOU AND YOUR ILK, I'LL TAKE OVER THE ENTIRETY OF THIS BASE.
BRUCE. BRUCE, YOU GOTTA TAKE CHARGE. YOU GOTTA COME BACK.
I TOLD YOU, STOP CALLING ME THAT. THE NAME IS BRIAN.
AND YOUR NAME IS MUD.
THOOOOM

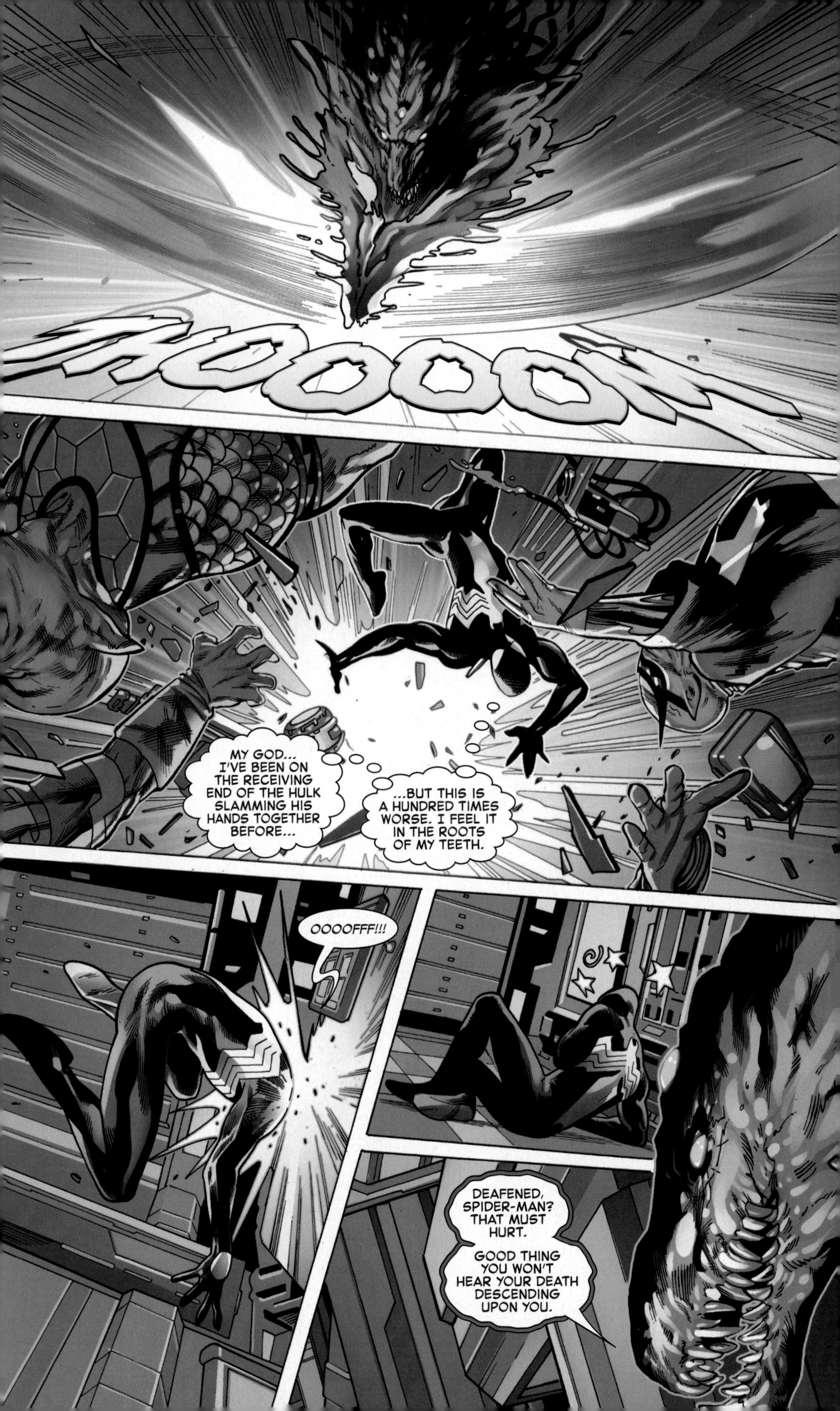
THOOOOM
MY GOD... I'VE BEEN ON THE RECEIVING END OF THE HULK SLAMMING HIS HANDS TOGETHER BEFORE...
...BUT THIS IS A HUNDRED TIMES WORSE. I FEEL IT IN THE ROOTS OF MY TEETH.
OOOOFFF!!!
DEAFENED, SPIDER-MAN? THAT MUST HURT.
GOOD THING YOU WON'T HEAR YOUR DEATH DESCENDING UPON YOU.

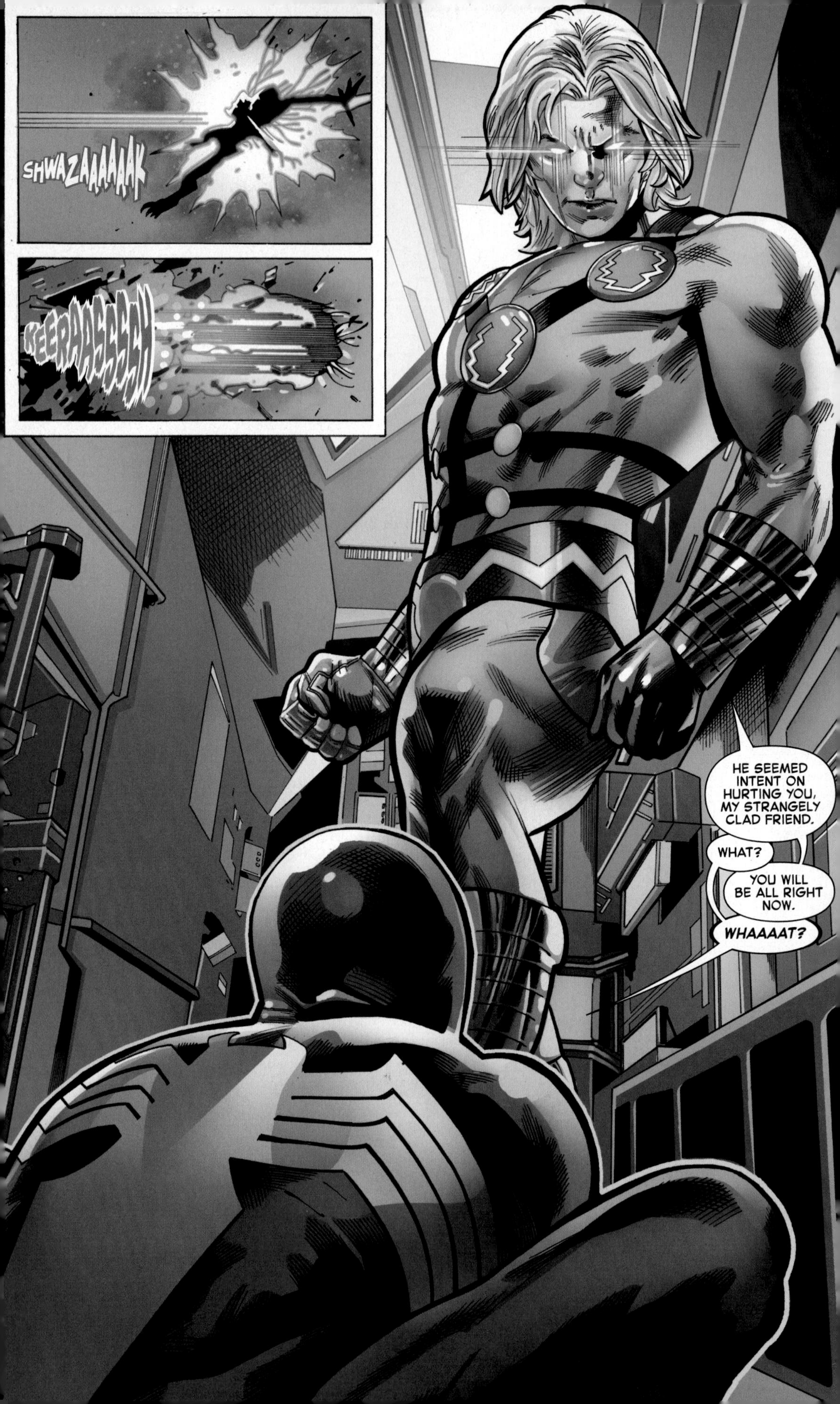
SHWAZAAAAAAK
KEERAASSSCH
HE SEEMED INTENT ON HURTING YOU, MY STRANGELY CLAD FRIEND.
WHAT?
YOU WILL BE ALL RIGHT NOW.
WHAAAAT?

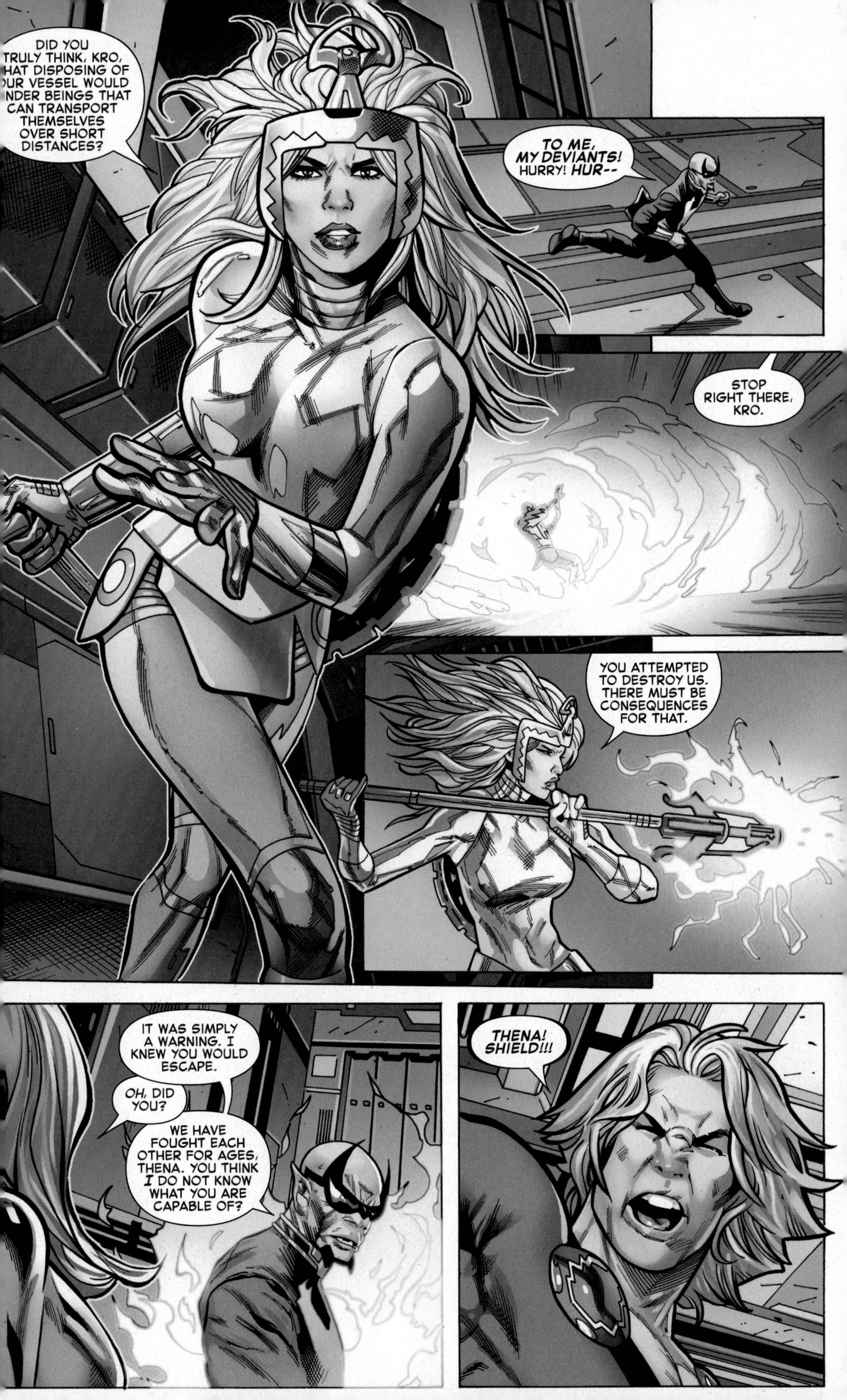

DID YOU TRULY THINK, KRO, THAT DISPOSING OF OUR VESSEL WOULD HINDER BEINGS THAT CAN TRANSPORT THEMSELVES OVER SHORT DISTANCES?
TO ME, MY DEVIANTS! HURRY! HUR--
STOP RIGHT THERE, KRO.
YOU ATTEMPTED TO DESTROY US. THERE MUST BE CONSEQUENCES FOR THAT.
IT WAS SIMPLY A WARNING. I KNEW YOU WOULD ESCAPE.
OH, DID YOU?
WE HAVE FOUGHT EACH OTHER FOR AGES, THENA. YOU THINK I DO NOT KNOW WHAT YOU ARE CAPABLE OF?
THENA! SHIELD!!!

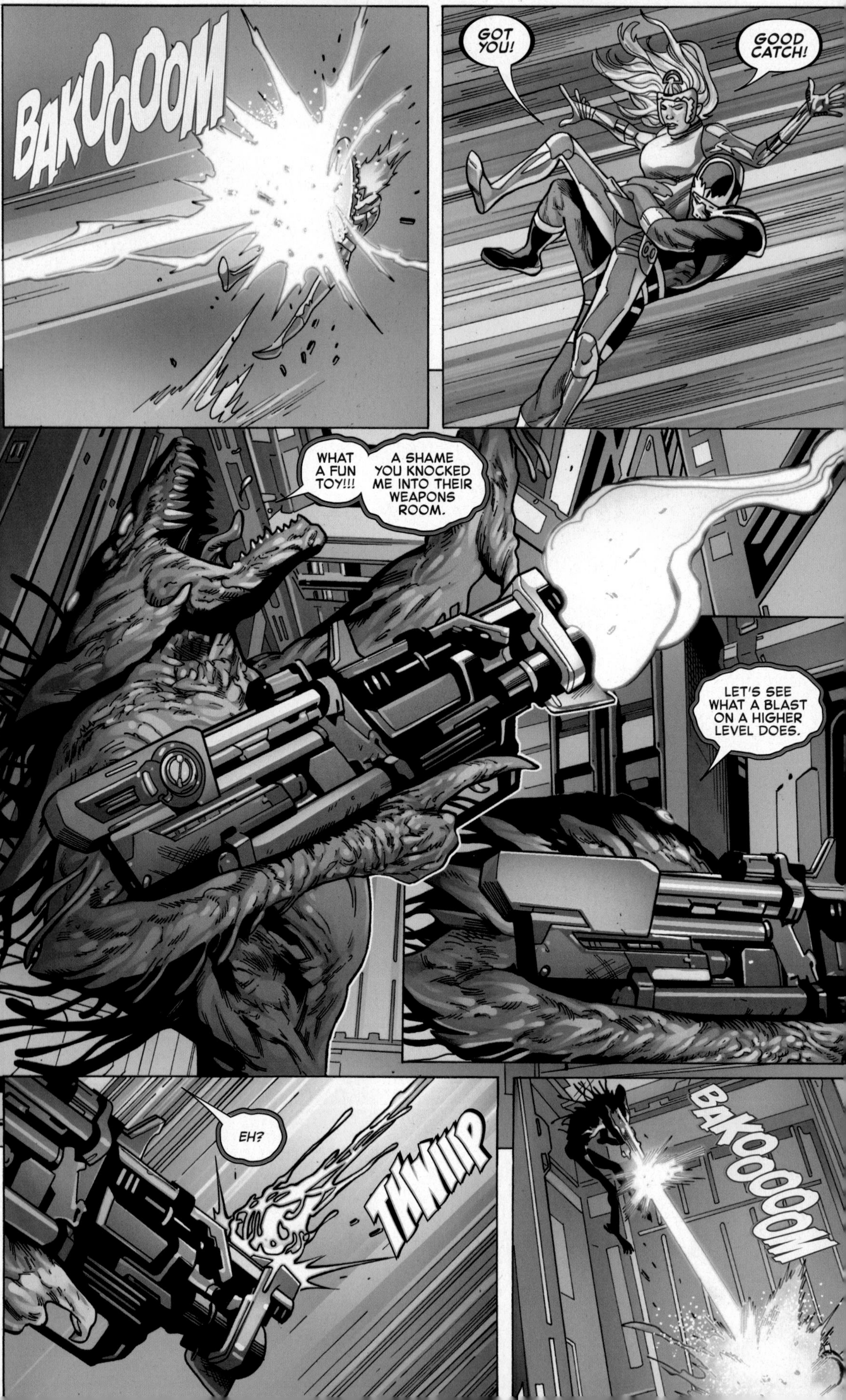

BAKOOOOM
GOT YOU!
GOOD CATCH!
WHAT A FUN TOY!!!
A SHAME YOU KNOCKED ME INTO THEIR WEAPONS ROOM.
LET'S SEE WHAT A BLAST ON A HIGHER LEVEL DOES.
EH?
THWIIP
BAKOOOOOM

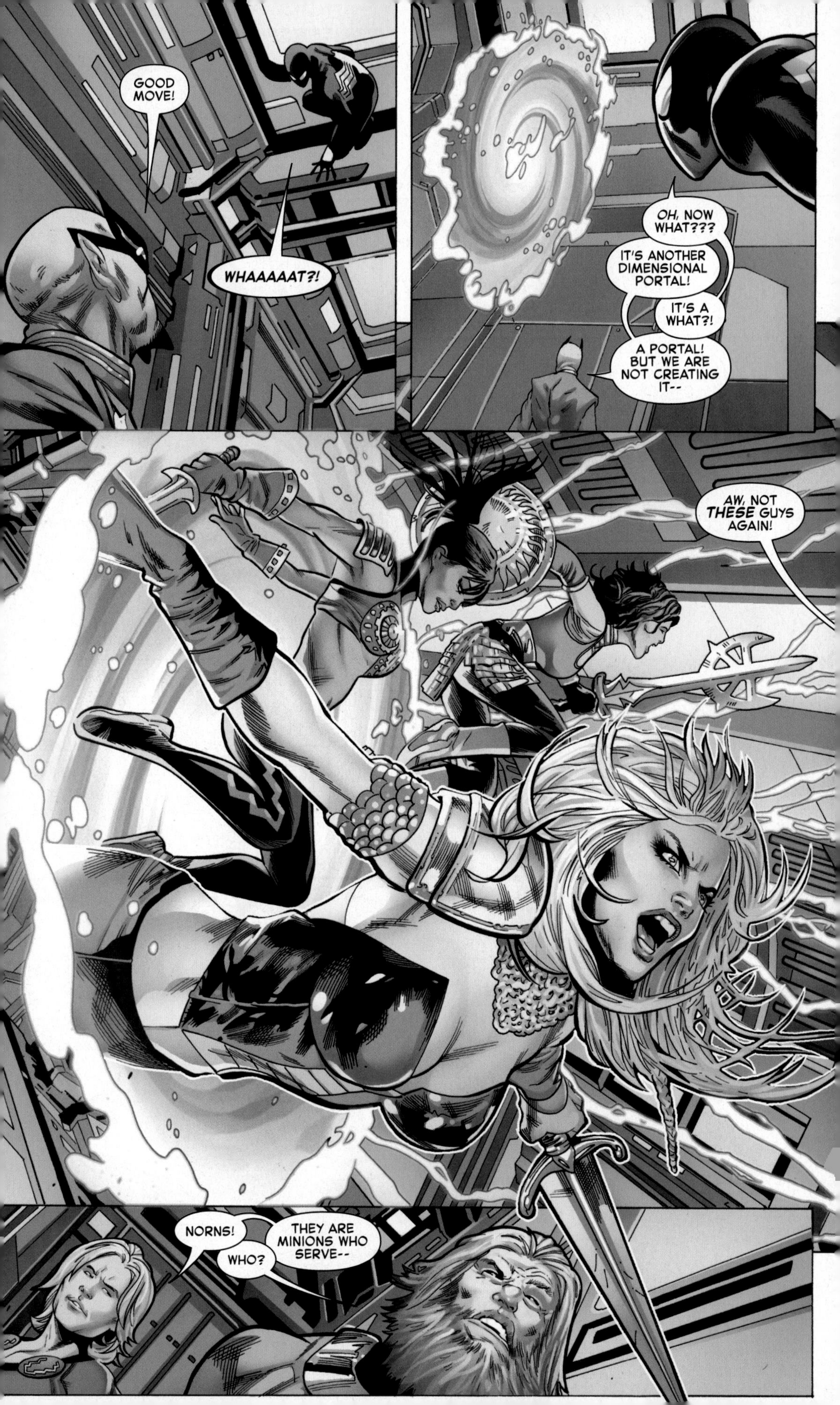
GOOD MOVE!
WHAAAAAT?!
OH, NOW WHAT???
IT'S ANOTHER DIMENSIONAL PORTAL!
IT'S A WHAT?!
A PORTAL! BUT WE ARE NOT CREATING IT--
AW, NOT THESE GUYS AGAIN!
NORNS!
WHO?
THEY ARE MINIONS WHO SERVE--

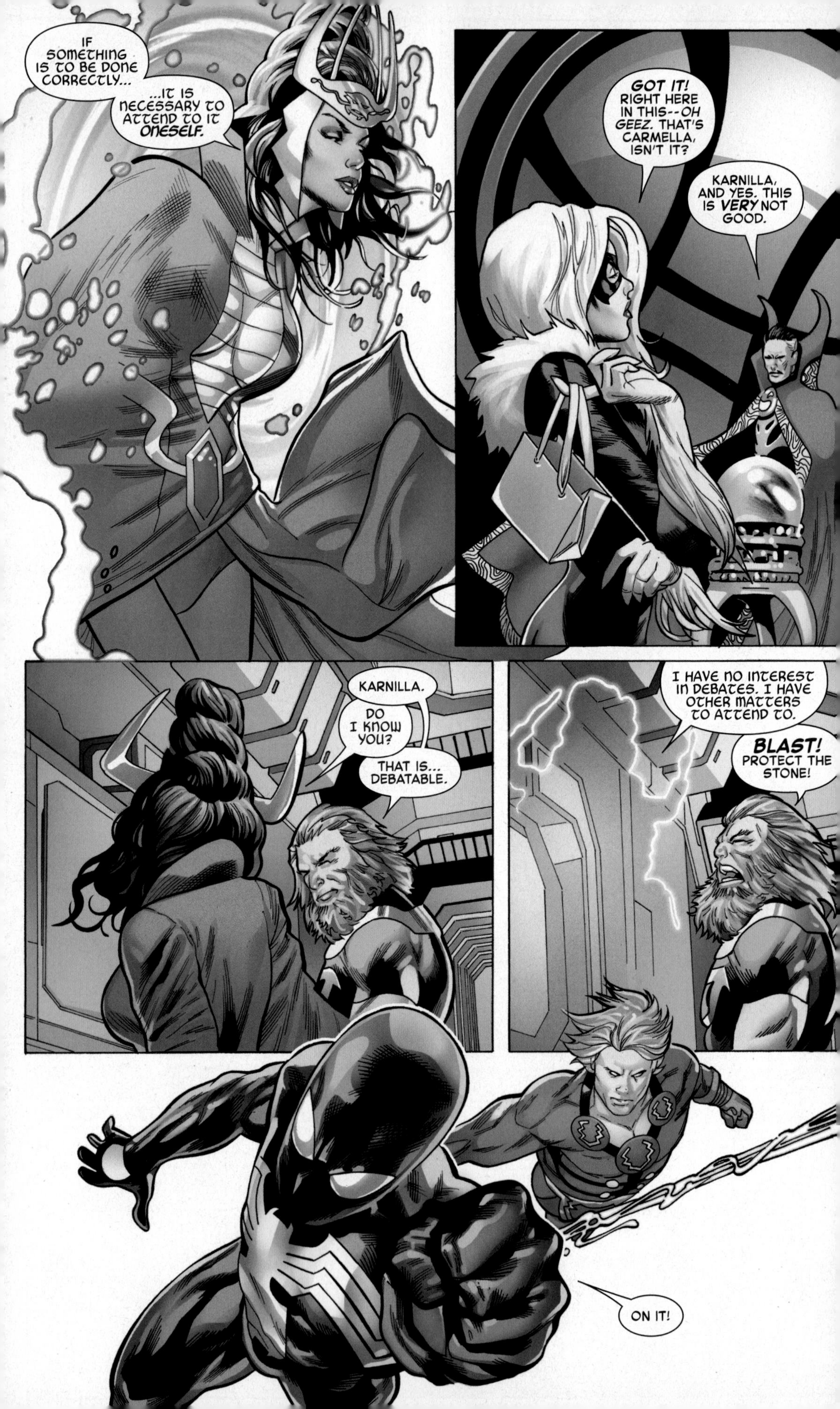
IF SOMETHING IS TO BE DONE CORRECTLY...
...IT IS NECESSARY TO ATTEND TO IT ONESELF.
GOT IT! RIGHT HERE IN THIS--OH GEEZ. THAT'S CARMELLA, ISN'T IT?
KARNILLA, AND YES. THIS IS VERY NOT GOOD.
KARNILLA.
DO I KNOW YOU?
THAT IS... DEBATABLE.
I HAVE NO INTEREST IN DEBATES. I HAVE OTHER MATTERS TO ATTEND TO.
BLAST! PROTECT THE STONE!
ON IT!

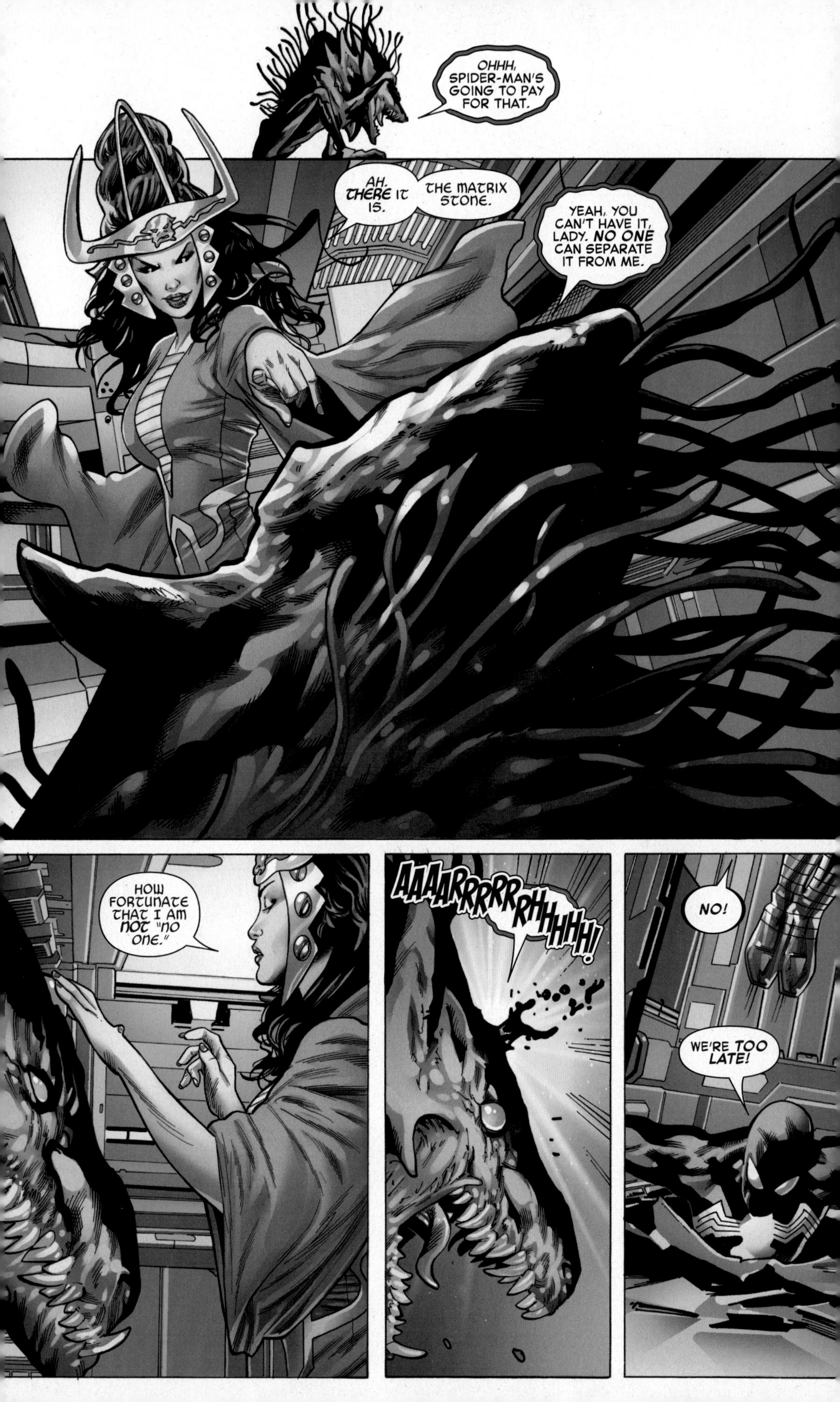
OHHH, SPIDER-MAN'S GOING TO PAY FOR THAT.
AH. THERE IT IS.
THE MATRIX STONE.
YEAH, YOU CAN'T HAVE IT, LADY. NO ONE CAN SEPARATE IT FROM ME.
HOW FORTUNATE THAT I AM NOT "NO ONE."
AAAARRRRRRHHHHHH!
NO!
WE'RE TOO LATE!

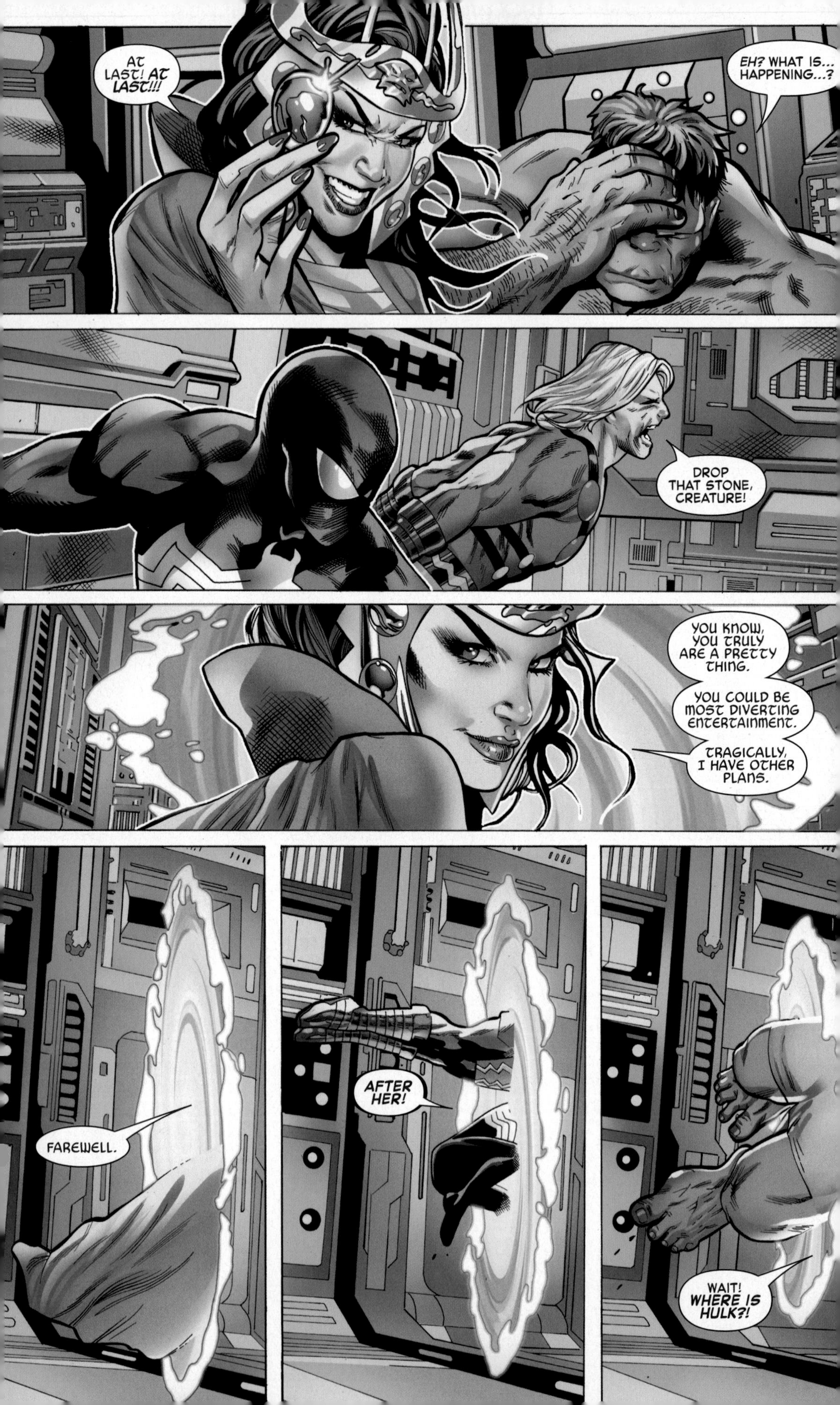
AT LAST! AT LAST!!!
EH? WHAT IS... HAPPENING...?
DROP THAT STONE, CREATURE!
YOU KNOW, YOU TRULY ARE A PRETTY THING.
YOU COULD BE MOST DIVERTING ENTERTAINMENT.
TRAGICALLY, I HAVE OTHER PLANS.
FAREWELL.
AFTER HER!
WAIT! WHERE IS HULK?!

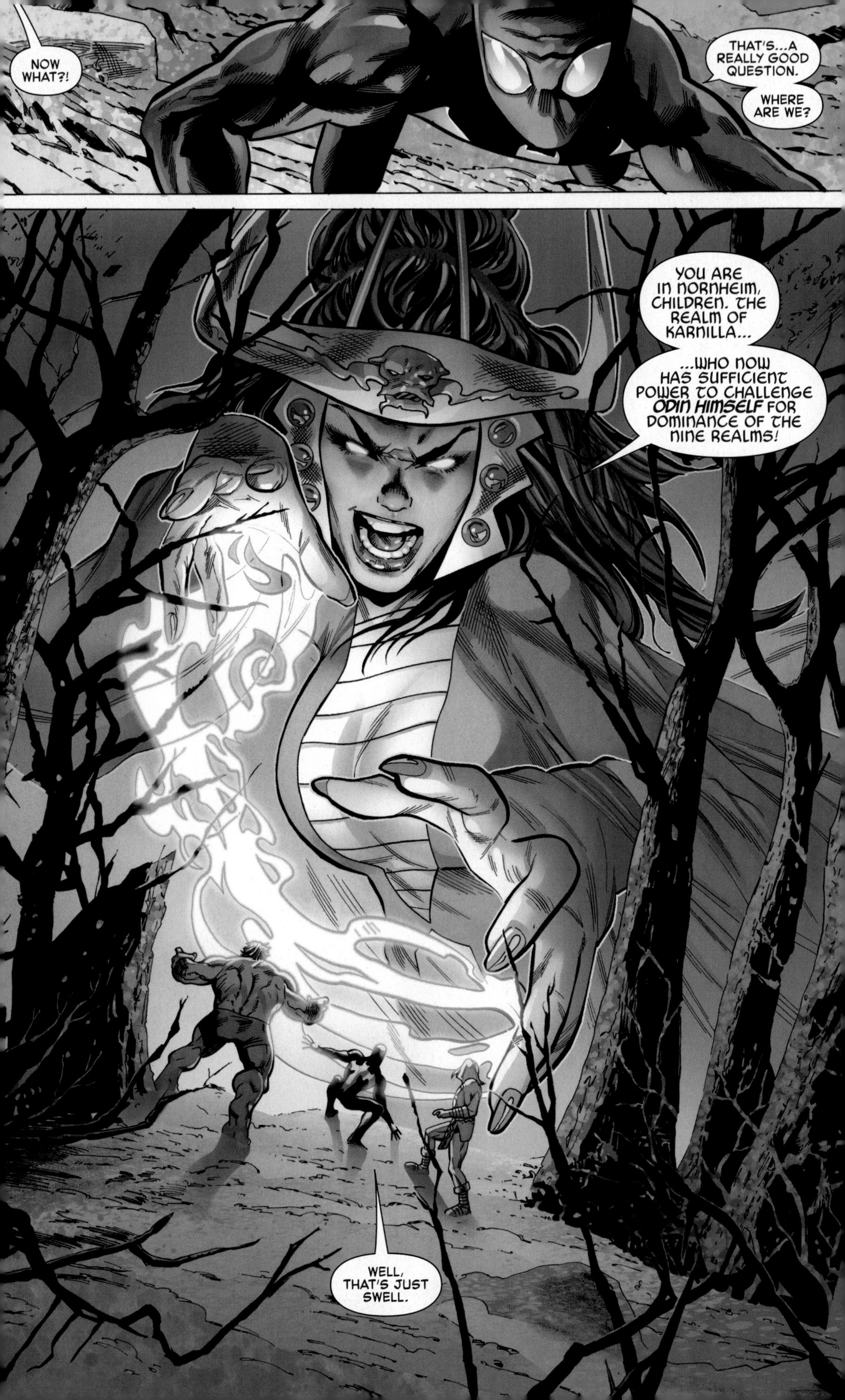
NOW WHAT?!
THAT'S...A REALLY GOOD QUESTION.
WHERE ARE WE?
YOU ARE IN NORNHEIM, CHILDREN. THE REALM OF KARNILLA...
...WHO NOW HAS SUFFICIENT POWER TO CHALLENGE ODIN HIMSELF FOR DOMINANCE OF THE NINE REALMS!
WELL, THAT'S JUST SWELL.

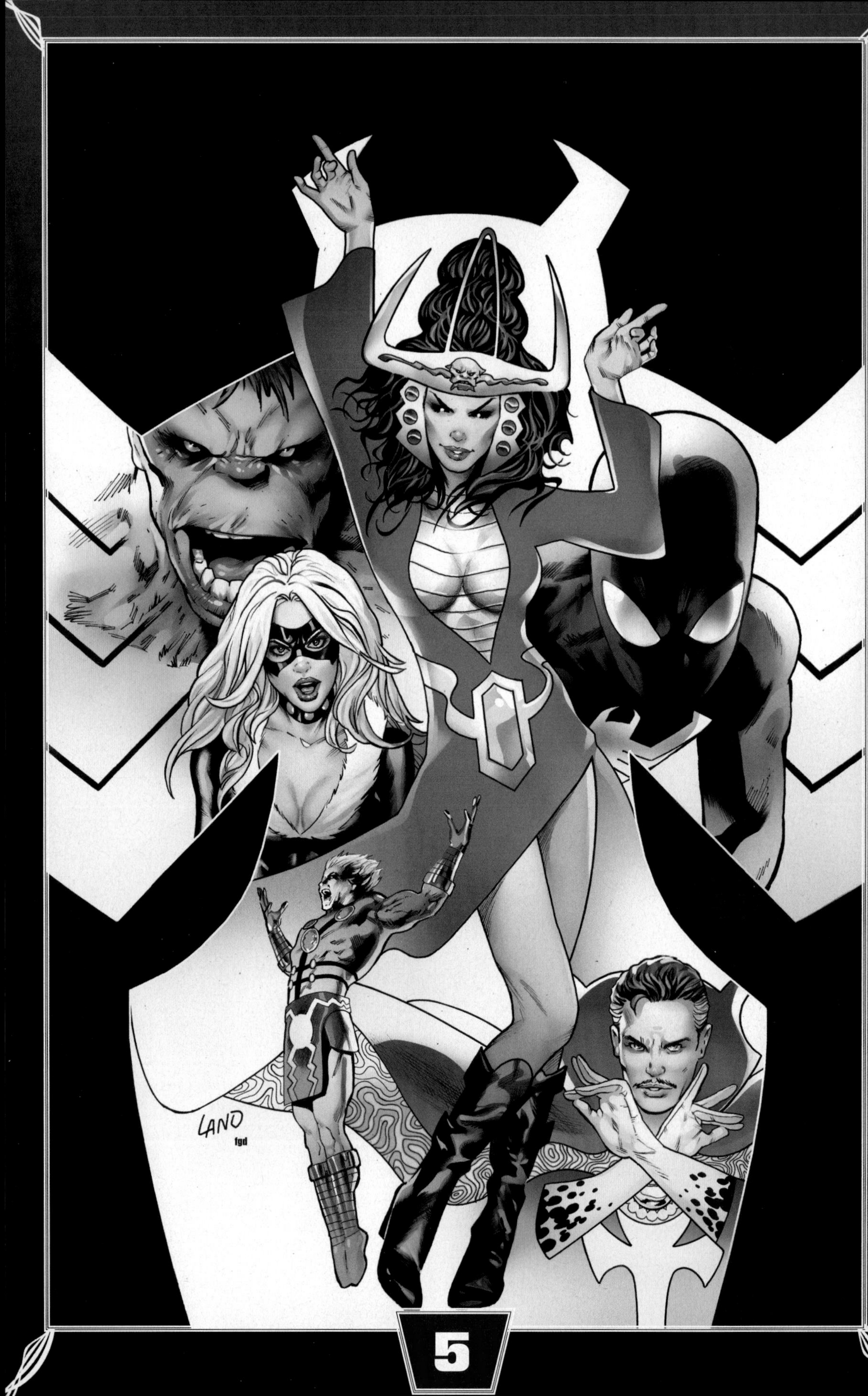
LANO
fgd

5

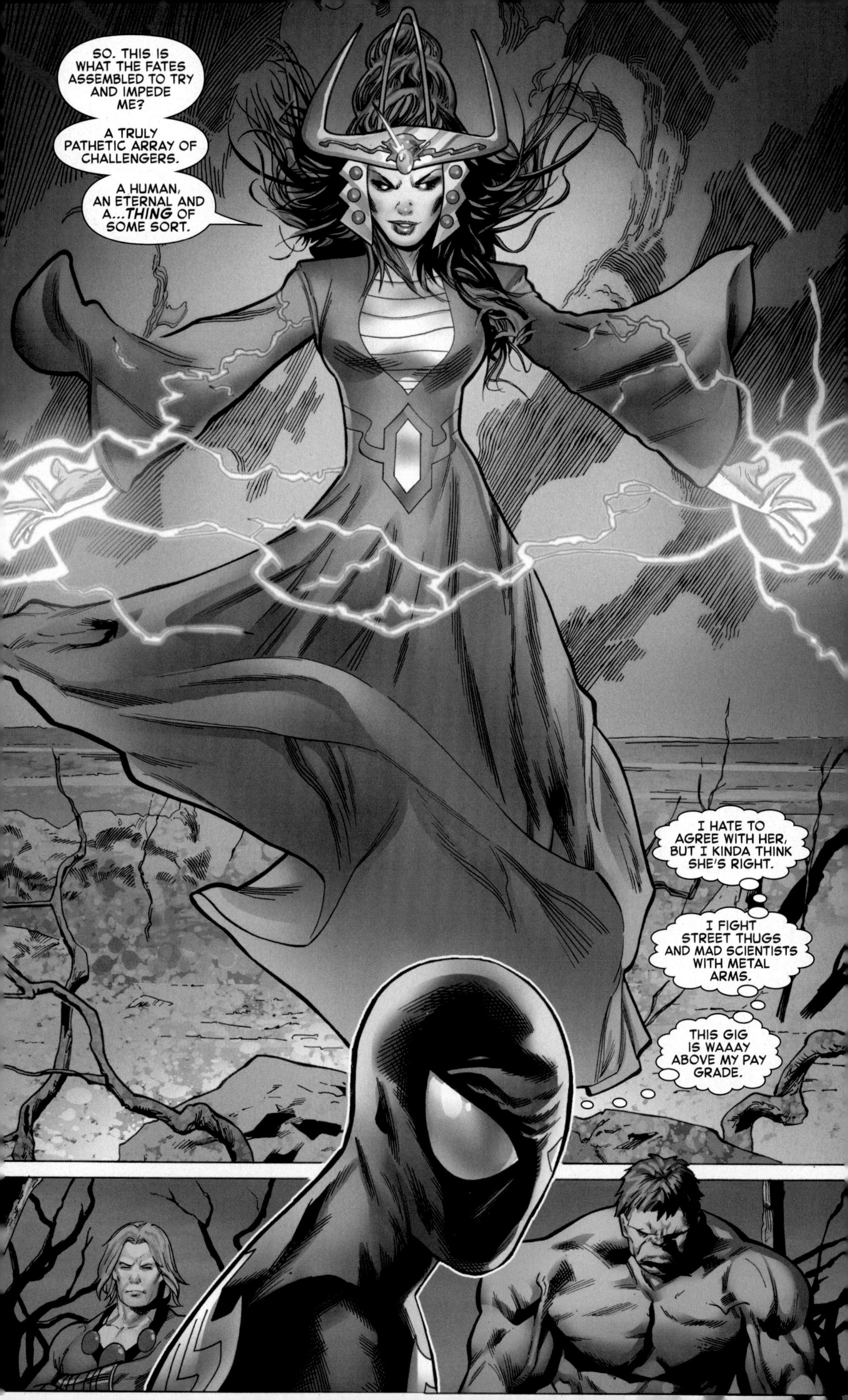
SO. THIS IS WHAT THE FATES ASSEMBLED TO TRY AND IMPEDE ME?
A TRULY PATHETIC ARRAY OF CHALLENGERS.
A HUMAN, AN ETERNAL AND A...THING OF SOME SORT.
I HATE TO AGREE WITH HER, BUT I KINDA THINK SHE'S RIGHT.
I FIGHT STREET THUGS AND MAD SCIENTISTS WITH METAL ARMS.
THIS GIG IS WAAAY ABOVE MY PAY GRADE.

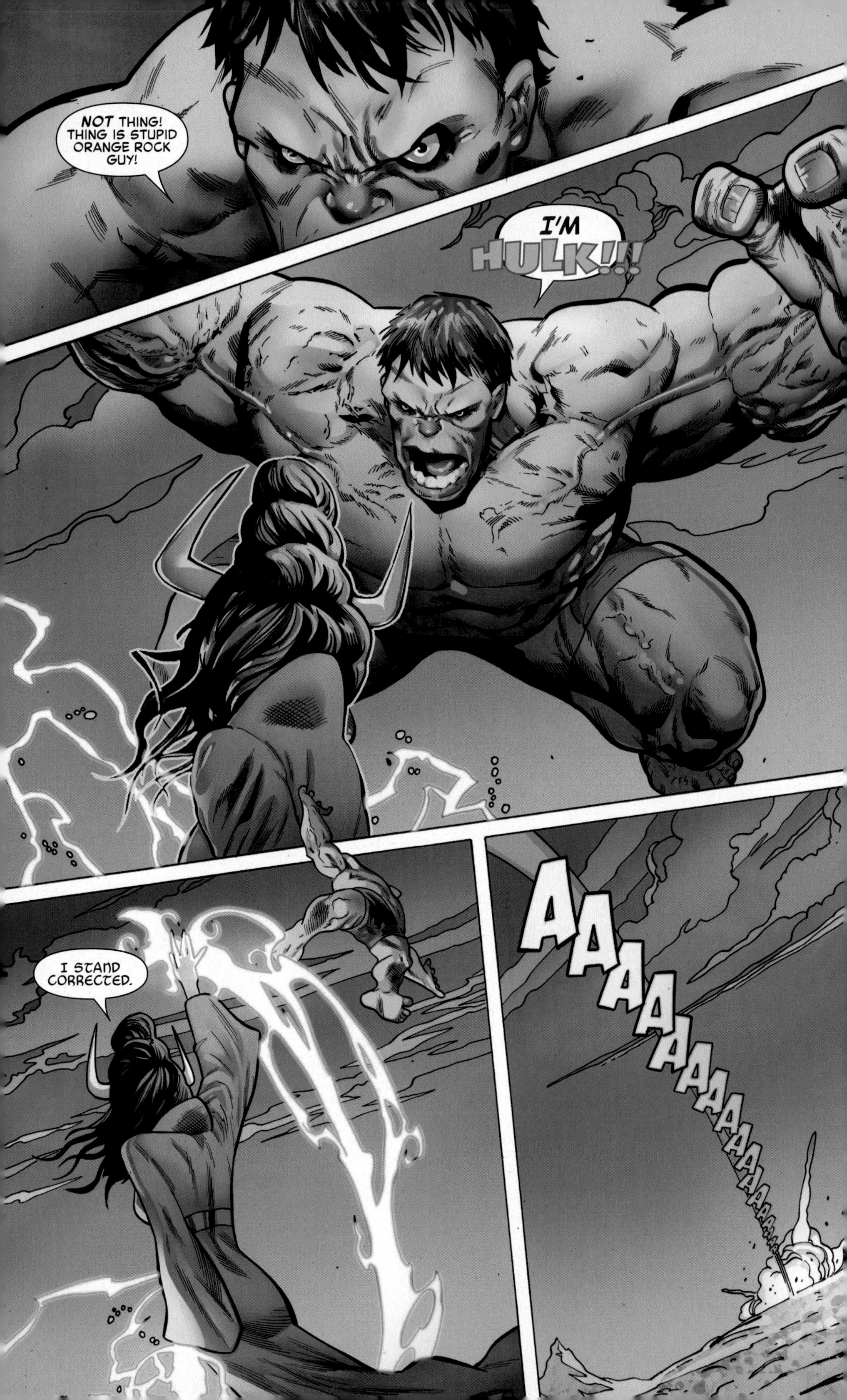
NOT THING! THING IS STUPID ORANGE ROCK GUY!
I'M HULK!!!
I STAND CORRECTED.
AAAAAAAAAAAAAAAAA

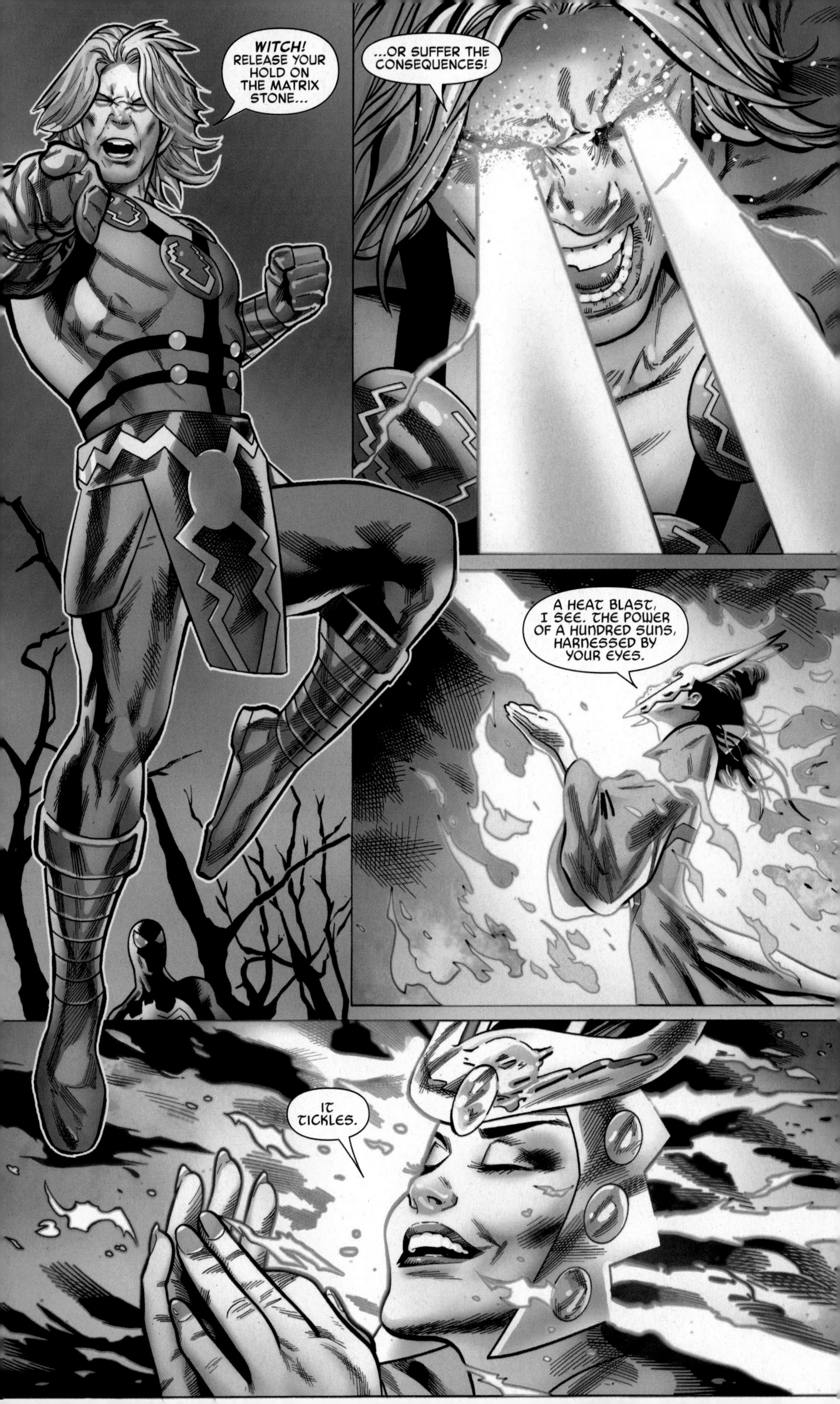
WITCH! RELEASE YOUR HOLD ON THE MATRIX STONE...
...OR SUFFER THE CONSEQUENCES!
A HEAT BLAST, I SEE. THE POWER OF A HUNDRED SUNS, HARNESSED BY YOUR EYES.
IT TICKLES.

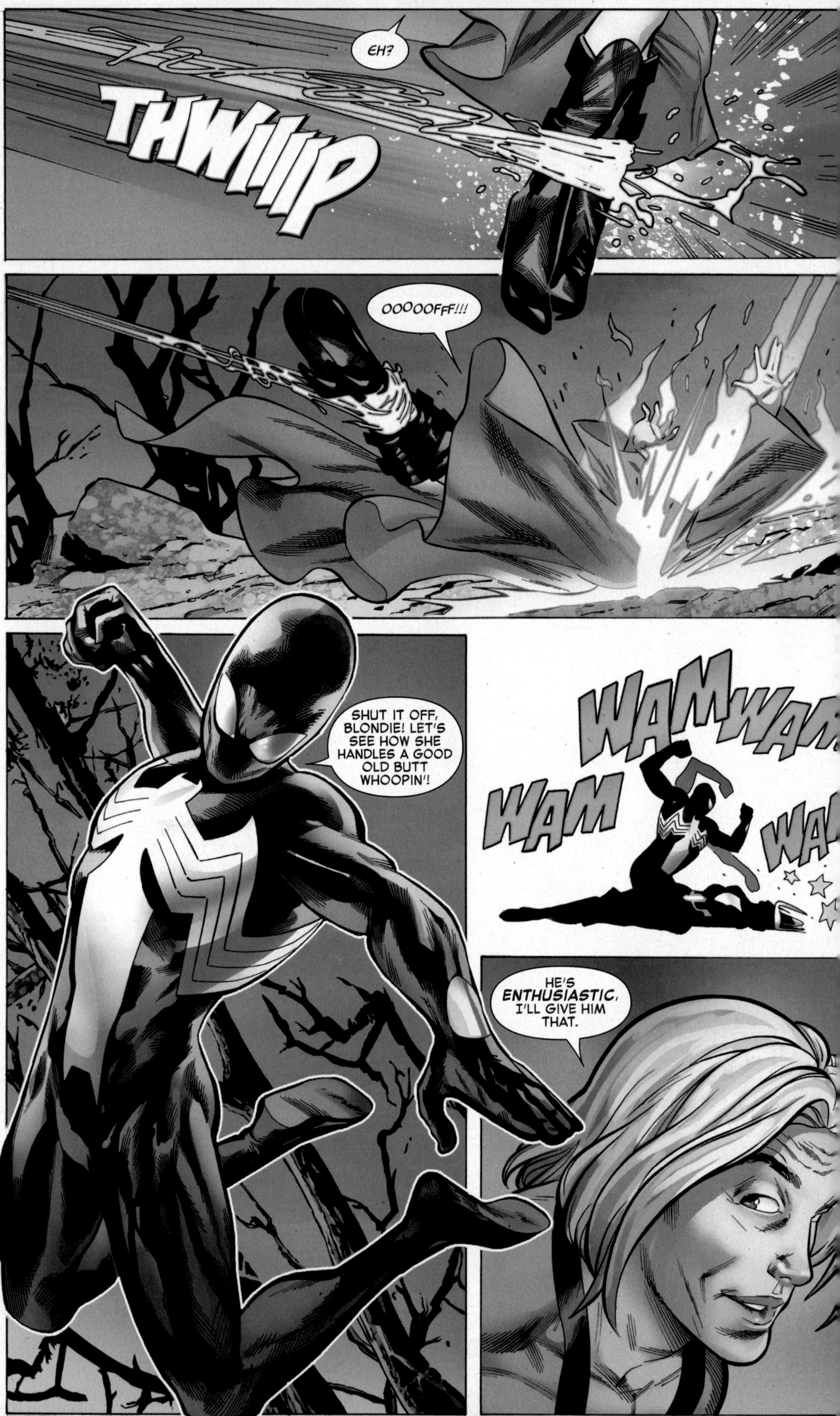
EH?
THWIIIP
OOOOOFFF!!!
SHUT IT OFF, BLONDIE! LET'S SEE HOW SHE HANDLES A GOOD OLD BUTT WHOOPIN'!
WAM
WAM
WAM
HE'S ENTHUSIASTIC, I'LL GIVE HIM THAT.

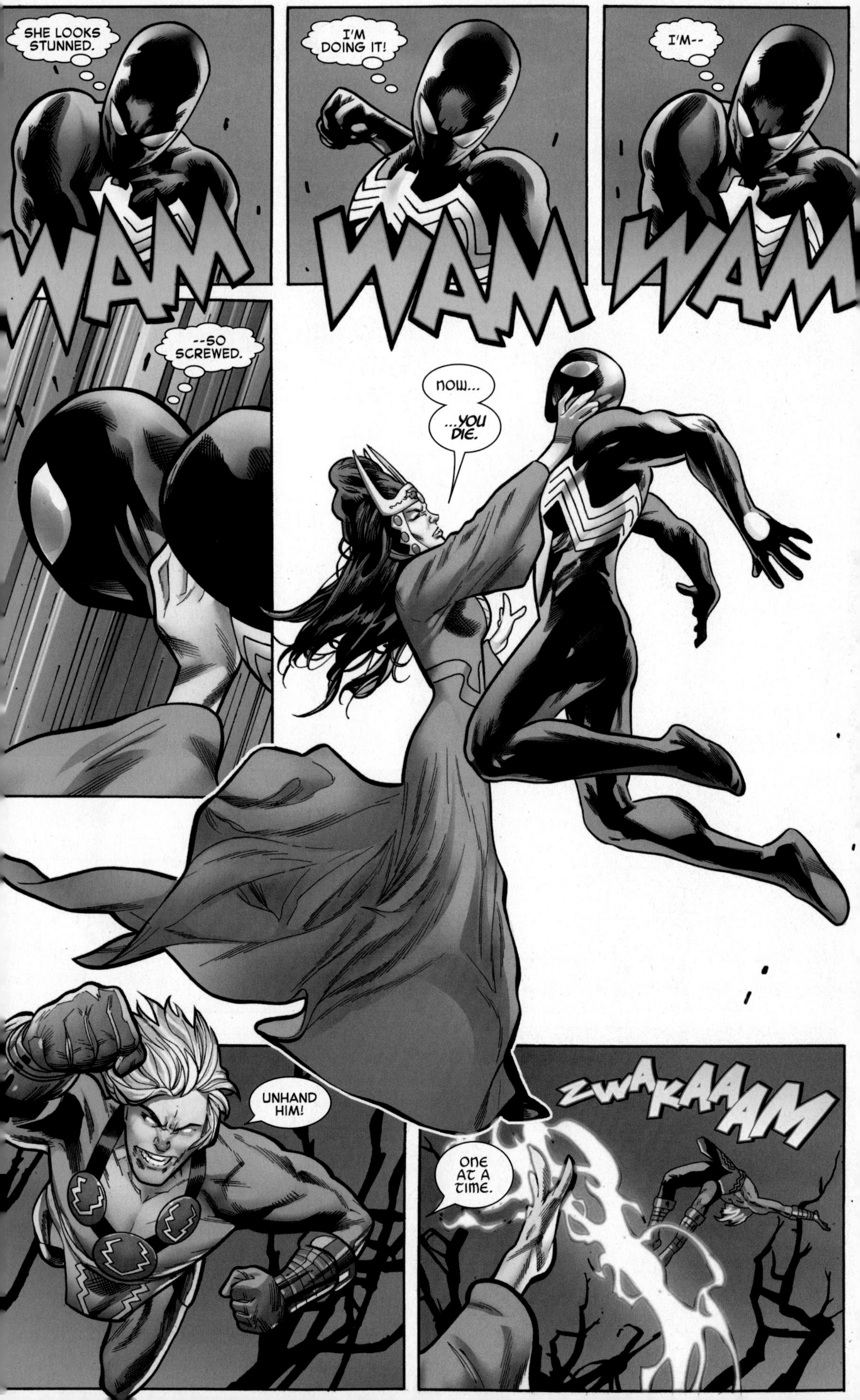
SHE LOOKS STUNNED.
WAM
I'M DOING IT!
WAM
I'M--
WAM
--SO SCREWED.
now...
...YOU DIE.
UNHAND HIM!
ZWAKAAAAM
ONE AT A TIME.

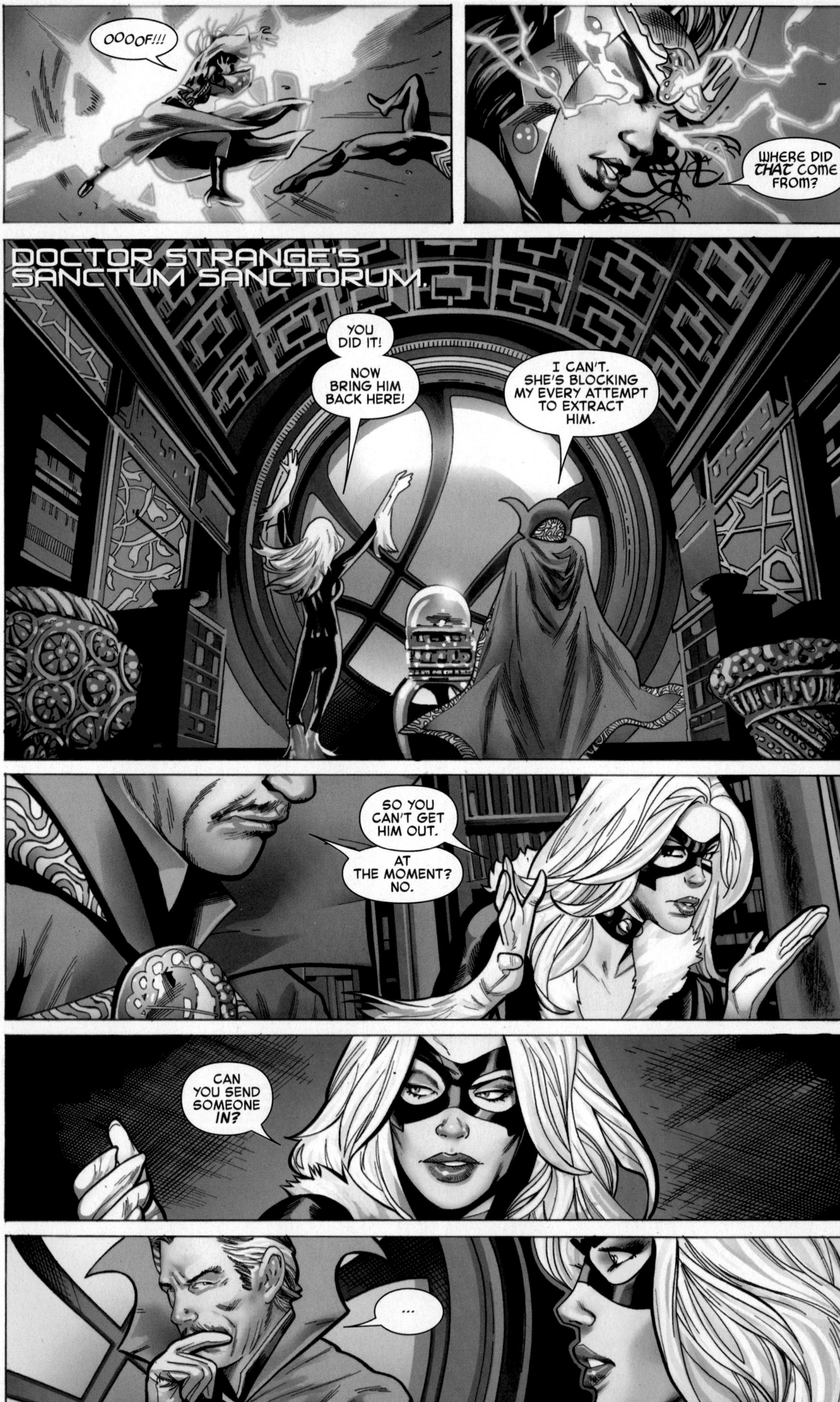
OOOOF!!!
WHERE DID THAT COME FROM?
DOCTOR STRANGE'S SANCTUM SANCTORUM.
YOU DID IT!
NOW BRING HIM BACK HERE!
I CAN'T. SHE'S BLOCKING MY EVERY ATTEMPT TO EXTRACT HIM.
SO YOU CAN'T GET HIM OUT.
AT THE MOMENT? NO.
CAN YOU SEND SOMEONE IN?
...

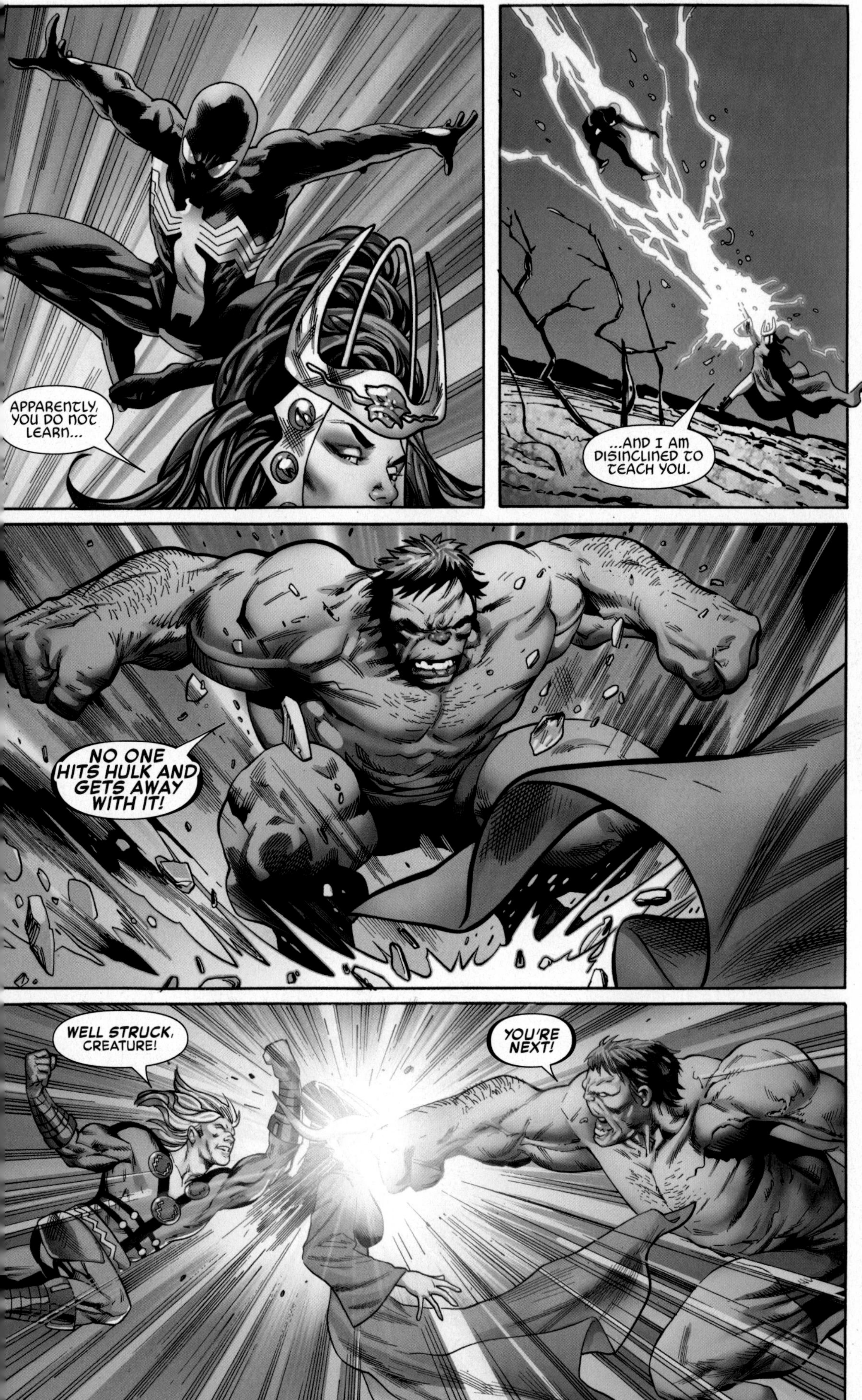

APPARENTLY, YOU DO NOT LEARN...
...AND I AM DISINCLINED TO TEACH YOU.
NO ONE HITS HULK AND GETS AWAY WITH IT!
WELL STRUCK, CREATURE!
YOU'RE NEXT!

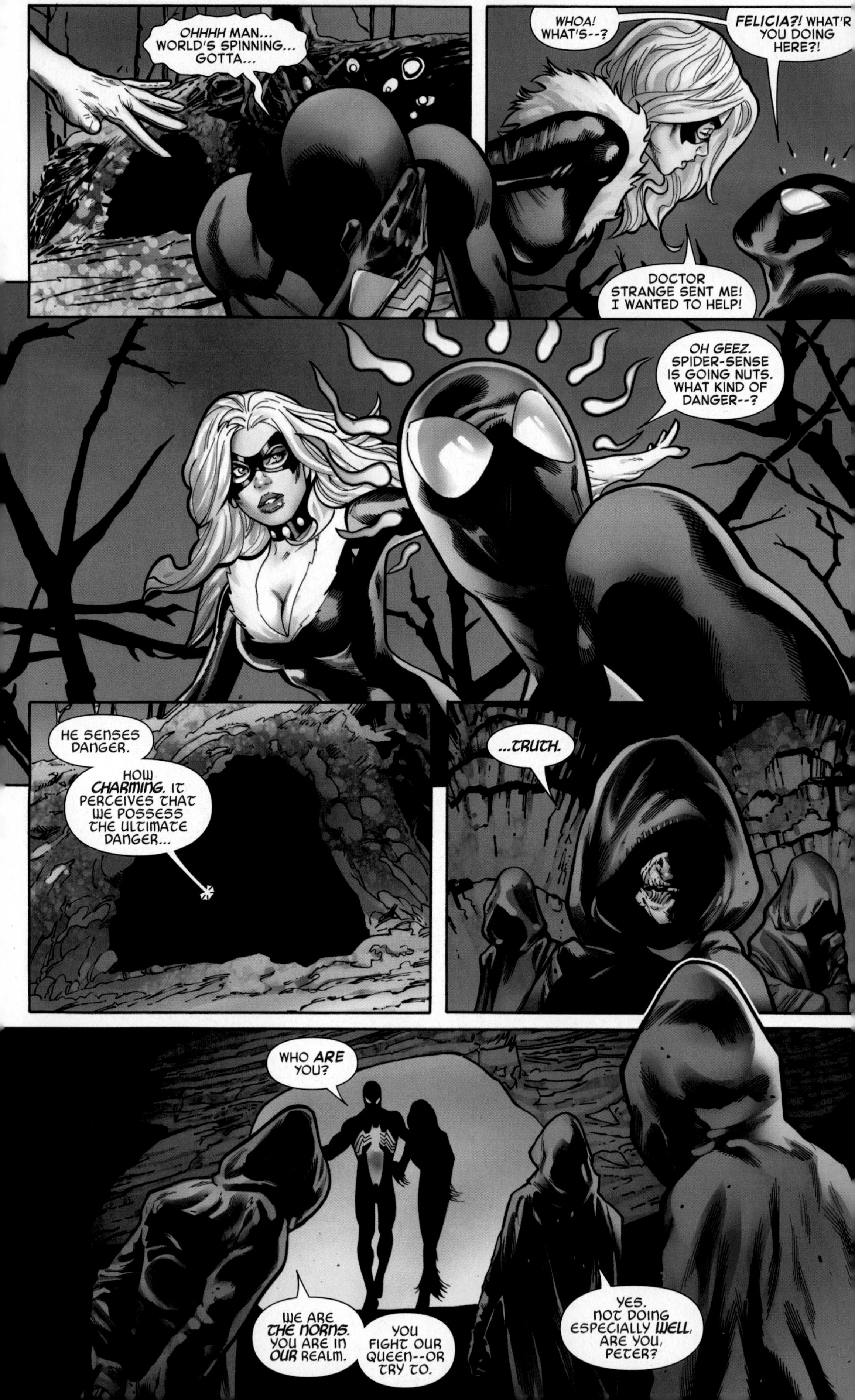

OHHHH MAN... WORLD'S SPINNING... GOTTA...
WHOA! WHAT'S--?
FELICIA?! WHAT'R YOU DOING HERE?!
DOCTOR STRANGE SENT ME! I WANTED TO HELP!
OH GEEZ. SPIDER-SENSE IS GOING NUTS. WHAT KIND OF DANGER--?
HE SENSES DANGER.
HOW CHARMING. IT PERCEIVES THAT WE POSSESS THE ULTIMATE DANGER...
...TRUTH.
WHO ARE YOU?
WE ARE THE NORNS. YOU ARE IN OUR REALM.
YOU FIGHT OUR QUEEN--OR TRY TO.
YES. NOT DOING ESPECIALLY WELL, ARE YOU, PETER?

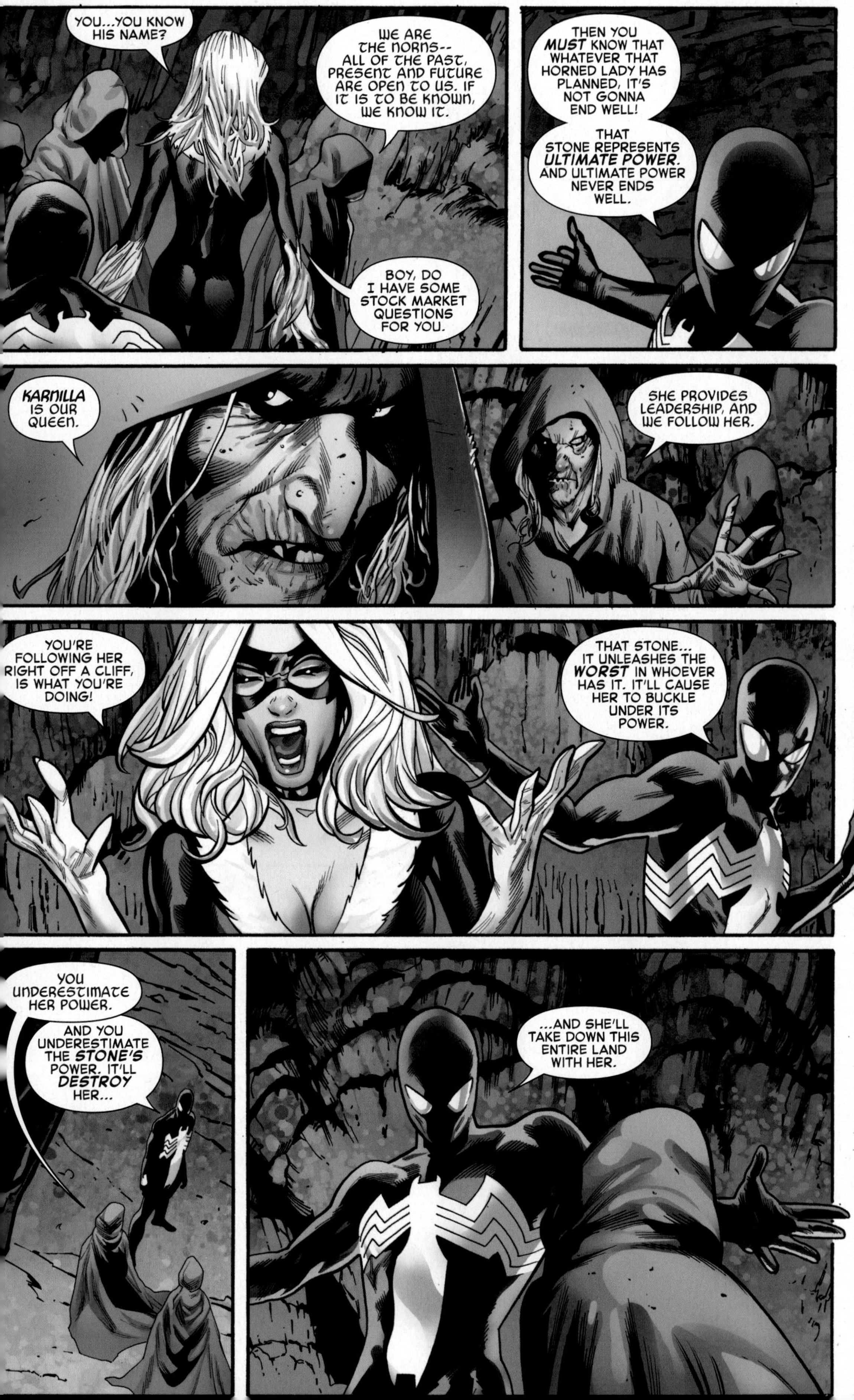
YOU...YOU KNOW HIS NAME?
WE ARE THE NORNS-- ALL OF THE PAST, PRESENT AND FUTURE ARE OPEN TO US. IF IT IS TO BE KNOWN, WE KNOW IT.
BOY, DO I HAVE SOME STOCK MARKET QUESTIONS FOR YOU.
THEN YOU MUST KNOW THAT WHATEVER THAT HORNED LADY HAS PLANNED, IT'S NOT GONNA END WELL!
THAT STONE REPRESENTS ULTIMATE POWER. AND ULTIMATE POWER NEVER ENDS WELL.
KARNILLA IS OUR QUEEN.
SHE PROVIDES LEADERSHIP, AND WE FOLLOW HER.
YOU'RE FOLLOWING HER RIGHT OFF A CLIFF, IS WHAT YOU'RE DOING!
THAT STONE... IT UNLEASHES THE WORST IN WHOEVER HAS IT. IT'LL CAUSE HER TO BUCKLE UNDER ITS POWER.
YOU UNDERESTIMATE HER POWER.
AND YOU UNDERESTIMATE THE STONE'S POWER. IT'LL DESTROY HER...
...AND SHE'LL TAKE DOWN THIS ENTIRE LAND WITH HER.

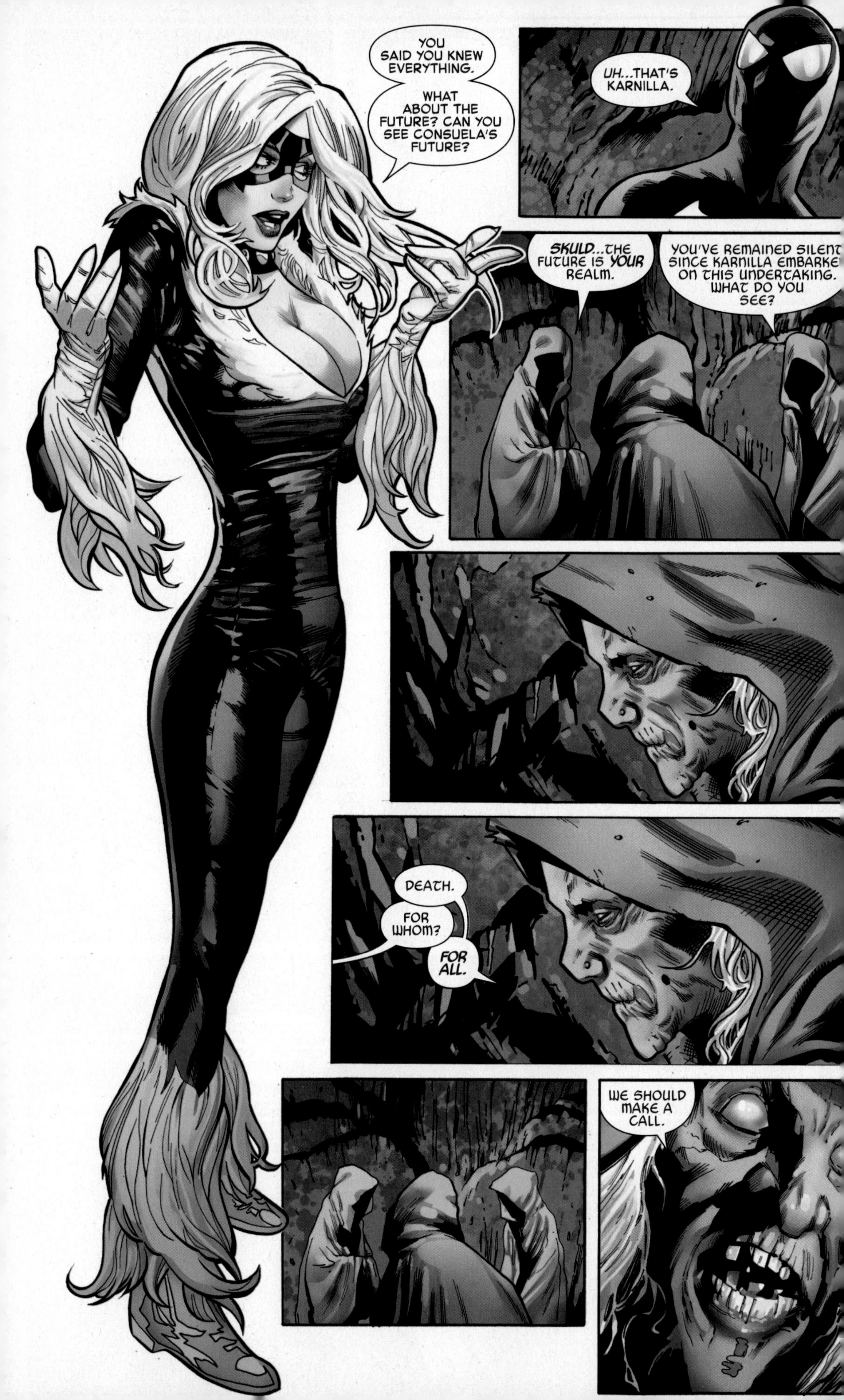

YOU SAID YOU KNEW EVERYTHING.
WHAT ABOUT THE FUTURE? CAN YOU SEE CONSUELA'S FUTURE?
UH...THAT'S KARNILLA.
SKULD...THE FUTURE IS YOUR REALM.
YOU'VE REMAINED SILENT SINCE KARNILLA EMBARKE ON THIS UNDERTAKING. WHAT DO YOU SEE?
DEATH.
FOR WHOM?
FOR ALL.
WE SHOULD MAKE A CALL.

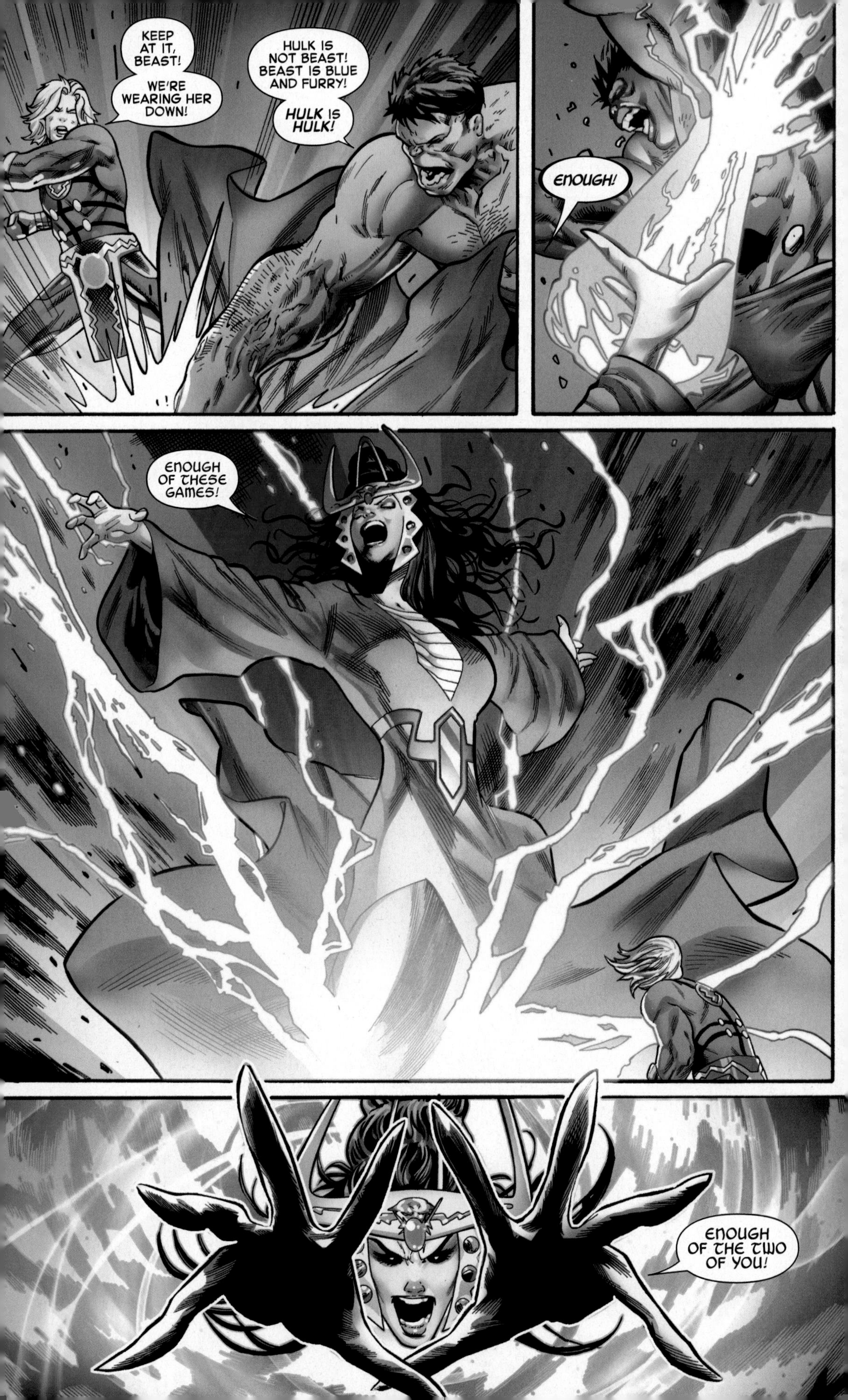
KEEP AT IT, BEAST!
WE'RE WEARING HER DOWN!
HULK IS NOT BEAST! BEAST IS BLUE AND FURRY!
HULK IS HULK!
ENOUGH!
ENOUGH OF THESE GAMES!
ENOUGH OF THE TWO OF YOU!

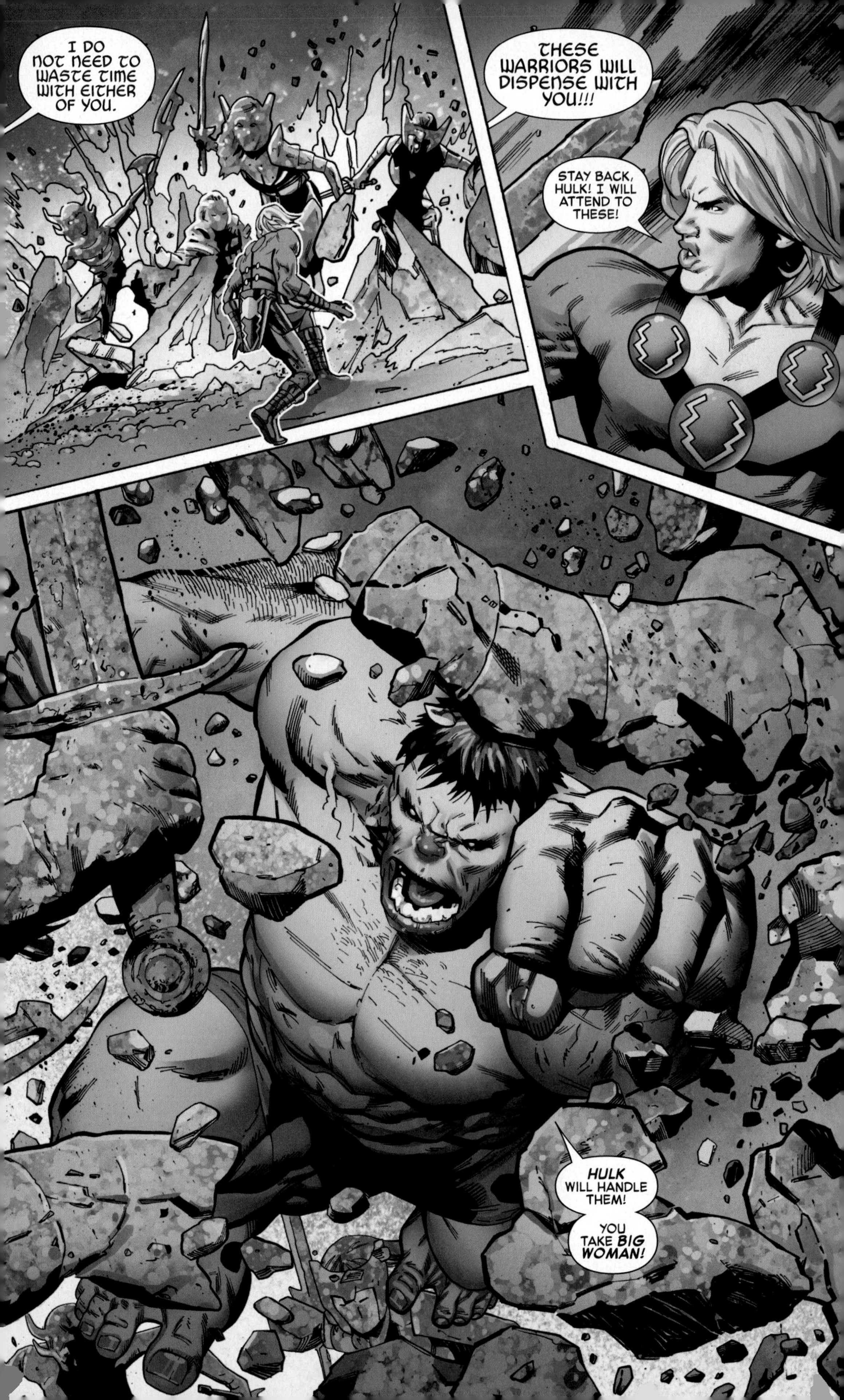
I DO NOT NEED TO WASTE TIME WITH EITHER OF YOU.
THESE WARRIORS WILL DISPENSE WITH YOU!!!
STAY BACK, HULK! I WILL ATTEND TO THESE!
HULK WILL HANDLE THEM!
YOU TAKE BIG WOMAN!

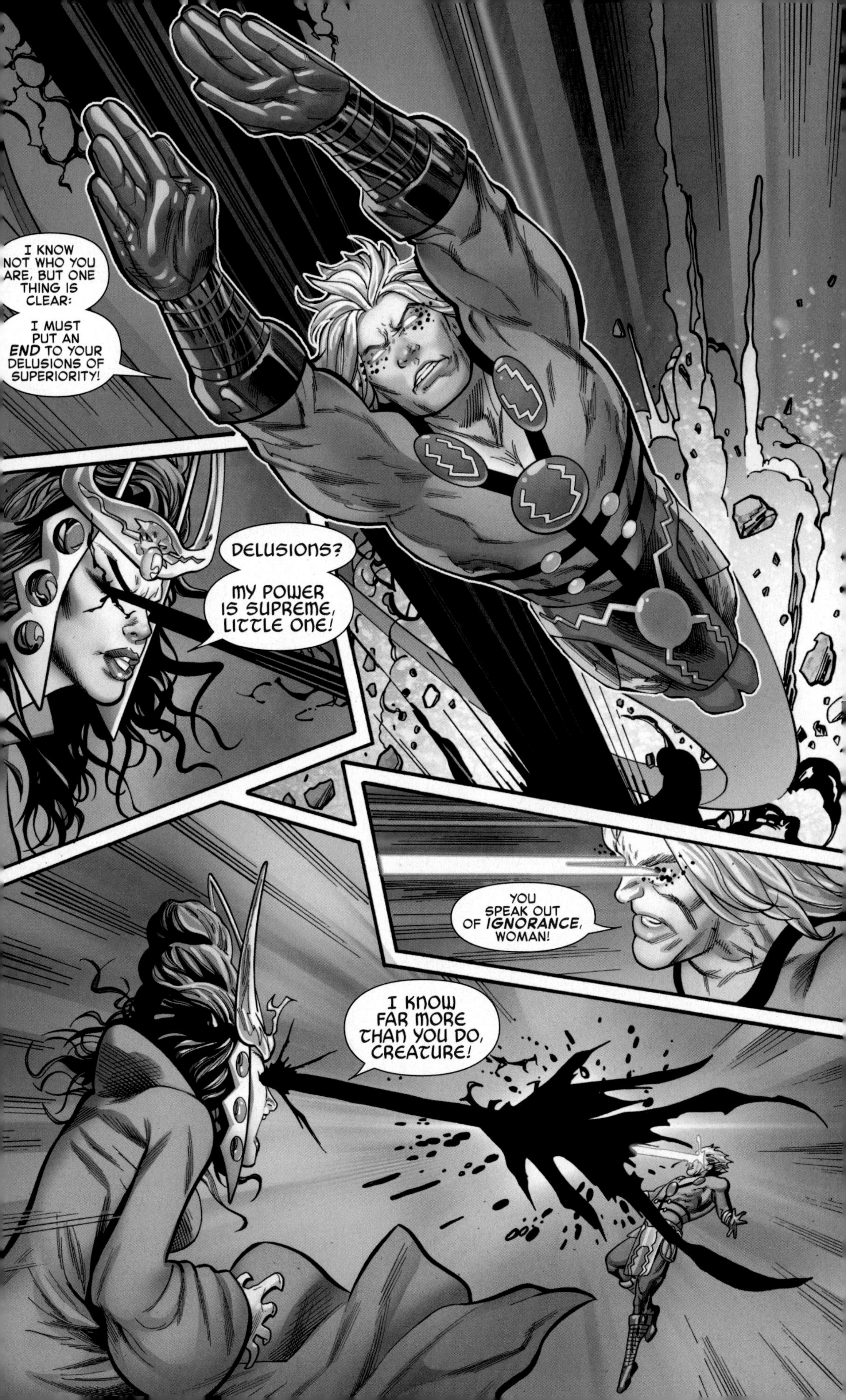
I KNOW NOT WHO YOU ARE, BUT ONE THING IS CLEAR:
I MUST PUT AN END TO YOUR DELUSIONS OF SUPERIORITY!
DELUSIONS?
MY POWER IS SUPREME, LITTLE ONE!
YOU SPEAK OUT OF IGNORANCE, WOMAN!
I KNOW FAR MORE THAN YOU DO, CREATURE!

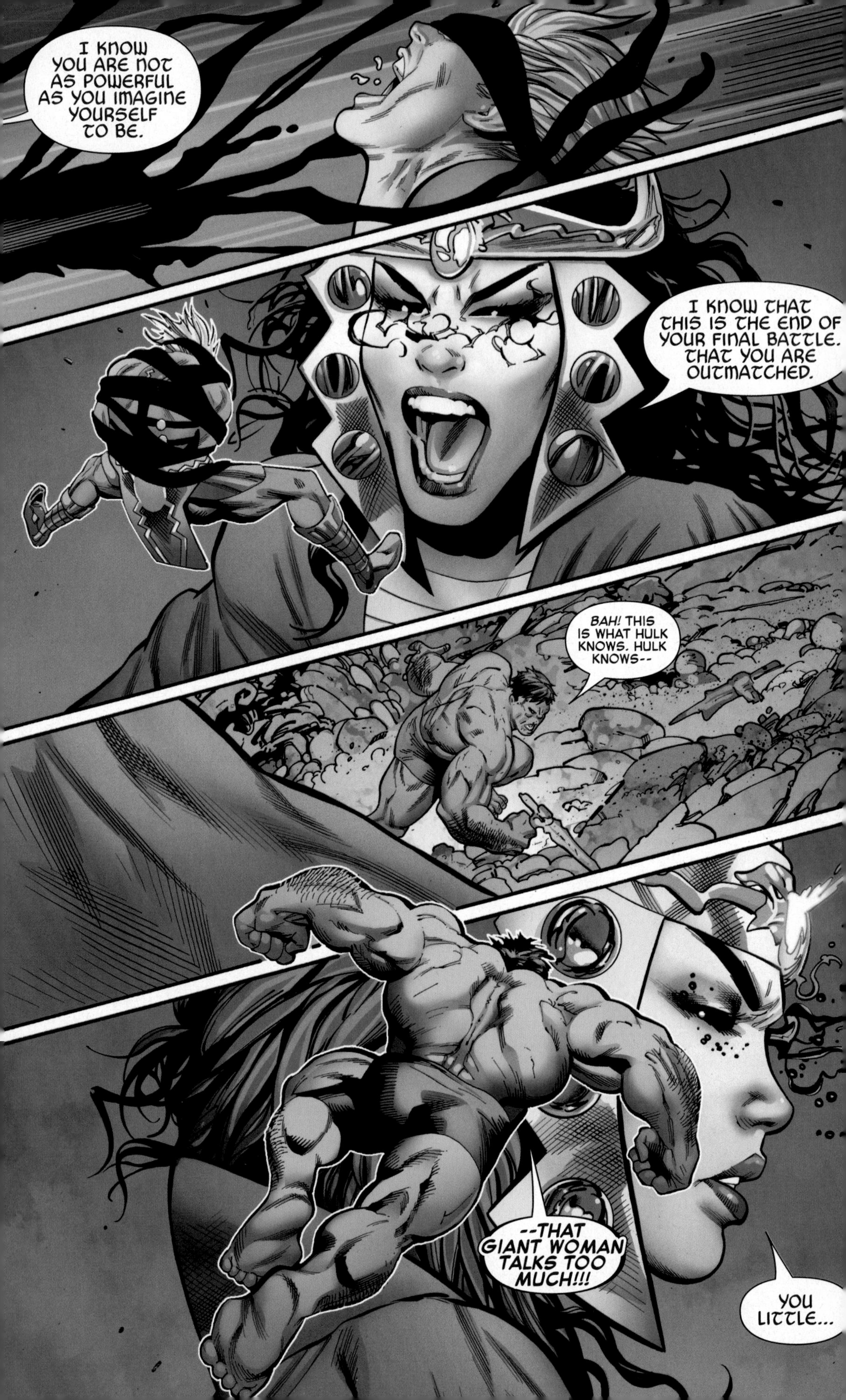
I KNOW YOU ARE NOT AS POWERFUL AS YOU IMAGINE YOURSELF TO BE.
I KNOW THAT THIS IS THE END OF YOUR FINAL BATTLE. THAT YOU ARE OUTMATCHED.
BAH! THIS IS WHAT HULK KNOWS. HULK KNOWS--
--THAT GIANT WOMAN TALKS TOO MUCH!!!
YOU LITTLE...

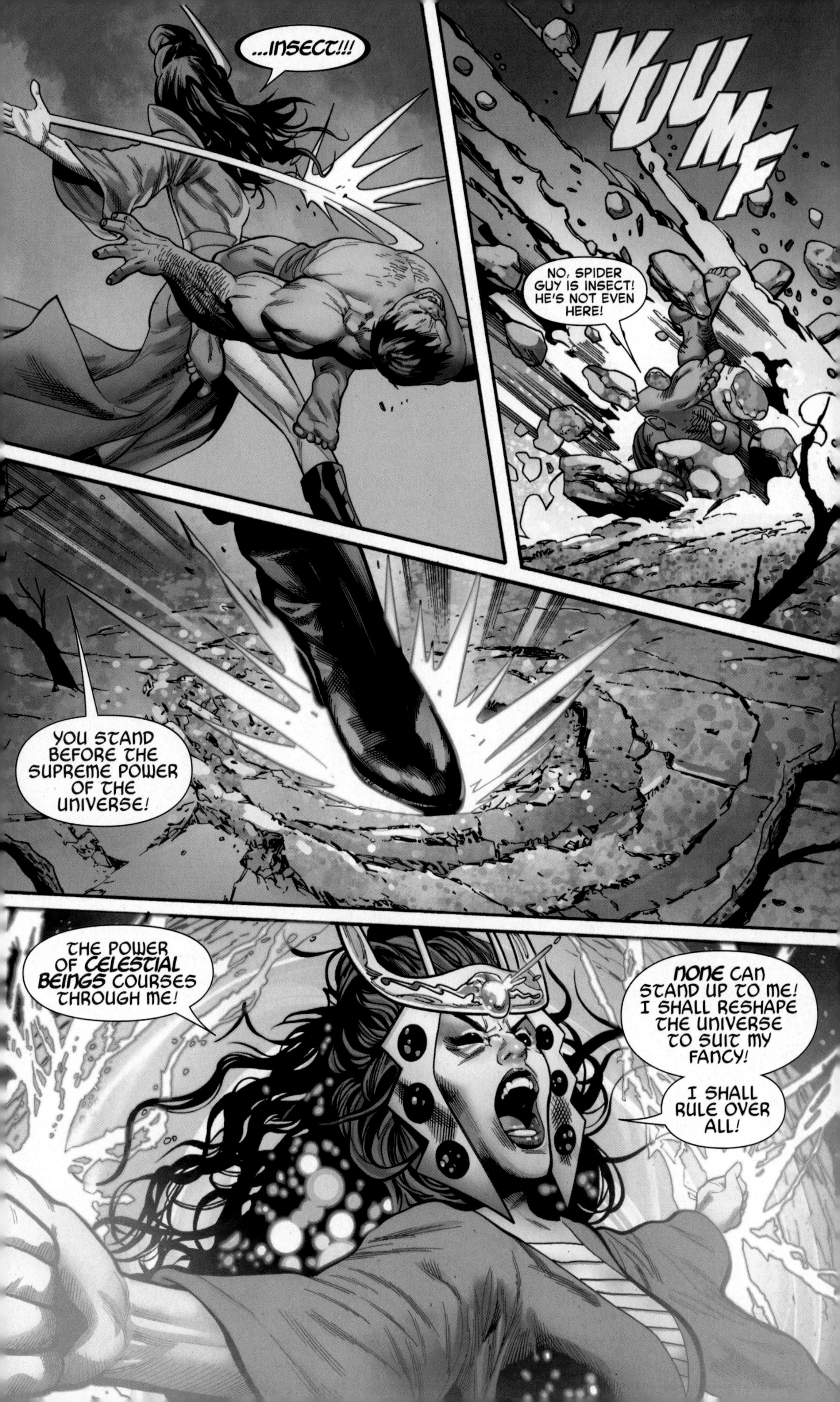
...INSECT!!!
WUUMF
NO, SPIDER GUY IS INSECT! HE'S NOT EVEN HERE!
YOU STAND BEFORE THE SUPREME POWER OF THE UNIVERSE!
THE POWER OF CELESTIAL BEINGS COURSES THROUGH ME!
NONE CAN STAND UP TO ME! I SHALL RESHAPE THE UNIVERSE TO SUIT MY FANCY!
I SHALL RULE OVER ALL!

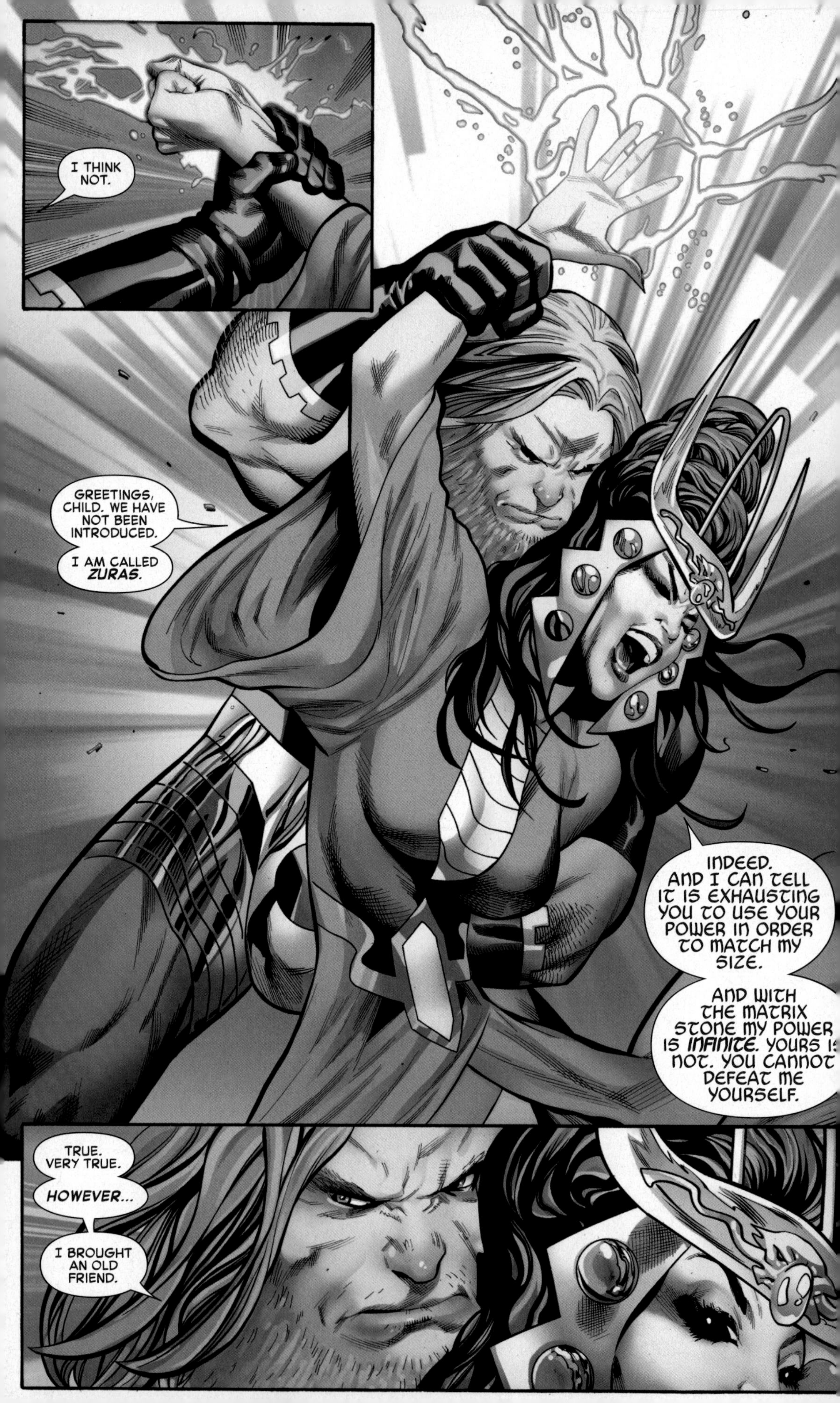
I THINK NOT.
GREETINGS, CHILD. WE HAVE NOT BEEN INTRODUCED.
I AM CALLED *ZURAS.*
INDEED. AND I CAN TELL IT IS EXHAUSTING YOU TO USE YOUR POWER IN ORDER TO MATCH MY SIZE.
AND WITH THE MATRIX STONE MY POWER IS *INFINITE.* YOURS IS NOT. YOU CANNOT DEFEAT ME YOURSELF.
TRUE. VERY TRUE.
HOWEVER...
I BROUGHT AN OLD FRIEND.

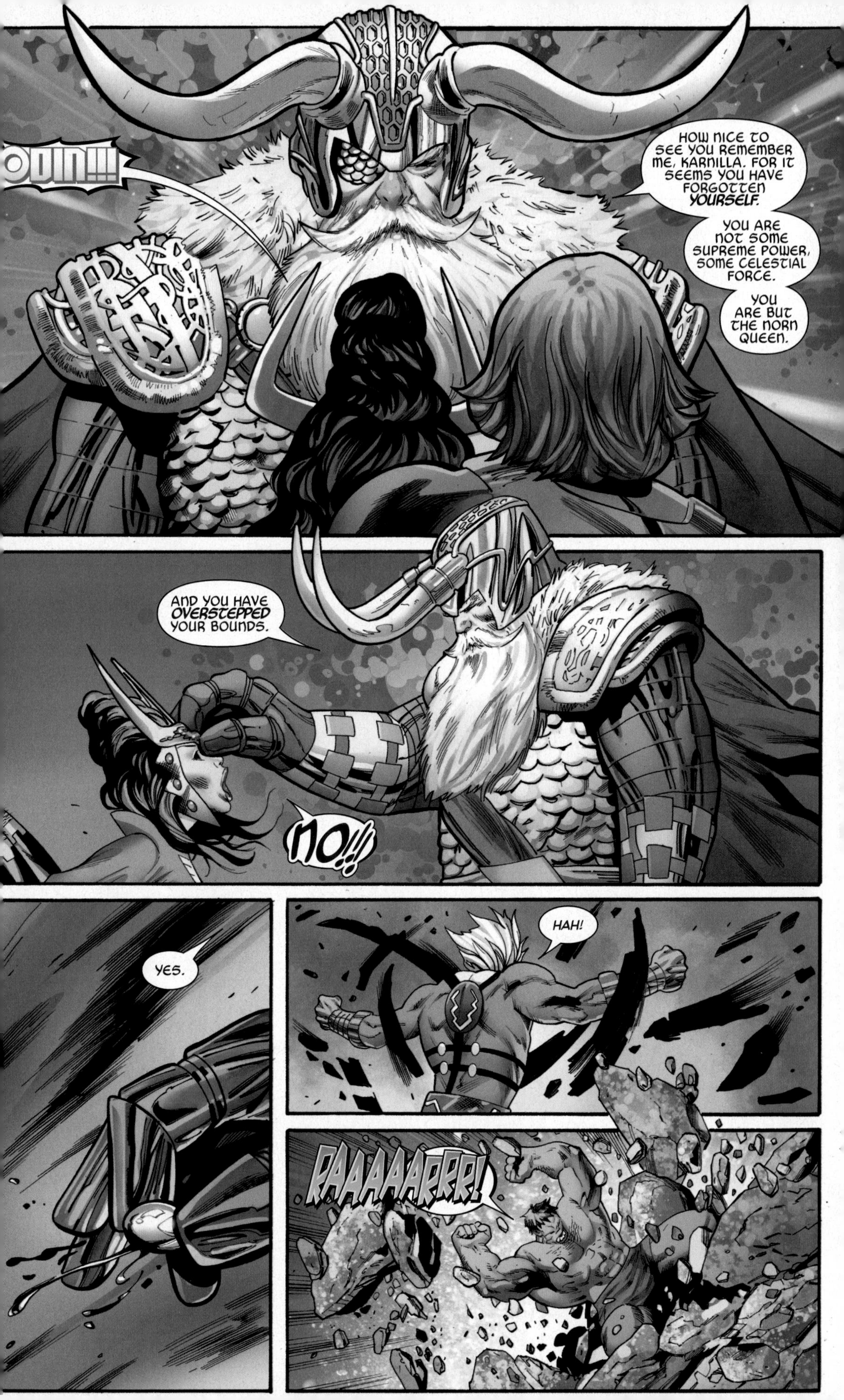
ODIN!!!
HOW NICE TO SEE YOU REMEMBER ME, KARNILLA. FOR IT SEEMS YOU HAVE FORGOTTEN *YOURSELF*.
YOU ARE NOT SOME SUPREME POWER, SOME CELESTIAL FORCE.
YOU ARE BUT THE NORN QUEEN.
AND YOU HAVE *OVERSTEPPED* YOUR BOUNDS.
NO!!!
YES.
HAH!
RAAAAARRR!

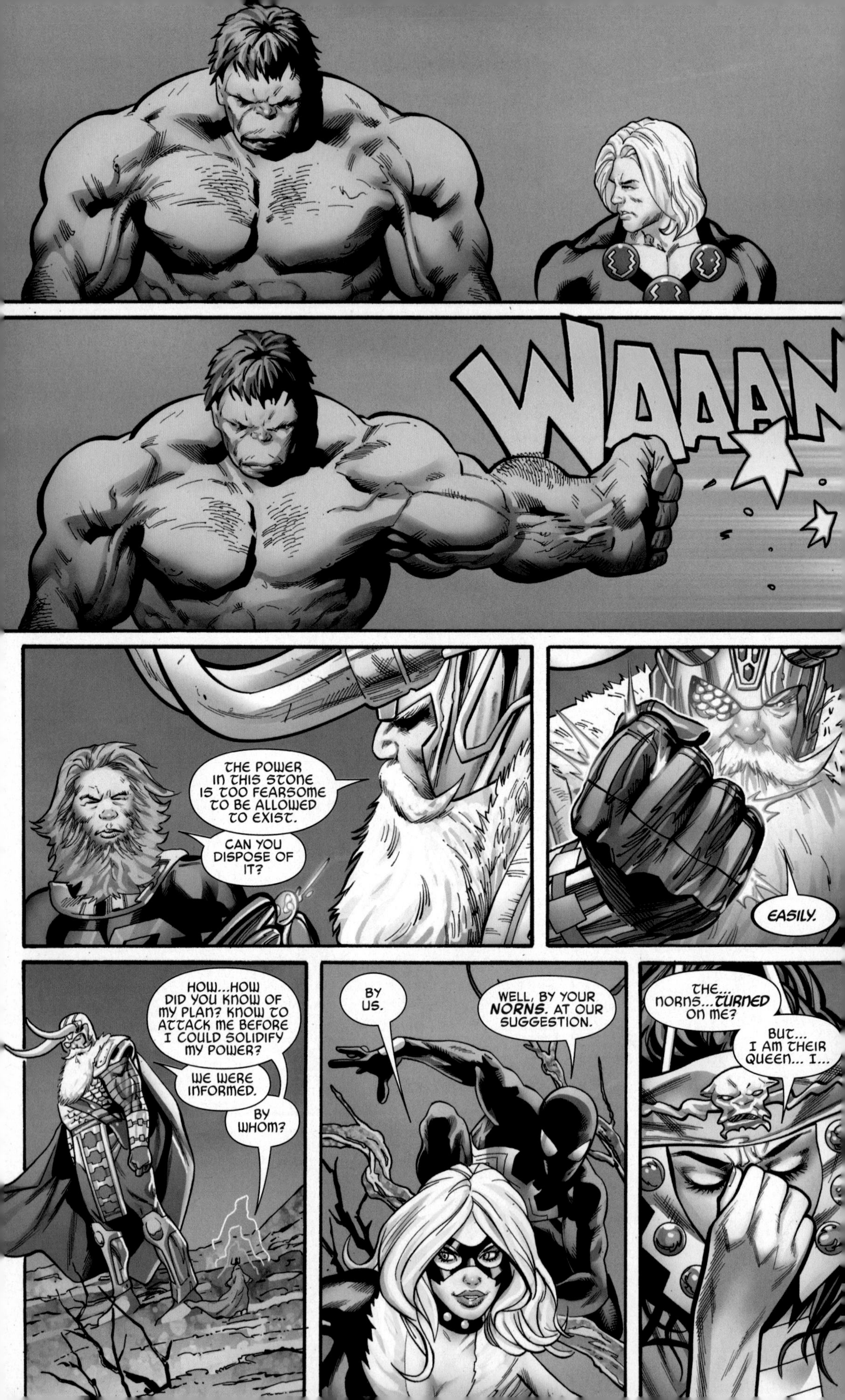
WAAAN
THE POWER IN THIS STONE IS TOO FEARSOME TO BE ALLOWED TO EXIST.
CAN YOU DISPOSE OF IT?
EASILY.
HOW...HOW DID YOU KNOW OF MY PLAN? KNOW TO ATTACK ME BEFORE I COULD SOLIDIFY MY POWER?
WE WERE INFORMED.
BY WHOM?
BY US.
WELL, BY YOUR NORNS. AT OUR SUGGESTION.
THE... NORNS...TURNED ON ME?
BUT... I AM THEIR QUEEN... I...

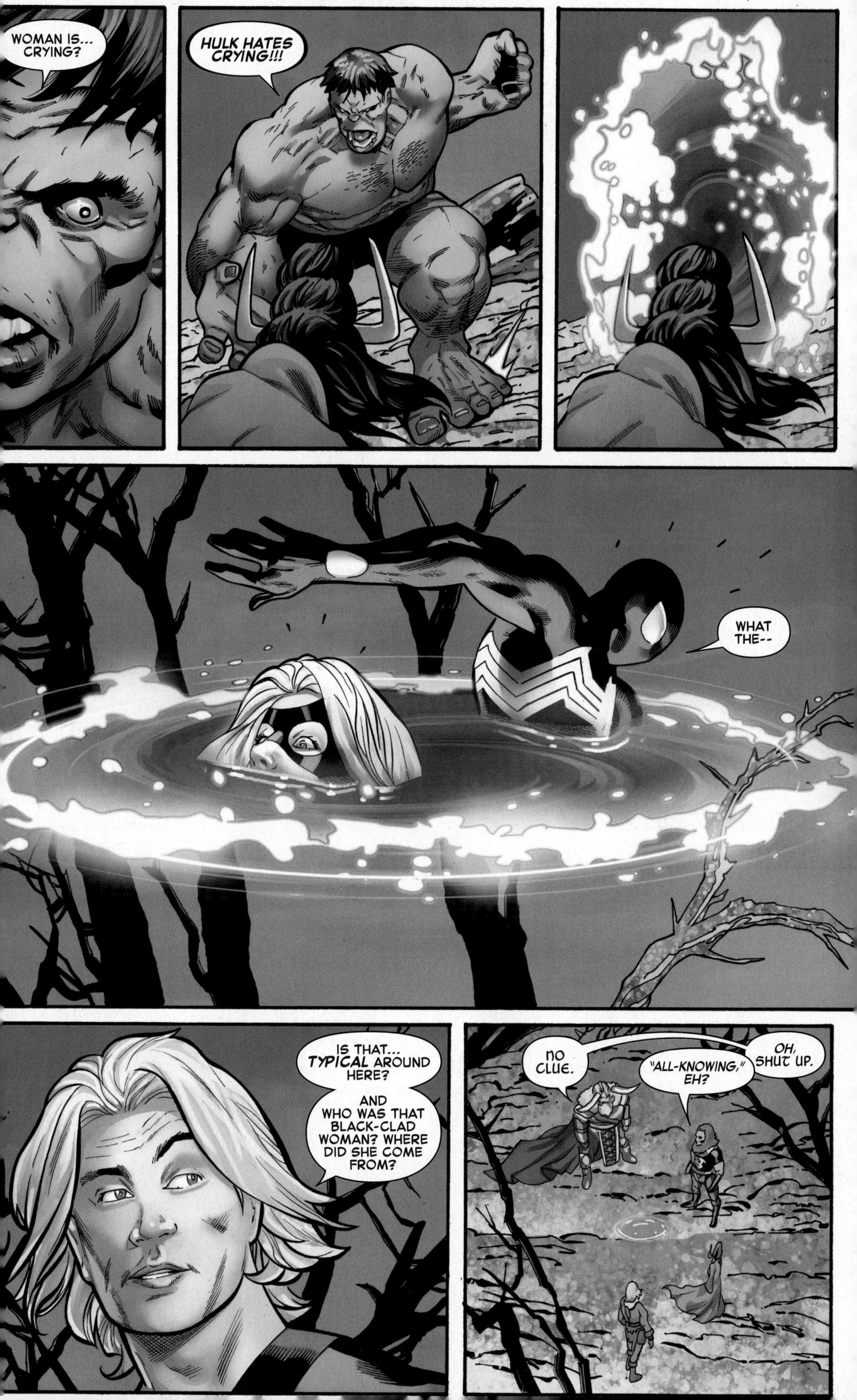
WOMAN IS... CRYING?
HULK HATES CRYING!!!
WHAT THE--
IS THAT... TYPICAL AROUND HERE?
AND WHO WAS THAT BLACK-CLAD WOMAN? WHERE DID SHE COME FROM?
NO CLUE.
"ALL-KNOWING," EH?
OH, SHUT UP.

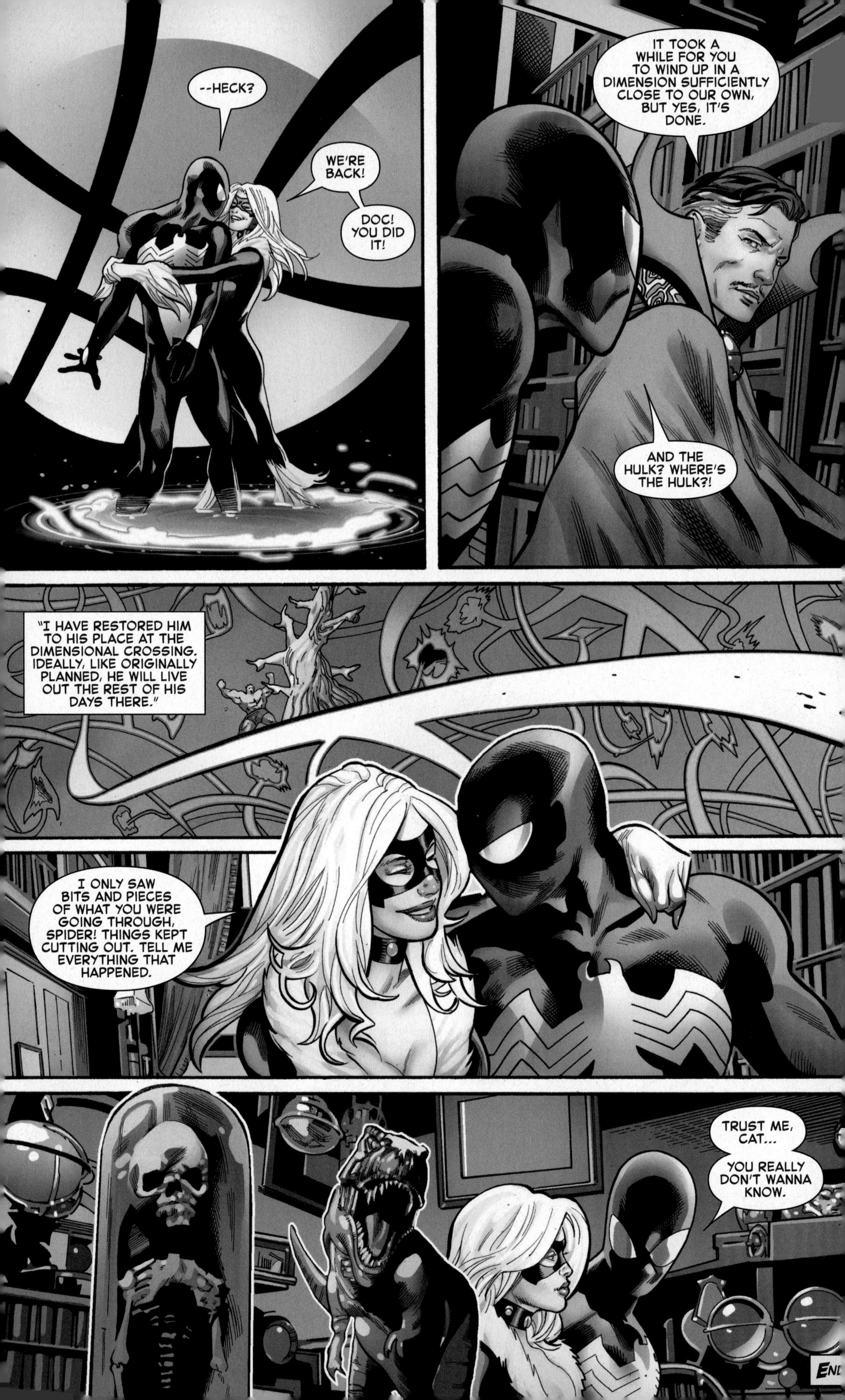
--HECK?
WE'RE BACK!
DOC! YOU DID IT!
IT TOOK A WHILE FOR YOU TO WIND UP IN A DIMENSION SUFFICIENTLY CLOSE TO OUR OWN, BUT YES, IT'S DONE.
AND THE HULK? WHERE'S THE HULK?!
"I HAVE RESTORED HIM TO HIS PLACE AT THE DIMENSIONAL CROSSING. IDEALLY, LIKE ORIGINALLY PLANNED, HE WILL LIVE OUT THE REST OF HIS DAYS THERE."
I ONLY SAW BITS AND PIECES OF WHAT YOU WERE GOING THROUGH, SPIDER! THINGS KEPT CUTTING OUT. TELL ME EVERYTHING THAT HAPPENED.
TRUST ME, CAT...
YOU REALLY DON'T WANNA KNOW.

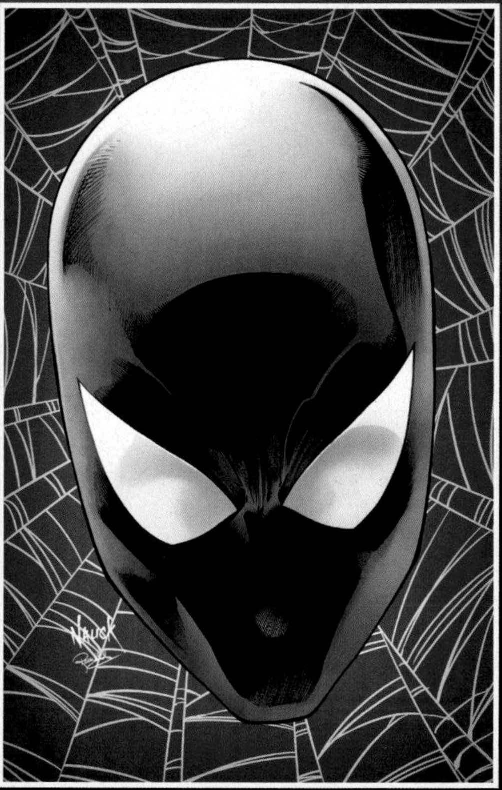
NAUCK

#1 HEADSHOT VARIANT BY
TODD NAUCK & **RACHELLE ROSENBERG**

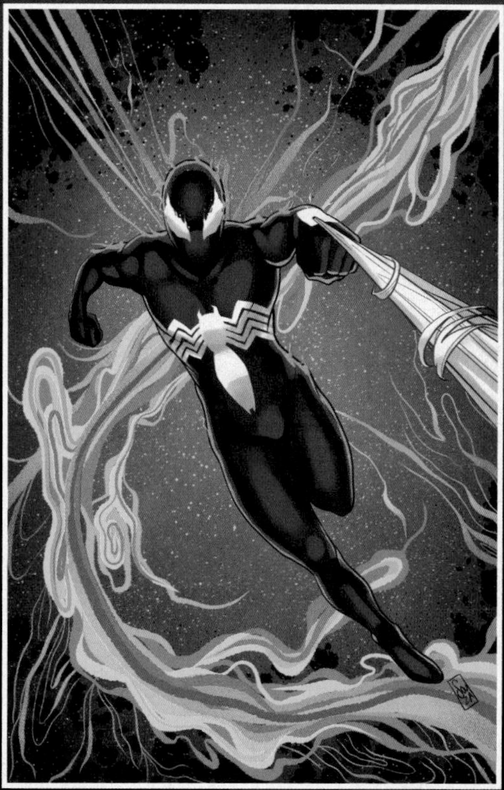

#1 VARIANT BY
ERNANDA SOUZA

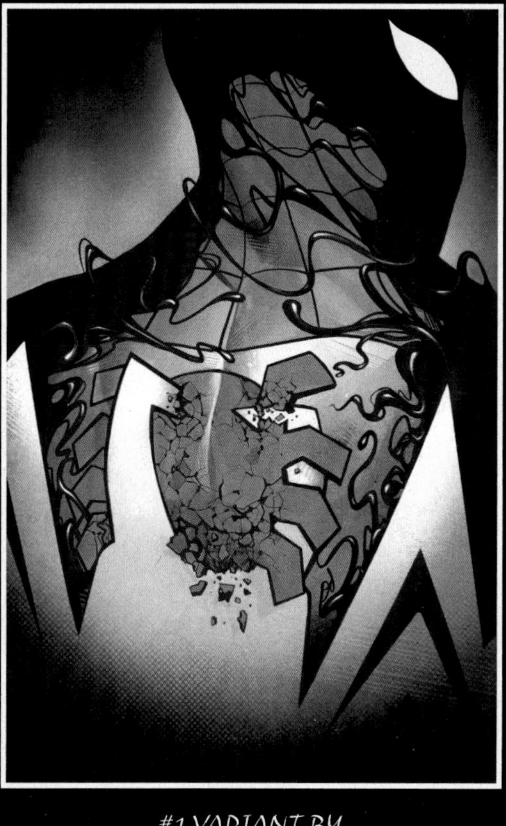

#1 VARIANT BY
MIKE DEL MUNDO

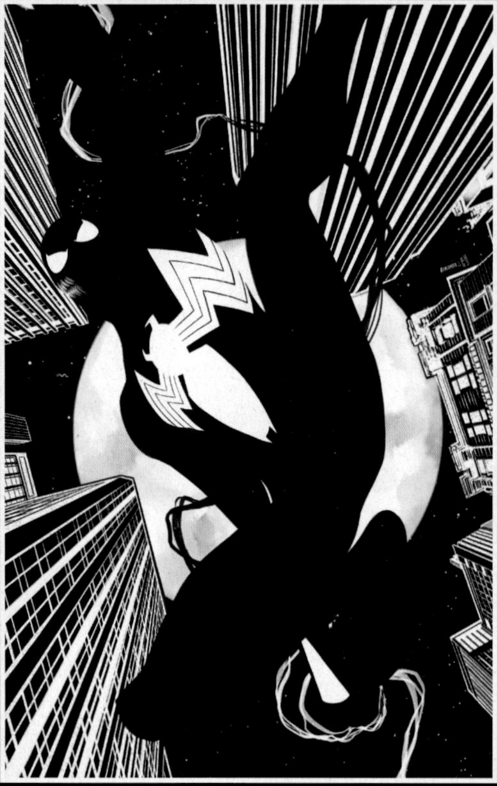

#2 VARIANT BY
DAVID BALDEÓN

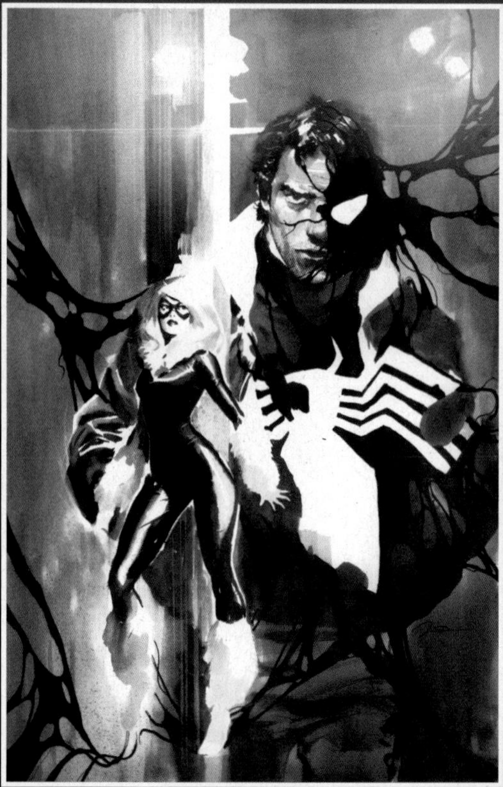

#3 VARIANT BY
GERALD PAREL

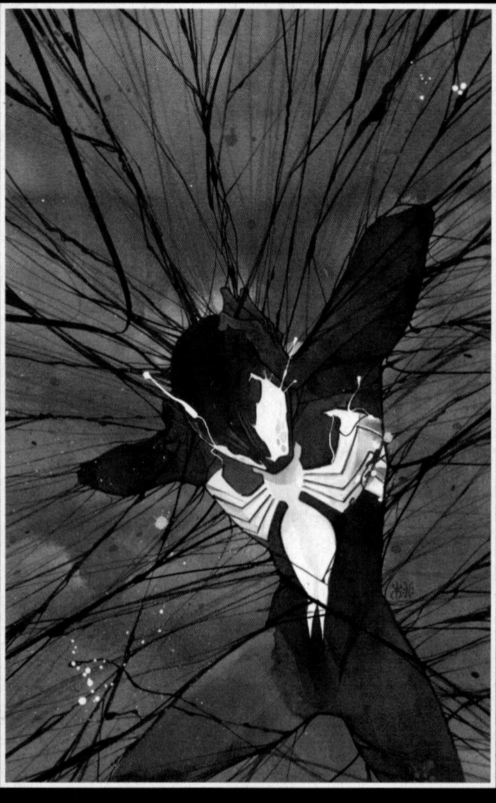

#4 VARIANT BY
PEACH MOMOKO

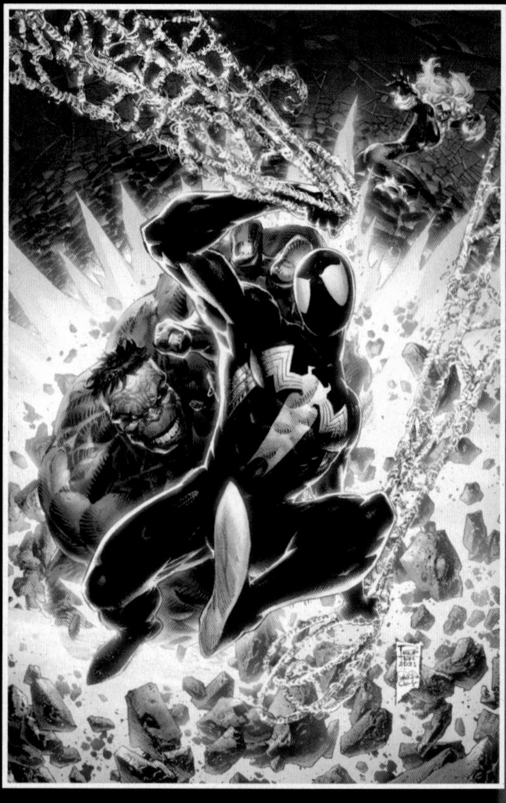

#5 VARIANT BY
PHILIP TAN & SEBASTIAN CHENG